Heinrich Heine

POETRY AND PROSE

The German Library: Volume 32

Volkmar Sander, General Editor

Heinrich Heine

POETRY
AND PROSE

Edited by Jost Hermand
and Robert C. Holub

Foreword by Alfred Kazin

CONTINUUM · NEW YORK

1992

The Continuum Publishing Company
370 Lexington Avenue, New York, NY 10017

Printed in the United States of America

Library of Congress Cataloging in Publication Data

Heine, Heinrich, 1797–1856.
Poetry and prose.

(The German library; v. 32)
I. Hermand, Jost.   II. Holub, Robert C.
III. Title.   IV. Series.
PT2316.A3H4   1982   831'.7   82-7981
ISBN 0-8264-0255-0   AACR2
ISBN 0-8264-0265-8 pbk

For acknowledgments of previous published material, please see page 300,
which constitutes an extension of the copyright page.

Contents

Foreword

In life (1797–1856) Heinrich Heine was generally admitted to be a superbly gifted but "difficult" man. In death his being "difficult" was so obstinately and even vindictively remembered that Hitler, flushed with triumph when he occupied Paris, ordered that Heine's grave in Montmartre be destroyed. This may have seemed extravagant to many "internal émigrés" in Germany at the time. But Heine was a problem and embarrassment to many Germans in the "educated classes."

Today opinion of Heine in Germany is more relaxed, more appreciative, but it is also distracted. Although the complexity of his character, the sharpness of his intellect, and the storminess of his life are hardly unknown, the real complaint against him now, especially in English-speaking countries where his early "romantic" poetry was once almost as popular as Longfellow's, is that he is not sufficiently "modern." The early twentieth-century modernist revolution (which now dominates literary opinion in the universities) revived many long-dead dramatists as incompatible as Büchner and Ibsen; fiction writers as opposed as Flaubert and Dostoevsky; seventeenth-century poets like Donne, visionary contemporaries like Blake and Hölderlin.

Goethe never needed to be "revived"; his place seemed immovable; his fame stretched from his own capacious lifetime to the twentieth century, not only as the supreme figure in German literature but as a wisdom figure that somehow redeemed German history from its more hideous recent episodes. But Heine—Heine had notoriously escaped many honors during his lifetime, and even now escapes the currently necessary distinction of being considered not just "modern" but *a* modern, one of the elect ahead of his time.

So Heine, unlucky fellow, was still not considered "one of us"— one of us in self-conscious, superior taste. No doubt one reason for this was a certain embarrassment at having to reclaim, for purely patriotic and remorseful reasons, someone who had been excluded from German history and literature, positively expunged from the noble record of German *Geist*. Although such classics as "Die Lorelei" were enshrined in German memory and affection even during the Hitler years, such poems fared better than their author. They were included in schoolbooks but attributed to "author unknown." To make amends after 1945 was not only necessary but easy. What was apparently *not* easy was how to fit the almost too-well-known Heine, the famously sentimental but also insurrectionary, bewilderingly contradictory Heine into the same modern canon that had no trouble accommodating Nietzsche, Kafka, Rilke.

The necessity of being "modern" has somehow been unquestioned in many Western literatures since T. S. Eliot in England, Paul Valéry in France seemed not only to establish the canon but pronounced the rules for belonging to it. No matter how far back he lived, a poet as venerable as Dante or Shakespeare was "modern" if he seemed to be talking to us of issues still unsettled, in language novel enough to provoke us still. The genius in each case had of course to be so unquestioned as to reach across the ages; only the absolutely first-rate need apply. But he/she had also to be so "complex," "difficult," "paradoxical," that we in our complex and difficult age could feel that these figures, by eluding the conventional taste of their own time, had become contemporaries of ours.

Now the very fact that Heine was so dear to some sentimental nineteenth-century taste that the Nazis could not obliterate him entirely has been held against Heine. In England and America Heine was a well-loved Victorian poet. He was so popular that a representative American Victorian (and a great arbiter of taste), the novelist and poet William Dean Howells, sadly said of his own verses that he could not tell where Heine's influence left off. At a time when that perennial "modern," Friedrich Nietzsche, said in praise of Heine that "he possessed that divine malice without which I cannot conceive perfection," certain early songs of Heine from the *Buch der Lieder* were proffered in courtship like flowers and boxes of candy.

And of course Heine's "songs" were put to ravishing music by Schubert, Mendelssohn, Schumann, Liszt, Brahms, and Richard Strauss. People who do not even know that Heine wrote "Die Lorelei" know as melody *Ich weiss nicht, was soll es bedeuten.* Heine in fact became such a classic of song, of sweetness and musicality, that his verses set to music by the greatest of German lyric composers made many of his works household names, an inspiration to lovers, but even more, a secure resource to all those who *liked* to say "I do not know why it should be that I am so sad."

The wonderful suppleness, the famous "inwardly expressive" genius of German lieder, no doubt rejoiced in all the wonderful opportunities that Heine's "heart laid bare" gave composers. The unembarrassed *Schmerz* could be irresistible. Schubert in "Der Atlas":

> *Ich unglückseliger Atlas! Eine Welt,*
> *Die ganze Welt der Schmerzen muss*
> *ich tragen.*

> (Unhappy Atlas that I am,
> I must bear a world,
> The whole world of sorrows.)

Schubert in "Das Fischermädchen" (The Fisher Maid):

> *Mein Herz gleicht ganz dem Meere,*
> *Hat Sturm und Ebb und Flut.*

> (My heart is just like the sea:
> It has its storms, its ebb, its flood.)

Mendelssohn in "Auf Flügeln des Gesanges" (On Wings of Song):

> *Dort wollen wir niedersinken*
> *Unter dem Palmenbaum*
> *Und Liebe und Ruhe trinken,*
> *Und träumen seligen Traum.*

(There we will sink down
Under the palm tree,
Drinking love and peace,
And dreaming a blessed dream.)

The equally well-known mischievousness, teasing, and surprise endings of so many of Heine's lyrics also lent him to the uses of a romanticism that vividly, even emphatically, knew how to rebound from aching *Schmerz* to mocking irony. Heine the sometimes too openly suffering love poet could also show himself the most derisive and painfully cutting satirist—often in the same poem or in the same sequence of poems—of love's self-centeredness and love's gushing trustfulness. Yet none of the poet's stabbing shifts of mood, his mordant wit, his fatalism—just the qualities that endeared Donne to Eliot and to the legion of Eliot's followers—managed to make Heine truly acceptable to self-conscious and exclusive modernist taste. It was as if Heine was almost too well known to need reclaiming.

Nor did the flightiness and even instability of Heine's views on mythology, religion, and politics endear him to twentieth-century taste. After all, Heine had condemned Christianity along with Judaism, because both formed the "Nazarene" personality that Heine disparaged in favor of the "Hellene." Heine's fellow Jews have never really succeeded in claiming Heine for their own. He entered the Lutheran church because baptism was "the entrance ticket to European civilization," but he hated himself for this, and in his last years, chained by spinal tuberculosis to his "mattress grave" in Paris, he wrote not just penitently but ecstatically of the Hebrew Bible, the Hebrew liturgy. In one of his most famous last poems he celebrated the life and death of the great, "sweet," medieval Hebrew poet of Spain, Judah Halevy, who in Jerusalem was slain by a "Saracen." Heine, near death, sought to identify himself with this greatest of medieval Hebrew poets.

Nevertheless, Heine's early and very German devotion to the pagan gods was just as real, and productive, as his yearning before death to return to the personal God of the Jews. Nor, despite his many rejections as a Jew, did he ever quite drop a scoffing tone at Jewish customs and rituals. Many brilliant Jewish writers and intellectuals have been more influenced by the Christian culture in which they live than by the Jewish religion in which they were reared. Heine never got over Germany.

At the same time his fellow Germans have not been able entirely to claim him as one of theirs; or, since 1945, fully to reclaim him. Some ancient wounds are still throbbing in the German body politic; Heine is often regarded as just that—a wound, an affront. Heine as revolutionary was, however, as unpredictable and contradictory in his rebelliousness against "Old Germany" as in everything else. With the Jews as with the Christians, the Germans as with the French, Heine no sooner smelled out a consensus anywhere than he left it.

Still, so far as he was anything for most of his life, Heine *was* (like the Napoleon-worshiping Stendhal whom he so much resembles) a rebel against the established order. He lived out the last twenty-five years of his life in Paris as a political exile (where despite his chauvinistic dislike of French poetry he was admired, supported, and translated by French poets); he was condemned and proscribed by the Prussian government of the time. A certain hesitation among Germans in accepting him even today may be due to the fact that to Marx, Nietzsche, and other rebellious Germans who admired him, Heine seemed far ahead of his country and his time; he was an everlasting antagonist of propriety and self-satisfaction who made things even more difficult for himself by being as hard on his friends as he was on his many enemies. And Heine not only had enemies everywhere; he never gave up the privilege of mocking even his friends.

Yet Nietzsche, the most farseeing, the most intelligent, the most mercilessly keen of modern German minds, said that Heine

> gave me the highest conception of the lyric poet. I seek in vain in all the realms [of time] for an equally sweet and passionate music. He possessed that divine malice without which I cannot conceive perfection. I estimate the value of human beings, of races, according to the necessity with which they cannot understand the god apart from the satyr. And how he handles his German! It will be said one day that Heine and I have been by far the first artists of the German language.

Even in the Victorian period, so ready to overemphasize the "sweet" Heine, Matthew Arnold, in what is probably the most penetrating appreciation of the poet in English, saw Heine's civic importance and quoted Heine's own words: "But lay on my coffin a *sword;* for I was a brave soldier in the Liberation War of humanity." Arnold, echoing these words, honored Heine not as a hero, "but preeminently [as] a brilliant, a most effective soldier in the Liberation War of humanity." By this Arnold meant not something political but what Goethe had said of himself: "If I were to say what I had really been to the Germans in general, and to the young German poets in particular, I should say I had been their *liberator.*" And what has "liberation," so often a necessary function in what Heine called the "dark night of Germany," a Germany so little affected by the great Paris revolution of 1830—what has it to do with the "modern," with those "modern times" that Heine felt he belonged to with all his heart and soul and mind? Arnold identified Heine entirely with "the awakening of the modern spirit."

> Modern times find themselves with an immense system of institutions, established facts, accredited dogmas, customs, rules, which have come to them from times not modern. In this system their life has to be carried forward; yet they have a sense that this system is not of their own creation, that it by no means corresponds exactly with the wants of their actual life, that, for them, it is customary, not rational. The modern spirit is now awake almost everywhere. . . . To remove this want of correspondence is beginning to be the settled endeavor of most persons of good sense. Dissolvents of the old European system of dominant ideas and facts we must all be, all of us who have any power of working; what we have to study is that we may not be acrid dissolvents of it.

Of course Arnold as a proper English gentleman could not approve of Heine's disorderly manner of life. He complained that while "Heine had all the culture of Germany; in his head fermented all the ideas of modern Europe," Heine in the end showed "want of moral balance, and of nobleness of soul and character." So the greatest of Victorian critics (but a minor poet) revenged himself in the end for having to recognize, as a far greater poet than himself, one who was truly what Arnold also was not—"a brave soldier in the Liberation War of humanity."

Yet Arnold saw Heine's greatness as a poet because, more than any other critic in English of his time, Arnold did have that fullness of historical grasp, that sense of the historical character of mankind, which Eliot defined as a criterion of greatness in his famous essay "Tradition and the Individual Talent." Eliot said that the "historical sense . . . we may call nearly indispensable to anyone who would continue to be a poet beyond his twenty-fifth year; and . . . the historical sense compels a man to write not merely with his own generation in his bones, but with a feeling that the whole of the literature of Europe from Homer and within it the whole of the literature of his own country has a simultaneous existence and composes a simultaneous order."

If this is "modernism," along with Arnold's prophetic understanding that the modern spirit consists in knowing how much of the past does *not* correspond with our lives, then Heine is truly a "modern" poet and a herald indeed of the modern spirit. In one of his most haunting poems, "Wo?" (Where?), he wrote the "dream of a summer night." In this dream, pale and weathered in the light of the moon, masonry lay about, remains of ancient glory, ruins of the Renaissance period. In an amazing dream through history, Heine went on to present Olympus, Adam and Eve, the destruction and fire of Troy, Paris and Helen, and Hector too; Moses and Aaron standing close by, Esther as well, Judith, Holofernes, and Haman; the god Amour, Phoebus Apollo, Vulcan and Venus, Pluto and Proserpina, Mercury, Bacchus the god, Priapus and Silenus; Balaam's ass, the temptation of Abraham, and Lot, who got drunk with his daughters.

And so on and on until this dream of history, this extraordinary procession that makes up history for a poet imbued with the mythological sense of things, ends with Balaam's ass braying, shouting down the gods and the saints. "And at last I myself cried out—and I woke up." This lovely dream of history ends indeed on a prophetic note. Joyce was to say in *Ulysses* that "history is a nightmare from which I am trying to awake." Heine woke up, and is perhaps still trying to wake us up. He may just be one of us.

ALFRED KAZIN

Introduction

Heinrich Heine was not a very prolific writer. Compared with the output of other literary giants such as Lessing, Goethe, Thomas Mann, or for that matter Brecht, his oeuvre is astonishingly small. Whereas their works fill twenty or fifty or even 250 volumes, Heine's complete works—in the definitive edition of Ernst Elster dated 1887—comprise only seven volumes. Almost everything Heine wrote is highly original, perceptive, touchingly beautiful, and/or maliciously ironic—and therefore worth preserving.

Hence the task of presenting Heine's oeuvre in only two volumes is a challenge. Too many important pieces and even small gems must be omitted. But once this job is completed, we are confronted with still another problem: there are almost no definable genres in Heine's oeuvre. True, there is a considerable amount of lyric poetry, but most of his other works are unique—strange, almost bizarre mixtures of journalistic, narrative, theoretical, and lyrical elements that defy any aesthetic categorization. Heine is not merely a poet; he is simultaneously a theoretician, a philosopher, a politician. To group his works in well-defined categories is therefore virtually impossible. But since only two volumes are at our disposal and both must have titles, we will refer to the first volume as "poetic works" and the second as "essays."

What are "poetic works"? In Heine's case, the term "poetic" applies first and foremost to his lyric poetry, as well as to his narrative prose, his verse epics, and his plays. But since the more poetic or aesthetically autonomous of these works are further removed from the unique spirit of their creator, we have chosen to omit his two plays (*Almansor* and *William Ratcliff*), one of his verse epics (*Atta Troll*), his novels and novellas (*Florentine Nights, The Rabbi of Bacherach,* and *The Memoirs of Count Schnabelewopski*), and many of his other tales, ballet scenarios, and ballads. What we have finally selected for inclusion are all those poetic works that reflect Heine's special style at its best. Most of them are highly autobiographical, a feature we have come to expect from modern writers or poets, but one that was unheard of in Biedermeier Germany of the 1820s and 1830s when Heine began publishing. Yet these autobiographical traces are exactly the elements that make Heine's work so sparkling and lively, so interesting and realistic in the best sense of the word.

Most of Heine's works are not conceived as timeless masterpieces, intended to last forever in unchanging beauty. Each was written for its own day—and precisely this fact makes the works so alive. While all consciously stylized works become stale after a certain time, subjectivity in revolt guarantees much greater durability. Throughout his life Heine spurned any categorization. For him, the personal truly was the political. He therefore made himself the main object of investigation. What makes him great is that, unlike so many of his bourgeois contemporaries, he never slipped into solipsism or aestheticism. Instead of becoming an aesthete, he remained a keen intellectual, a *philosophe* or *citoyen* in the sense of the Enlightenment, interested in everything around him and placing himself at the center of society. His subjective experiences are thus seen in the light of larger political, social, philosophical, aesthetic, and even economic developments, which makes them objective in a general historical sense without reifying them.

This intention is discernable in Heine's very earliest writing—he sees himself as an outsider *and* representative at the same time. Born in Düsseldorf—in all probability in 1797—the son of a Jewish textile merchant, he grew up in an atmosphere of admiration for all things French as embodied in the figure of Napoleon Bonaparte, the great liberator (especially for the Jews).

In contrast to this liberal spirit, Heine was exposed during his early student years to the more reactionary side of German Romanticism through August Wilhelm von Schlegel and other members of the Romantic school. Ultimately Heine went on to study with Hegel in Berlin, thus acquiring an entirely new outlook on history, philosophy, and aesthetics. Even his early work, apart from his rather conventional lyric poetry and his two tragedies, is therefore characterized by an extremely stimulating mixture of philosophical ideas, learned quotations, keen social observations, aesthetic reflections, lapses into brooding melancholy, snide remarks about the ruling classes, open hatred for German chauvinism, sarcastic comments about other writers, and a variety of other ingredients, resulting at times in a peculiar potpourri of mutually illuminating elements. Like most brilliantly talented young men, Heine wanted to express everything all at once in these writings. In this respect he goes far beyond the fragmentarism of the Romantics. He shunned in his early writing the pseudoreligious universalism of most of his contemporaries, primarily because of his familiarity with the Hegelian precept that everything is connected with everything else and can be judged only in its dialectical interrelationships. Especially in his journalistic pieces from this early period— such as the *Letters from Berlin* of 1822—Heine touches upon virtually everything of note at the time in the sphere of politics, society, and culture.

In the 1820s, Heine was a man on the move. He traveled to all parts of Germany, from Alps to ocean, and also to Poland, England, Italy, and finally France. He yielded fully to all new impressions, simultaneously reflecting upon them, trying to see everything in its proper social and political context, and putting all his thoughts down on paper in a series of serious yet highly amusing travel sketches. Apart from the *Book of Songs,* which came out in 1827, his most important publications during this period are the four volumes of *Travel Sketches* [*Reisebilder*] (1826–32), which contain, among other things, *The Harz Journey* and *Ideas— Book Le Grand,* works that made him famous overnight.

After Heine arrived in Paris in 1831, where he remained for the rest of his life, the so-called poetic elements in his works diminished for a while. The next ten years were devoted mainly to political and philosophical debates, resulting in a series of long essays and monographs replete with theoretical reflections. These works comprise the major part of the second volume of Heine's writings in this series. In them Heine finally overcomes his limitations as a German and a Jew and develops into a figure of international stature, recognized by friend and foe alike as one of the most influential writers in the field of aesthetic, intellectual, and political debate. His involvement with day-to-day politics led, perhaps unavoidably, to spectacular feuds with other authors and the authorities, in which Heine honed his already highly developed polemical and satirical style into a lethal weapon.

During these altercations, which reached a peak in his *Börne* book of 1840, Heine became increasingly aware that he should not neglect his poetic production merely because of such vicissitudes. He therefore returned in the early 1840s, almost unexpectedly, to poetry and even verse epics, demonstrating two things to his amazed contemporaries: first, that he was still the leading poet of his time; second, that even political polemics can be expressed in a highly poetic manner. The best proof of the truth of these assertions is his poetic masterwork, *Germany: A Winter's Tale,* of 1844, a work filled with personal invective against political enemies, realistic travel sketches, and, at the same time, fictional elements, and even visions and dreams. This work is journalism and poetry, politics and fiction, detached irony and unrestrained involvement all at once. *A Winter's Tale* is a work whose quality can only be described in seemingly contradictory terms, for underlying it is a love-hate relationship with Germany that remains unresolved to the end—and to the end of Heine's life. It is the only work from this period that presents the concept of the German *misère* developed by Marx and Engels during the same years. Their concept of German *misère,* along with Heine's *A Winter's Tale,* established a model for leftist criticism of German backwardness—a model still useful for Heinrich Mann's *Untertan* (1918), Tucholsky's *Deutschland, Deutschland über alles* (1929), or Brecht's *The Private Life of the Master Race* (1938).

In the final ten years of his life, Heine continued writing in almost every imaginable form, though he produced relatively little. Apart from some extremely interesting autobiographical statements, what stands out during this period, when he was increasingly bedridden due to an incurable illness, are his last poems, many of which are reprinted in this volume. There is a tone of sadness, of nearness to death, in these poems that is unique in German literature of the nineteenth century. But instead of succumbing to sadness and only lamenting his pains, his increasing blindness, and his general disability, Heine fills even his last poems with his accustomed rebelliousness, wit, and sarcasm. Even now he does not shy away from attacking his old enemies: aristocrats, slave-traders, religious hypocrites, and all the other reactionary forces that conspire to make life so miserable for the poor, the outcast, and the oppressed.

Heine died in 1856, leaving a poetic legacy whose liberal spirit and poetic quality are (with the exception of Georg Büchner) unparalleled in German literature of the nineteenth century. For this reason, Heine is the sole German writer during the period between Goethe and Thomas Mann who has long been accepted in the canon of world literature. He is thus not an author who must be rescued from oblivion. The French, the English, the Italians, the Spaniards, the Americans, the Russians—all cherished his works as early as the second half of the nineteenth century and considered him a classic. But this canonization is fraught with certain dangers, since it tends to mummify him as an author. It is high time, therefore, to remove Heine from his pedestal and put him back into real life. He is not a high priest of poetry. On the contrary. He is an advocate of the immediacy of life, of political awareness, of constant struggle against the forces of reaction that ever seek to defend their privileges or expand their power. In this sense Heine is still one of us.

J.H.

Part One

LYRIC
POETRY

Die Grenadiere

Nach Frankreich zogen zwei Grenadier,
Die waren in Russland gefangen.
Und als sie kamen ins deutsche Quartier,
Sie liessen die Köpfe hangen.

Da hörten sie beide die traurige Mär:
Dass Frankreich verloren gegangen,
Besiegt und zerschlagen das grosse Heer—
Und der Kaiser, der Kaiser gefangen.

Da weinten zusammen die Grenadier
Wohl ob der kläglichen Kunde.
Der eine sprach: Wie weh wird mir,
Wie brennt meine alte Wunde!

Der andre sprach: Das Lied ist aus,
Auch ich möcht mit dir sterben,
Doch hab ich Weib und Kind zu Haus,
Die ohne mich verderben.

Was schert mich Weib, was schert mich Kind,
Ich trage weit bessres Verlangen;
Lass sie betteln gehn, wenn sie hungrig sind—
Mein Kaiser, mein Kaiser gefangen!

Gewähr mir, Bruder, eine Bitt:
Wenn ich jetzt sterben werde,
So nimm meine Leiche nach Frankreich mit,
Begrab mich in Frankreichs Erde.

Das Ehrenkreuz am roten Band
Sollst du aufs Herz mir legen;
Die Flinte gib mir in die Hand,
Und gürt mir um den Degen.

The Grenadiers

Toward France there wandered two grenadiers;
  In Russia they had been taken.
And as they reached the German frontiers,
  Body and spirit were shaken.

For there they learned the tragic tale
  That France had been lost and forsaken;
The Army had suffered to no avail,
  And the Emperor, the Emperor was taken!

They wept together, those two grenadiers;
  To one thing their thoughts kept returning.
Alas, said one, half choked with tears,
  That old wound of mine keeps burning.

The other said, This is the end;
  With you I'd gladly perish.
But there's the homeland to defend,
  And wife and child to cherish.

What matters wife? What matters child?
  With far greater cares I am shaken.
Let them go and beg with hunger wild.
  My Emperor, my Emperor is taken!

And, brother, this my only prayer,
  Now I am dying, grant me:
You'll bear my body to France, and there
  In the soil of France you'll plant me.

The cross of honor with crimson band
  Lay on my heart that bound me;
Then put the musket in my hand
  And strap my saber round me.

So will ich liegen und horchen still,
Wie eine Schildwach, im Grabe,
Bis einst ich höre Kanonengebrüll
Und wiehernder Rosse Getrabe.

Dann reitet mein Kaiser wohl über mein Grab,
Viel Schwerter klirren und blitzen;
Dann steig ich gewaffnet hervor aus dem Grab—
Den Kaiser, den Kaiser zu schützen.

Die Welt ist dumm, die Welt ist blind,
Wird täglich abgeschmackter!
Sie spricht von dir, mein schönes Kind,
Du hast keinen guten Charakter.

Die Welt ist dumm, die Welt ist blind,
Und dich wird sie immer verkennen;
Sie weiss nicht, wie süss deine Küsse sind,
Und wie sie beseligend brennen.

Ein Fichtenbaum steht einsam
Im Norden auf kahler Höh.
Ihn schläfert; mit weisser Decke
Umhüllen ihn Eis und Schnee.

Er träumt von einer Palme,
Die, fern im Morgenland,
Einsam und schweigend trauert
Auf brennender Felsenwand.

Then I will lie and listen and wait,
  A sentinel, down in the grass there,
Till I hear the roar of the guns and the great
  Thunder of hoofs as they pass there.

The Emperor will come and the columns will wave;
  The swords will be flashing and rending;
And I will arise, full-armed, from the grave,
  My Emperor, my Emperor defending!

Translated by Louis Untermeyer

The world is dumb, the world is blind,
I see it daily worsen;
It says of you and of your kind
You're not so refined a person.

The world is dumb, the world is blind
To your way of being and living;
Instead of your kisses, it judges your mind,
Unaware of the bliss you're giving.

Translated by Felix Pollak

A spruce is standing lonely
In the north on a barren height.
It drowses; ice and snowflakes
Wrap it in a blanket of white.

It dreams about a palm tree
In a distant, eastern land,
That languishes lonely and silent
Upon the scorching sand.

Translated by Max Knight

Ein Jüngling liebt ein Mädchen,
Die hat einen andern erwählt;
Der andre liebt eine andre,
Und hat sich mit dieser vermählt.

Das Mädchen heiratet aus Ärger
Den ersten besten Mann,
Der ihr in den Weg gelaufen;
Der Jüngling ist übel dran.

Es ist eine alte Geschichte,
Doch bleibt sie immer neu;
Und wem sie just passieret,
Dem bricht das Herz entzwei.

Sie sassen und tranken am Teetisch,
Und sprachen von Liebe viel.
Die Herren die waren ästhetisch,
Die Damen von zartem Gefühl.

Die Liebe muss sein platonisch,
Der dürre Hofrat sprach.
Die Hofrätin lächelt ironisch,
Und dennoch seufzet sie: Ach!

Der Domherr öffnet den Mund weit:
Die Liebe sei nicht zu roh,
Sie schadet sonst der Gesundheit.
Das Fräulein lispelt: Wie so?

Die Gräfin spricht wehmütig:
Die Liebe ist eine Passion!
Und präsentieret gütig
Die Tasse dem Herren Baron.

A young man loves a maiden,
　Whose heart for another has yearned;
This other loves another
　By whom his love is returned.

The maiden weds in anger
　The first good man she espies
Who runs into her pathway;
　The youth grows bitter and wise.

It is an old, old story
　But one that's always new;
And every time it happens
　It breaks a heart in two.

Translated by Louis Untermeyer

They drank tea and waxed theoretic
About love and its sinful allure;
The gentlemen stressed the aesthetic,
The ladies were all for *l'amour.*

Love must be strictly Platonic,
The emaciated Councilor cried.
His spouse smiled slightly ironic,
And murmured, Oh dear me! and sighed.

The Prelate shrieked like a buzzard,
Love must not be rough, don't you know,
Or else it becomes a health hazard!
The little miss whispered, How so?

The Countess sighed soulful and tender.
True love is a passion, she trilled,
As with a sweet smile of surrender
The Baron's cup she refilled.

Am Tische war noch ein Plätzchen;
Mein Liebchen, da hast du gefehlt.
Du hättest so hübsch, mein Schätzchen,
Von deiner Liebe erzählt.

Ich weiss nicht was soll es bedeuten,
Dass ich so traurig bin;
Ein Märchen aus alten Zeiten,
Das kommt mir nicht aus dem Sinn.

Die Luft ist kühl und es dunkelt,
Und ruhig fliesst der Rhein;
Der Gipfel des Berges funkelt
Im Abendsonnenschein.

Die schönste Jungfrau sitzet
Dort oben wunderbar;
Ihr goldnes Geschmeide blitzet,
Sie kämmt ihr goldenes Haar.

Sie kämmt es mit goldenem Kamme
Und singt ein Lied dabei;
Das hat eine wundersame,
Gewaltige Melodei.

Den Schiffer im kleinen Schiffe
Ergreift es mit wildem Weh;
Er schaut nicht die Felsenriffe,
Er schaut nur hinauf in die Höh.

Ich glaube, die Wellen verschlingen
Am Ende Schiffer und Kahn;
Und das hat mit ihrem Singen
Die Lore-Ley getan.

There was still a place at the table,
That should have been yours, my dove;
You'd have been so eager and able
To tell them about your love.

Translated by Felix Pollak

I don't know the reason why
I should be feeling so sad;
A tale of times gone by
Keeps running through my head.

The air is cool, day is sinking,
And quiet flows the Rhine;
The mountain peak is glinting
In the evening's parting shine.

The loveliest maiden is sitting
Above there, wondrously fair;
Her golden jewels aglitter,
She is combing her golden hair.

The comb she is holding is golden,
She is singing a song so weird,
So eerie and so bold,
As never an ear has heard.

In his little craft the boatman
Is seized by a woeful love;
He sees not the cliffs approaching,
His eyes are fastened above.

I fancy the waves will cover
Both boatman and boat before long;
And that was done to her lover
By the Lorelei and her song.

Translated by Felix Pollak

Mein Herz, mein Herz ist traurig,
Doch lustig leuchtet der Mai;
Ich stehe, gelehnt an der Linde,
Hoch auf der alten Bastei.

Da drunten fliesst der blaue
Stadtgraben in stiller Ruh;
Ein Knabe fährt im Kahne,
Und angelt und pfeift dazu.

Jenseits erheben sich freundlich,
In winziger, bunter Gestalt,
Lusthäuser, und Gärten, und Menschen,
Und Ochsen, und Wiesen, und Wald.

Die Mägde bleichen Wäsche,
Und springen im Gras herum:
Das Mühlrad stäubt Diamanten,
Ich höre sein fernes Gesumm.

Am alten grauen Turme
Ein Schilderhäuschen steht;
Ein rotgeröckter Bursche
Dort auf und nieder geht.

Er spielt mit seiner Flinte,
Die funkelt im Sonnenrot,
Er präsentiert und schultert—
Ich wollt, er schösse mich tot.

My heart, my heart is saddened,
But May glows joyously,
I lean at the high old bastion
Against a linden tree.

Below me the blue waters
Flow gently in the moat.
A boy is fishing and whistling,
Leisurely rowing his boat.

And colorful in the distance,
Friendly and small, one sees
Cottages, gardens, and people,
And oxen, and meadows, and trees.

In the grass some maids bleach laundry
Joyful and frolicsome.
The mill wheel sprays clear diamonds,
I hear its distant hum.

There's a sentry box by the tower
That's gray and of old renown;
A lad with a scarlet tunic
Is pacing up and down.

He's playing with his rifle,
It shines in the sun so red,
He shoulders and presents it—
I wish he would shoot me dead.

Translated by Max Knight

Still ist die Nacht, es ruhen die Gassen,
In diesem Hause wohnte mein Schatz;
Sie hat schon längst die Stadt verlassen,
Doch steht noch das Haus auf demselben Platz.

Da steht auch ein Mensch und starrt in die Höhe,
Und ringt die Hände, vor Schmerzensgewalt;
Mir graust es, wenn ich sein Antlitz sehe—
Der Mond zeigt mir meine eigne Gestalt.

Du Doppeltgänger! du bleicher Geselle!
Was äffst du nach mein Liebesleid,
Das mich gequält auf dieser Stelle,
So manche Nacht, in alter Zeit?

Und als ich euch meine Schmerzen geklagt,
Da habt ihr gegähnt und nichts gesagt;
Doch als ich sie zierlich in Verse gebracht,
Da habt ihr mir grosse Elogen gemacht.

Du bist wie eine Blume,
So hold und schön und rein;
Ich schau dich an, und Wehmut
Schleicht mir ins Herz hinein.

Mir ist, als ob ich die Hände
Aufs Haupt dir legen sollt,
Betend, dass Gott dich erhalte
So rein und schön und hold.

The night is calm; the streets quiet down;
Here lived a lass who was dear to me.
Long years ago she left the town,
But here is her house, as it used to be.

And here is a creature who stares into space
And wrings his hands in a storm of pain.
I shudder when I see his face:
It is my own self the moon shows plain.

You double! You comrade ghostly white!
Why have you come to ape the woe
That tortured me, night after night,
Under these windows—long ago?

Translated by Aaron Kramer

And when my woes I did report,
You yawned and did not say a word;
But when I put them in fancy rhymes,
You called me the laureate of all times.

Translated by Felix Pollak

You're lovely as a flower,
So pure and fair to see;
I look at you, and sadness
Comes stealing over me.

I feel my hands should gently
Cover your head in prayer—
That God may always keep you
So lovely, pure, and fair.

Translated by Aaron Kramer

Und bist du erst mein ehlich Weib,
Dann bist du zu beneiden,
Dann lebst du in lauter Zeitvertreib,
In lauter Pläsier und Freuden.

Und wenn du schiltst und wenn du tobst,
Ich werd es geduldig leiden;
Doch wenn du meine Verse nicht lobst,
Lass ich mich von dir scheiden.

Die Götter Griechenlands

Vollblühender Mond! In deinem Licht,
Wie fliessendes Gold, erglänzt das Meer;
Wie Tagesklarheit, doch dämmrig verzaubert,
Liegts über der weiten Strandesfläche;
Und am hellblaun, sternlosen Himmel
Schweben die weissen Wolken,
Wie kolossale Götterbilder
Von leuchtendem Marmor.

Nein, nimmermehr, das sind keine Wolken!
Das sind sie selber, die Götter von Hellas,
Die einst so freudig die Welt beherrschten,
Doch jetzt, verdrängt und verstorben,
Als ungeheure Gespenster dahinziehn
Am mitternächtlichen Himmel.

Staunend, und seltsam geblendet, betracht ich
Das luftige Pantheon,
Die feierlich stummen, graunhaft bewegten
Riesengestalten.
Der dort ist Kronion, der Himmelskönig,
Schneeweiss sind die Locken des Haupts,
Die berühmten, olymposerschütternden Locken.

Once you become my wedded wife,
Ah! Then you'll envied be;
You'll lead the very merriest life,
All jest and jollity.

And should you scold and fume, or worse,
I'll keep a patient heart;
But should you fail to praise my verse,
Then you and I must part!

Translated by Robert Levy

The Gods of Greece

Full-blooming moon! In your light,
Like flowing gold, sparkles the sea;
Like clearness of day, yet dimly enchanted,
It lies on the level expanse of bay;
And in the clear blue, starless heaven
Hover the white clouds,
Like colossal figures of gods
In shining marble.

No, no longer, those are no clouds.
Those are they themselves, the gods of Hellas,
Who once so joyfully ruled the world.
But now, driven out and wasted in death,
As huge apparitions wander away
In the midnight heaven.

Marveling and strangely dazzled, I watch
The airy Pantheon,
The solemnly mute, horribly stirred,
Gigantic shapes.
He there is Cronos, the king of heaven,
Snow-white are the locks of his head,
The renowned, Olympus-shaking locks.

Er hält in der Hand den erloschenen Blitz,
In seinem Antlitz liegt Unglück und Gram,
Und doch noch immer der alte Stolz.
Das waren bessere Zeiten, o Zeus,
Als du dich himmlisch ergötztest
An Knaben und Nymphen und Hekatomben;
Doch auch die Götter regieren nicht ewig,
Die jungen verdrängen die alten,
Wie du einst selber den greisen Vater
Und deine Titanen-Öhme verdrängt hast,
Jupiter Parricida!
Auch dich erkenn ich, stolze Juno!
Trotz all deiner eifersüchtigen Angst,
Hat doch eine andre das Zepter gewonnen,
Und du bist nicht mehr die Himmelskönigin,
Und dein grosses Aug ist erstarrt,
Und deine Liljenarme sind kraftlos,
Und nimmermehr trifft deine Rache
Die gottbefruchtete Jungfrau
Und den wundertätigen Gottessohn.
Auch dich erkenn ich, Pallas Athene!
Mit Schild und Weisheit konntest du nicht
Abwehren das Götterverderben?
Auch dich erkenn ich, auch dich, Aphrodite,
Einst die goldene! jetzt die silberne!
Zwar schmückt dich noch immer des Gürtels Liebreiz,
Doch graut mir heimlich vor deiner Schönheit,
Und wollt mich beglücken dein gütiger Leib,
Wie andere Helden, ich stürbe vor Angst—
Als Leichengöttin erscheinst du mir,
Venus Libitina!
Nicht mehr mit Liebe blickt nach dir,
Dort, der schreckliche Ares.
Es schaut so traurig Phöbos Apollo,
Der Jüngling. Es schweigt seine Leir,
Die so freudig erklungen beim Göttermahl.
Noch trauriger schaut Hephaistos,
Und wahrlich, der Hinkende! nimmermehr

He holds in his hand the extinguished lightning,
In his countenance lurk misfortune and grief,
And yet still ever the ancient pride.
Those were better times, O Zeus,
When you delighted yourself in heaven,
With boys and nymphs and hecatombs;
Yet even the gods rule not forever,
The young drive out the old,
As you yourself the hoary father
And your Titan-mother drove out,
Jupiter Parricida!
You, too, I recognize, haughty Juno!
In spite of all your jealous fear
Another has won the scepter,
And you are no longer the queen of heaven,
And your great eye is frozen,
And your lily arms are powerless,
And nevermore your vengeance pursues
The god-impregnated virgin
And the wonder-working son of the god.
You, too, I recognize, Pallas Athene!
Could you not, then, with shield and wisdom,
Ward off the decay of the gods?
You, too, I see there, you, too, Aphrodite,
Once the golden one, now the silver one!
Indeed still adorns you the girdle's love charm,
Yet I shudder secretly at your beauty,
And if your good body desired to delight me,
Like other heroes, I would die of anguish—
As corpse-goddess you appear to me,
Venus Libitina!
No more with love looks toward you
There, the terrible Ares.
There gazes so mournfully Phoebus Apollo,
The youth. His lyre is silent
That played with such joy at the meal of the gods.
More mournfully still gazes Hephäestus,
And in truth nevermore the lame one

Fällt er Heben ins Amt,
Und schenkt geschäftig, in der Versammlung,
Den lieblichen Nektar—Und längst ist erloschen
Das unauslöschliche Göttergelächter.

Ich hab euch niemals geliebt, ihr Götter!
Denn widerwärtig sind mir die Griechen,
Und gar die Römer sind mir verhasst.
Doch heilges Erbarmen und schauriges Mitleid
Durchströmt mein Herz,
Wenn ich euch jetzt da droben schaue,
Verlassene Götter,
Tote, nachtwandelnde Schatten,
Nebelschwache, die der Wind verscheucht—
Und wenn ich bedenke, wie feig und windig
Die Götter sind, die euch besiegten,
Die neuen, herrschenden, tristen Götter,
Die schadenfrohen im Schafspelz der Demut—
O, da fasst mich ein düsterer Groll,
Und brechen möcht ich die neuen Tempel,
Und kämpfen für euch, ihr alten Götter,
Für euch und eur gutes, ambrosisches Recht,
Und vor euren hohen Altären,
Den wiedergebauten, den opferdampfenden,
Möcht ich selber knieen und beten,
Und flehend die Arme erheben—

Denn immerhin, ihr alten Götter,
Habt ihrs auch ehmals, in Kämpfen der Menschen,
Stets mit der Partei der Sieger gehalten,
So ist doch der Mensch grossmütger als ihr,
Und in Götterkämpfen halt ich es jetzt
Mit der Partei der besiegten Götter.
Also sprach ich, und sichtbar erröteten
Droben die blassen Wolkengestalten,
Und schauten mich an wie Sterbende,
Schmerzenverklärt, und schwanden plötzlich.

Assumes the office of Hebe
And busily pours, in the assembly,
The lovely nectar. And long is extinguished
The inextinguishable laughter of gods.

You I have never loved, you gods!
For contrary to me are the Greeks,
And even the Romans to me are hateful.
Yet holy compassion and shuddering pity
Stream through my heart
As I watch you now, up there,
Abandoned gods,
Dead, night-wandering shadows,
Mist-frail, that the wind in terror scatters,
And when I consider how cowardly and windy
Are the gods who conquered you,
The new, ruling, wistful gods,
The malicious ones in humility's sheepskin—
Oh, then a gloomy resentment seizes me,
And then I could break the new temples,
And fight for you, you ancient gods,
For you and your good, ambrosial right,
And before your lofty altars,
All built again, all smoking with sacrifice,
I myself could kneel and pray
And lift up my arms beseeching—

For always, far back, you ancient gods,
In earlier times, in battles of men
You constantly held to the side of the victors.
So man is, then, more generous than you,
And now in battles of gods I hold
To the side of the vanquished gods.
So I spoke, and visibly flushed
Up there, the pallid cloud shapes,
And looked at me like dying ones,
Transfigured with pain, and vanished suddenly.

Der Mond verbarg sich eben
Hinter Gewölk, das dunkler heranzog;
Hochaufrauschte das Meer,
Und siegreich traten hervor am Himmel
Die ewigen Sterne.

Fragen

Am Meer, am wüsten, nächtlichen Meer
Steht ein Jüngling-Mann,
Die Brust voll Wehmut, das Haupt voll Zweifel,
Und mit düstern Lippen fragt er die Wogen:

"O löst mir das Rätsel des Lebens,
Das qualvoll uralte Rätsel,
Worüber schon manche Häupter gegrübelt,
Häupter in Hieroglyphenmützen,
Häupter in Turban and schwarzem Barett,
Perückenhäupter und tausend andre
Arme, schwitzende Menschenhäupter—
Sagt mir, was bedeutet der Mensch?
Woher ist er kommen? Wo geht er hin?
Wer wohnt dort oben auf goldenen Sternen?"

Es murmeln die Wogen ihr ewges Gemurmel,
Es wehet der Wind, es fliehen die Wolken,
Es blinken die Sterne, gleichgültig und kalt,
Und ein Narr wartet auf Antwort.

The moon hid itself now
Behind thick clouds that loomed darkly nearer.
Loud rose the rushing sound of the sea,
And victorious stood forth in the heavens
The eternal stars.

Translated by Vernon Watkins

Questions

By the sea, by the desolate nocturnal sea,
Stands a youthful man,
His breast full of sadness, his head full of doubt.
And with bitter lips he questions the waves:

"Oh, solve me the riddle of life!
The cruel, world-old riddle,
Concerning which already many a head hath been racked.
Heads in hieroglyphic hats,
Heads in turbans and in black caps,
Periwigged heads, and a thousand other
Poor, sweating human heads.
Tell me, what signifies man?
Whence does he come? Whither does he go?
Who dwells yonder above the golden stars?"

The waves murmur their eternal murmur,
The winds blow, the clouds flow past.
Cold and indifferent twinkle the stars,
And a fool awaits an answer.

Translated by Emma Lazarus

Himmlisch wars, wenn ich bezwang
Meine sündige Begier,
Aber wenns mir nicht gelang,
Hatt ich doch ein gross Pläsier.

Auf diesem Felsen bauen wir
Die Kirche von dem dritten,
Dem dritten neuen Testament;
Das Leid ist ausgelitten.

Vernichtet ist das Zweierlei,
Das uns so lang betöret;
Die dumme Leiberquälerei
Hat endlich aufgehöret.

Hörst du den Gott im finstern Meer?
Mit tausend Stimmen spricht er.
Und siehst du über unserm Haupt
Die tausend Gotteslichter?

Der heilge Gott der ist im Licht
Wie in den Finsternissen;
Und Gott ist alles was da ist;
Er ist in unsern Küssen.

Das Fräulein stand am Meere
Und seufzte lang und bang,
Es rührte sie so sehre
Der Sonnenuntergang.

Mein Fräulein! sein Sie munter,
Das ist ein altes Stück;
Hier vorne geht sie unter
Und kehrt von hinten zurück.

It was heaven to abstain
And keep my sinful greed at bay;
But when my efforts were in vain,
I had great pleasure anyway.

Translated by Felix Pollak

Upon these rocks we'll build a church
To celebrate the splendid,
The third and final testament;
Our sufferings are ended.

Destroyed is the duality
That long has bound us fast;
The stupid torment of the flesh
Is flung aside at last.

Do you hear God's word in the darkened sea?
In a thousand voices He exclaims.
And can't you see above our heads
The thousand God-lit flames?

The holy Lord is in the light
And in the night's abysses;
And God is everything that is:
He throbs in our kisses.

Translated by Aaron Kramer

The young miss stood by the ocean
And sighed an anxious sigh;
She felt such deep emotion
Seeing the sunlight die.

My dear, it's an age-old number,
Don't let it weigh on your mind;
Here in front it goes under,
And wheels right back from behind.

Translated by Aaron Kramer

Wenn ich, beseligt von schönen Küssen,
In deinen Armen mich wohl befinde,
Dann musst du mir nie von Deutschland reden;—
Ich kanns nicht vertragen—es hat seine Gründe.

Ich bitte dich, lass mich mit Deutschland in Frieden!
Du musst mich nicht plagen mit ewigen Fragen
Nach Heimat, Sippschaft und Lebensverhältnis;—
Es hat seine Gründe—ich kanns nicht vertragen.

Die Eichen sind grün, und blau sind die Augen
Der deutschen Frauen; sie schmachten gelinde
Und seufzen von Liebe, Hoffnung und Glauben;—
Ich kanns nicht vertragen—es hat seine Gründe.

Schaff mich nicht ab, wenn auch den Durst
Gelöscht der holde Trunk;
Behalt mich noch ein Vierteljahr,
Dann hab auch ich genung.

Kannst du nicht mehr Geliebte sein,
Sei Freundin mir sodann;
Hat man die Liebe durchgeliebt,
Fängt man die Freundschaft an.

Jugend, die mir täglich schwindet,
Wird durch raschen Mut ersetzt,
Und mein kühnrer Arm umwindet
Noch viel schlankre Hüften jetzt.

Tat auch manche sehr erschrocken,
Hat sie doch sich bald gefügt;
Holder Zorn, verschämtes Stocken
Wird von Schmeichelei besiegt.

When in your arms and in our kisses
   I find love's sweet and happiest season,
My Germany you must never mention—
   I cannot bear it: there is a reason.

Oh, silence your chatter on anything German;
   You must not plague me or ask me to share it.
Be still when you think of my home or my kindred—
   There is a reason: I cannot bear it.

The oaks are green, and the German women
   Have smiling eyes that know no treason;
They speak of love and faith and honor.
   I cannot bear it: there is a reason.

Translated by Louis Untermeyer

Don't send me off, now that your thirst
   Is quenched, and all seems stale to you;
Keep me a short three months or more,
   Then I'll be sated, too.

If now you will not be my love
   Then try to be my friend;
Friendship is something that may come
   When love comes to an end.

Translated by Louis Untermeyer

Youth is leaving me; but daily
   By new courage it's replaced;
And my bold arm circles gaily
   Many a young and slender waist.

Some were shocked and others pouted;
   Some grew wroth—but none denied.
Flattery has always routed
   Lovely shame and stubborn pride.

Doch, wenn ich den Sieg geniesse,
Fehlt das Beste mir dabei.
Ist es die verschwundne, süsse,
Blöde Jugendeselei?

Der Tannhäuser

1

Ihr guten Christen, lasst Euch nicht
Von Satans List umgarnen!
Ich sing Euch das Tannhäuserlied,
Um Eure Seelen zu warnen.

Der edle Tannhäuser, ein Ritter gut,
Wollt Lieb und Lust gewinnen,
Da zog er in den Venusberg,
Blieb sieben Jahre drinnen.

Frau Venus, meine schöne Frau,
Leb wohl, mein holdes Leben!
Ich will nicht länger bleiben bei dir,
Du sollst mir Urlaub geben.

"Tannhäuser, edler Ritter mein,
Hast heut mich nicht geküsset;
Küss mich geschwind, und sage mir:
Was du bei mir vermisset?

Habe ich nicht den süssesten Wein
Tagtäglich dir kredenzet?
Und hab ich nicht mit Rosen dir
Tagtäglich das Haupt bekränzet?"

Yet the best is gone. Too late, I'd
　　Give my soul for it, in truth.
Can it be the blundering, great-eyed,
　　Sweet stupidity of youth?

Translated by Louis Untermeyer

Tannhäuser

1

Good Christians, beware of Satan, the fiend,
　　The wily advocate!
I'm going to sing you the Tannhäuser song,
　　An earnest *caveat.*

Tannhäuser dreamed, the noble knight,
　　Of love and how to win it,
So into the mountain of Venus he moved,
　　And for seven years stayed in it.

O Venus, my dear and precious love,
　　Farewell, I'm leaving your nest!
I don't want to stay any longer with you,
　　You ought to grant me some rest.

Tannhäuser, noble knight of mine,
　　You haven't kissed me today!
Come, kiss me quickly and tell me straight
　　How I've caused your dismay.

Haven't I daily the sweetest wine
　　Poured you with loving care?
And haven't I daily with roses red
　　Adorned your fragrant hair?

Frau Venus, meine schöne Frau,
Von süssem Wein und Küssen
Ist meine Seele geworden krank;
Ich schmachte nach Bitternissen.

Wir haben zuviel gescherzt und gelacht,
Ich sehne mich nach Tränen,
Und statt mit Rosen möcht ich mein Haupt
Mit spitzigen Dornen krönen.

"Tannhäuser, edler Ritter mein,
Du willst dich mit mir zanken;
Du hast geschworen viel tausendmal,
Niemals von mir zu wanken.

Komm, lass uns in die Kammer gehn,
Zu spielen der heimlichen Minne;
Mein schöner liljenweisser Leib
Erheitert deine Sinne."

Frau Venus, meine schöne Frau,
Dein Reiz wird ewig blühen;
Wie viele einst für dich geglüht,
So werden noch viele glühen.

Doch denk ich der Götter und Helden, die einst
Sich zärtlich daran geweidet,
Dein schöner liljenweisser Leib,
Er wird mir schier verleidet.

Dein schöner liljenweisser Leib
Erfüllt mich fast mit Entsetzen,
Gedenk ich, wie viele werden sich
Noch späterhin dran ergetzen!

"Tannhäuser, edler Ritter mein,
Das sollst du mir nicht sagen,
Ich wollte lieber, du schlügest mich,
Wie du mich oft geschlagen.

O Venus, my dear and precious love,
Your sweet wines and caresses
Have made my soul quite gravely ill;
I'm yearning for bitternesses.

We have joked too much and laughed too much,
I'm longing for one who adorns,
Instead of with roses fragrant and soft,
My head with a crown of thorns.

Tannhäuser, noble knight of mine,
I fear you want to grieve me;
You've sworn to me a thousand times,
Never to up and leave me.

Come, let us go to the little room
And be each the other's lover;
My beautiful and lily-white limbs
Will soon your sense recover.

O Venus, my dear and precious love,
Your charms will be always enchanting;
So many have often yearned for you,
Now others won't be wanting.

But when I think of the heroes and gods,
With whom you in past times were lusting,
Your beautiful and lily-white limbs
Become to me nearly disgusting.

Your beautiful and lily-white limbs
Fill me with a virtual dread,
When I imagine how many will
Possess and caress them yet!

Tannhäuser, noble knight of mine,
Don't say such words to me.
I'd rather you beat me, as you often have,
When you laid me across your knee.

Ich wollte lieber, du schlügest mich,
Als dass du Beleidigung sprächest,
Und mir, undankbar kalter Christ,
Den Stolz im Herzen brächest.

Weil ich dich geliebet gar zu sehr,
Hör ich nun solche Worte—
Leb wohl, ich gebe Urlaub dir,
Ich öffne dir selber die Pforte."

2

Zu Rom, zu Rom, in der heiligen Stadt,
Da singt es und klingelt und läutet:
Da zieht einher die Prozession,
Der Papst in der Mitte schreitet.

Das ist der fromme Papst Urban,
Er trägt die dreifache Krone,
Er trägt ein rotes Purpurgewand,
Die Schleppe tragen Barone.

"O heiliger Vater, Papst Urban,
Ich lass dich nicht von der Stelle,
Du hörest zuvor meine Beichte an,
Du rettest mich von der Hölle!"

Das Volk es weicht im Kreis zurück,
Es schweigen die geistlichen Lieder:—
Wer ist der Pilger bleich und wüst,
Vor dem Papste kniet er nieder?

"O heiliger Vater, Papst Urban,
Du kannst ja binden und lösen,
Errette mich von der Höllenqual
Und von der Macht des Bösen.

Rather than take your insults in stride,
I wish you'd break me apart;
But, cold and ungrateful Christian, don't try
To break the pride in my heart!

Because I've loved you all too much,
I am now being hurt to the core.
All right, I'll give you the leave you crave,
I'll show you myself to the door.

2

In Rome, in Rome, the holy place,
There's singing, bell-ringing, loud banter;
A pious procession is moving along,
The Pope astride in the center.

He is the holy Pope Urban,
The three-tiered crown on his head;
Barons are carrying his velvet train,
His robes are purple and red.

O Holy Father, Pope Urban,
Pray stop and briefly dwell;
I beseech you, hear my confession right now,
And save my soul from hell!

The circle around the Pope draws back,
The sacred chants have ceased;
Who is this pilgrim so savage and pale,
Who kneels before the priest?

O Holy Father, Pope Urban,
You can ban and absolve from bans;
Oh, rescue me from the tortures of hell
And the Evil One's fiendish plans!

Ich bin der edle Tannhäuser genannt,
Wollt Lieb und Lust gewinnen,
Da zog ich in den Venusberg,
Blieb sieben Jahre drinnen.

Frau Venus ist eine schöne Frau,
Liebreizend und anmutreiche;
Wie Sonnenschein und Blumenduft
Ist ihre Stimme, die weiche.

Wie der Schmetterling flattert um eine Blum,
Am zarten Kelch zu nippen,
So flattert meine Seele stets
Um ihre Rosenlippen.

Ihr edles Gesicht umringeln wild
Die blühend schwarzen Locken;
Schaun dich die grossen Augen an,
Wird dir der Atem stocken.

Schaun dich die grossen Augen an,
So bist du wie angekettet;
Ich habe nur mit grosser Not
Mich aus dem Berg gerettet.

Ich hab mich gerettet aus dem Berg,
Doch stets verfolgen die Blicke
Der schönen Frau mich überall,
Sie winken: komm zurücke!

Ein armes Gespenst bin ich am Tag,
Des Nachts mein Leben erwachet,
Dann träum ich von meiner schönen Frau,
Sie sitzt bei mir und lachet.

Sie lacht so gesund, so glücklich, so toll,
Und mit so weissen Zähnen!
Wenn ich an dieses Lachen denk,
So weine ich plötzliche Tränen.

I am Tannhäuser, a knight, who dreamed
Of love and how to win it,
So into the mountain of Venus I moved,
And for seven years stayed in it.

My Venus is a beautiful girl,
Enchanting, yet graced with poise;
Like sunshine, like a flower's sweet scent
Is her melodious voice.

As the butterfly flutters about a bud
And into its nectar dips,
So my soul must forever flutter about
Her tempting rosebud lips.

Framing her noble face, behold
Dark locks in wild array;
When her big eyes are looking at you,
They take your breath away.

When her big eyes are looking at you,
You've lost your liberty;
It took me years and all my might
From that magic mountain to flee.

I finally did from that mountain escape,
Yet I'm still on the rack,
For those eyes are pursuing me everywhere
And call to me, Come back!

By day, I am a mere poor ghost,
My life begins at night;
Then I dream of a beautiful girl,
Who sits laughing at my side.

Her laugh is so healthy, so happy, so free,
Her teeth are white as snow;
When I think of that laughter, my tears
Are suddenly starting to flow.

Ich liebe sie mit Allgewalt,
Nichts kann die Liebe hemmen!
Das ist wie ein wilder Wasserfall,
Du kannst seine Fluten nicht dämmen;

Er springt von Klippe zu Klippe herab,
Mit lautem Tosen und Schäumen,
Und bräch er tausendmal den Hals,
Er wird im Laufe nicht säumen.

Wenn ich den ganzen Himmel besäss,
Frau Venus schenkt ich ihn gerne;
Ich gäb ihr die Sonne, ich gäb ihr den Mond,
Ich gäbe ihr sämtliche Sterne.

Ich liebe sie mit Allgewalt,
Mit Flammen, die mich verzehren,—
Ist das der Hölle Feuer schon,
Die Gluten, die ewig währen?

O heiliger Vater, Papst Urban,
Du kannst ja binden und lösen!
Errette mich von der Höllenqual
Und von der Macht des Bösen."

Der Papst hub jammernd die Händ empor,
Hub jammernd an zu sprechen:
"Tannhäuser, unglückselger Mann,
Der Zauber ist nicht zu brechen.

Der Teufel, den man Venus nennt,
Er ist der Schlimmste von allen;
Erretten kann ich dich nimmermehr
Aus seinen schönen Krallen.

Mit deiner Seele musst du jetzt
Des Fleisches Lust bezahlen,
Du bist verworfen, du bist verdammt
Zu ewigen Höllenqualen."

I love her wildly, with all my heart,
Such love no one can stem;
It is like the flood of a waterfall
That will break through every dam.

It cascades down from rock to rock,
With roaring and with boiling,
It may break its neck a thousand times,
It keeps on foaming and toiling.

If all the heavens were my own,
I'd give them to Venus with pleasure;
I'd give her the sun, I'd give her the moon,
I'd give her the stars beyond measure.

My love is consuming me, body and soul,
With flames that are burning infernal!
Are these already the fires of hell,
The blaze that is blazing eternal?

O Holy Father, Pope Urban,
You can ban and absolve from bans;
Oh, rescue me from the tortures of hell
And the Evil One's fiendish plans!

The Pope deploringly raised his hands,
His words were deploringly spoken:
Tannhäuser, most unfortunate man,
That magic cannot be broken.

The devil, whom as Venus we know,
Is the worst one who ever was;
Nevermore can I rescue you
From her cruel beautiful claws.

Now with your soul you have to pay
For all your fleshly vice!
Eternally damned to suffer hell's pains,
This is your heavy price.

3

Der Ritter Tannhäuser er wandelt so rasch,
Die Füsse die wurden ihm wunde.
Er kam zurück in den Venusberg
Wohl um die Mitternachtstunde.

Frau Venus erwachte aus dem Schlaf,
Ist schnell aus dem Bette gesprungen;
Sie hat mit ihrem weissen Arm
Den geliebten Mann umschlungen.

Aus ihrer Nase rann das Blut,
Den Augen die Tränen entflossen;
Sie hat mit Tränen und Blut das Gesicht
Des geliebten Mannes begossen.

Der Ritter legte sich ins Bett,
Er hat kein Wort gesprochen.
Frau Venus in die Küche ging,
Um ihm eine Suppe zu kochen.

Sie gab ihm Suppe, sie gab ihm Brot,
Sie wusch seine wunden Füsse,
Sie kämmte ihm das struppige Haar,
Und lachte dabei so süsse.

"Tannhäuser, edler Ritter mein,
Bist lange ausgeblieben,
Sag an, in welchen Landen du dich
So lange herumgetrieben?"

Frau Venus, meine schöne Frau,
Ich hab in Welschland verweilet;
Ich hatte Geschäfte in Rom und bin
Schnell wieder hierher geeilet.

3

The knight Tannhäuser traveled so fast,
His feet were bloody and sore;
It was well around midnight when he reached
The mountain of Venus once more.

Lady Venus awoke from sleep,
And sprang from her bed in haste:
She clasped the knight in her lily-white arms,
And they tenderly embraced.

Blood ran down from her nose, and tears
Fell from her eyes in a flood!
She drenched the face of her darling spouse
With a stream of tears and blood.

The knight spoke not a single word,
But lay down on the bed.
Into the kitchen Venus went
To fix him soup and bread.

She gave him soup, she gave him bread,
She washed his wounded feet.
She combed his bristly hair, and laughed
In a voice that was honey-sweet.

Tannhäuser, noble knight of mine,
How long you've been away!
Where've you been roving all this time?
In what far lands did you stay?

Lady Venus, my beautiful wife,
I had some business in Rome;
But just as soon as my work was done,
I left, and hurried home.

Auf sieben Hügeln ist Rom gebaut,
Die Tiber tut dorten fliessen;
Auch hab ich in Rom den Papst gesehn,
Der Papst er lässt dich grüssen.

Auf meinem Rückweg sah ich Florenz,
Bin auch durch Mailand gekommen,
Und bin alsdann mit raschem Mut
Die Schweiz hinaufgeklommen.

Und als ich über die Alpen zog,
Da fing es an zu schneien,
Die blauen Seen die lachten mich an,
Die Adler krächzen und schreien.

Und als ich auf dem Sankt-Gotthard stand,
Da hört ich Deutschland schnarchen;
Es schlief da unten in sanfter Hut
Von sechsunddreissig Monarchen.

In Schwaben besah ich die Dichterschul,
Gar liebe Geschöpfchen und Tröpfchen!
Auf kleinen Kackstühlchen sassen sie dort,
Fallhütchen auf den Köpfchen.

Zu Frankfurt kam ich am Schabbes an,
Und ass dort Schalet und Klöse;
Ihr habt die beste Religion,
Auch lieb ich das Gänsegekröse.

In Dresden sah ich einen Hund,
Der einst gehört zu den Bessern,
Doch fallen ihm jetzt die Zähne aus,
Er kann nur bellen und wässern.

Zu Weimar, dem Musenwitwensitz,
Da hört ich viel Klagen erheben,
Man weinte und jammerte: Goethe sei tot,
Und Eckermann sei noch am Leben!

Rome is built on seven hills;
You can see the Tiber flow.
I also saw the Pope in Rome,
He sends you a warm hello!

I passed through Florence, coming back,
And skirted Milan, too,
And then climbed over Switzerland
So fast I fairly flew.

And as I moved across the Alps,
The snow began to fall:
Blue lakes laughed up at me, I heard
The eagles croak and call.

And, standing on Saint Gotthard Peak,
I heard old Germany snore;
In the gentle guard of thirty-six kings
It was sleeping just as before.

I saw the Swabian poets' school,
Those darling little fools!
With caps upon their heads, they sat
On little toilet stools.

I got to Frankfurt on Saturday,
Ate *sholet* and dumplings there;
Not only is their religion best;
Their giblets, too, are rare.

In Dresden I saw a poor old dog
Who'd made quite a stir in his youth;
But now he can only bark and piss,
Having lost his one last tooth.

In Weimar, home of the widowed muse,
The moans were loud and long.
The people lamented: "Goethe is dead,
But Eckermann's going strong!"

Zu Potsdam vernahm ich ein lautes Geschrei—
Was gibt es? rief ich verwundert.
"Das ist der Gans in Berlin, der liest
Dort über das letzte Jahrhundert."

Zu Göttingen blüht die Wissenschaft,
Doch bringt sie keine Früchte.
Ich kam dort durch in stockfinstrer Nacht,
Sah nirgendswo ein Lichte.

Zu Celle im Zuchthaus sah ich nur
Hannoveraner—O Deutsche!
Uns fehlt ein Nationalzuchthaus
Und eine gemeinsame Peitsche!

Zu Hamburg frug ich: warum so sehr
Die Strassen stinken täten?
Doch Juden und Christen versicherten mir,
Das käme von den Fleeten.

Zu Hamburg, in der guten Stadt,
Wohnt mancher schlechte Geselle;
Und als ich auf die Börse kam,
Ich glaubte, ich wär noch in Celle.

Zu Hamburg sah ich Altona,
Ist auch eine schöne Gegend;
Ein andermal erzähl ich dir
Was mir alldort begegent.

In Potsdam I heard a noisy yell,
And cried: "What can it be?"
"It's Dr. Gans in Berlin; he speaks
On the eighteenth century."

Science blooms in Göttingen,
But every branch is bare;
I hurried through in pitch-black night—
Not a light shone anywhere.

Hanoverians fill the Celle jail;
O Germans—hear my call:
We need a *national* house of reform,
And one great whip for us all!

In Hamburg I asked: "How come the streets
Stink so? Is something dead?"
But Jews and Christians gently smiled:
"It's from the sewers," they said.

In Hamburg, in that worthy town,
Some evil creatures dwell.
And when I came along the bourse
I thought I was still in Celle.

In Hamburg I visited Altona,
—Now *that's* a place to see!
Some other time I'll let you know
What happened there to me.

Parts 1 and 2 translated by Felix Pollak
Part 3 translated by Aaron Kramer

Anno 1839

O, Deutschland, meine ferne Liebe,
Gedenk ich deiner, wein ich fast!
Das muntre Frankreich scheint mir trübe,
Das leichte Volk wird mir zur Last.

Nur der Verstand, so kalt und trocken,
Herrscht in dem witzigen Paris—
O, Narrheitsglöcklein, Glaubensglocken,
Wie klingelt ihr daheim so süss!

Höfliche Männer! Doch verdrossen
Geb ich den artgen Gruss zurück.—
Die Grobheit, die ich einst genossen
Im Vaterland, das war mein Glück!

Lächelnde Weiber! Plappern immer,
Wie Mühlenräder stets bewegt!
Da lob ich Deutschlands Frauenzimmer,
Das schweigend sich zu Bette legt.

Und alles dreht sich hier im Kreise,
Mit Ungestüm, wie 'n toller Traum!
Bei uns bleibt alles hübsch im Gleise,
Wie angenagelt, rührt sich kaum.

Mir ist, als hört ich fern erklingen
Nachtwächterhörner, sanft und traut;
Nachtwächterlieder hör ich singen,
Dazwischen Nachtigallenlaut.

Dem Dichter war so wohl daheime,
In Schildas teurem Eichenhain!
Dort wob ich meine zarten Reime
Aus Veilchenduft und Mondenschein.

Anno 1839

Germany, distant love of mine!
When I remember you, I pine.
Gay France is dull—this flippant folk
Bears down my spirit like a yoke.

In witty Paris nothing rules
But mind. O little bells of fools,
O bells of faith!—How dear, how sweet
You sound above the German street!

Courteous men! Yet I reply
To their *bonjour* with jaundiced eye.
The rudest treatment I was given
In Germany now seems like heaven.

These smiling women! Never still,
Forever churning—like a mill.
I'll take the German girls instead.
They never talk when they're in bed.

And here in France our whole life seems
To spin around like frenzied dreams.
At home all things are in a groove,
As though nailed down—they scarcely move.

From far away I seem to hear
Night-watchman bugles, soft and clear;
Night-watchman songs are sweetly ringing,
And far-off nightingales are singing.

At home, in Schilda's oaken grove,
How well the poet thrived! I wove
My tenderhearted verses there,
Of moonlight and of violet air.

Translated by Aaron Kramer

Doktrin

Schlage die Trommel und fürchte dich nicht,
Und küsse die Marketenderin!
Das ist die ganze Wissenschaft,
Das ist der Bücher tiefster Sinn.

Trommle die Leute aus dem Schlaf,
Trommle Reveille mit Jugendkraft,
Marschiere trommelnd immer voran,
Das ist die ganze Wissenschaft.

Das ist die Hegelsche Philosophie,
Das ist der Bücher tiefster Sinn!
Ich hab sie begriffen, weil ich gescheit,
Und weil ich ein guter Tambour bin.

Adam der Erste

Du schicktest mit dem Flammenschwert
Den himmlischen Gendarmen,
Und jagtest mich aus dem Paradies,
Ganz ohne Recht und Erbarmen!

Ich ziehe fort mit meiner Frau
Nach andren Erdenländern;
Doch dass ich genossen des Wissens Frucht,
Das kannst du nicht mehr ändern.

Du kannst nicht ändern, dass ich weiss,
Wie sehr du klein und nichtig,
Und machst du dich auch noch so sehr
Durch Tod und Donnern wichtig.

Doctrine

Beat the drum and don't be afraid,
And kiss the pretty peddler girl!
This is the ultimate wisdom,
This is the books' most precious pearl.

Drum the people out of their sleep,
Drum reveille with youthful aplomb,
And drumming march ahead of all,
That is the ultimate wisdom.

This is the Hegelian philosophy,
This is the books' most secret seed!
I have grasped it because I am bright,
And because I am a good tambour indeed.

Translated by Felix Pollak

Adam the First

You sent forth, with their swords of flame,
The guards of your heavenly city,
And chased me out of paradise
With neither justice nor pity.

I trudge along beside my wife
Toward regions far and strange;
But I have fed on wisdom's fruit,
And this you cannot change.

You cannot steal what I have learned:
How weak you are, and small,
Trying to prove, with thunder and death,
That you are Lord of all!

O Gott! wie erbärmlich ist doch dies
Consilium-abeundi!
Das nenne ich einen Magnifikus
Der Welt, ein Lumen-Mundi!

Vermissen werde ich nimmermehr
Die paradiesischen Räume;
Das war kein wahres Paradies—
Es gab dort verbotene Bäume.

Ich will mein volles Freiheitsrecht!
Find ich die gringste Beschränknis,
Verwandelt sich mir das Paradies
In Hölle und Gefängnis.

Die Tendenz

Deutscher Sänger! sing und preise
Deutsche Freiheit, dass dein Lied
Unsrer Seelen sich bemeistre
Und zu Taten uns begeistre,
In Marseillerhymnenweise.

Girre nicht mehr wie ein Werther,
Welcher nur für Lotten glüht—
Was die Glocke hat geschlagen,
Sollst du deinem Volke sagen,
Rede Dolche, rede Schwerter!

Sei nicht mehr die weiche Flöte,
Das idyllische Gemüt—
Sei des Vaterlands Posaune,
Sei Kanone, sei Kartaune,
Blase, schmettre, donnre, töte!

O God! How wretched is this deed,
This awful condemnation!
I call it worthy of heaven's dean,
A brilliant inspiration!

I'll never yearn for paradise;
Your Eden wasn't much:
I found some lovely trees, whose fruit
I was not allowed to touch.

My freeman's right must be complete!
If I should ever feel
The slightest limit—Heaven would be
A hell and a Bastille!

Translated by Aaron Kramer

The Message

German singers! sing and praise
German freedom—till your song
Takes possession of our souls,
And inspires us to goals,
As the noble Marseillaise.

No more Werthers need be heard—
We have cooed and wooed too long—
Be your people's guide and rock—
Tell them that the hour has struck;
Speak the sword, the dagger word!

Do not be the tender flute,
The idyllic soul. Be strong.
Be the trumpet of the land!
Be the cannon—take your stand—
Shatter, thunder, blare, uproot!

Blase, schmettre, donnre täglich,
Bis der letzte Dränger flieht—
Singe nur in dieser Richtung,
Aber halte deine Dichtung
Nur so allgemein als möglich.

Nachtgedanken

Denk ich an Deutschland in der Nacht,
Dann bin ich um den Schlaf gebracht,
Ich kann nicht mehr die Augen schliessen,
Und meine heissen Tränen fliessen.

Die Jahre kommen und vergehn!
Seit ich die Mutter nicht gesehn,
Zwölf Jahre sind schon hingegangen;
Es wächst mein Sehnen und Verlangen.

Mein Sehnen und Verlangen wächst.
Die alte Frau hat mich behext,
Ich denke immer an die alte,
Die alte Frau, die Gott erhalte!

Die alte Frau hat mich so lieb,
Und in den Briefen, die sie schrieb,
Seh ich, wie ihre Hand gezittert,
Wie tief das Mutterherz erschüttert.

Die Mutter liegt mir stets im Sinn.
Zwölf lange Jahre flossen hin,
Zwölf lange Jahre sind verflossen,
Seit ich sie nicht ans Herz geschlossen.

Shatter, thunder, night and day—
Till you've righted every wrong!
Sing to waken, to incite!
—But be careful that you write
In the vaguest sort of way . . .

Translated by Aaron Kramer

Night Thoughts

At night I think of Germany,
And then there is no sleep for me:
I cannot shut my eyes at all,
And down my cheeks the hot tears fall.

The seasons come and pass away!
Twelve years have vanished since the day
I told my mother I must go;
My yearnings and desires grow.

My yearnings and desires swell.
I'm under the old lady's spell;
My mother's always in my mind—
May God be close to her, and kind!

My dear old lady loves me so!
And all her tender letters show
How dreadfully her hand was shaking;
And how her mother-heart is aching.

I think of her both night and day.
Full twelve long years have flown away,
Full twelve long years have drifted past
Since I embraced my mother last.

Deutschland hat ewigen Bestand,
Es ist ein kerngesundes Land,
Mit seinen Eichen, seinen Linden,
Werd ich es immer wiederfinden.

Nach Deutschland lechzt ich nicht so sehr,
Wenn nicht die Mutter dorten wär;
Das Vaterland wird nie verderben,
Jedoch die alte Frau kann sterben.

Seit ich das Land verlassen hab,
So viele sanken dort ins Grab,
Die ich geliebt—wenn ich sie zähle,
So will verbluten meine Seele.

Und zählen muss ich—Mit der Zahl
Schwillt immer höher meine Qual,
Mir ist, als wälzten sich die Leichen,
Auf meine Brust—Gottlob! sie weichen!

Gottlob! durch meine Fenster bricht
Französisch heitres Tageslicht;
Es kommt mein Weib, schön wie der Morgen,
Und lächelt fort die deutschen Sorgen.

The German nation will not fail—
It is a sturdy land, and hale,
And with its towering oak and lime
Will prosper till the end of time.

I would not give it half a care
If mother weren't living there;
The homeland never will decay;
My mother, though, might pass away.

Since my departure, many fell
Of those I knew and loved so well—
When I begin to count the toll
The blood is driven from my soul.

Yet I must count—and with the count
I feel my pangs begin to mount.
My breast is crushed, as though the dead
Roll over it. Thank God! They've fled.

Thank God! At last the morning light
Bursts through my windows: French and bright.
My wife is coming—fair as day—
And smiles my German cares away.

Translated by Aaron Kramer

Die schlesischen Weber

Im düstern Auge keine Träne,
Sie sitzen am Webstuhl und fletschen die Zähne:
Deutschland, wir weben dein Leichentuch,
Wir weben hinein den dreifachen Fluch—
    Wir weben, wir weben!

Ein Fluch dem Gotte, zu dem wir gebeten
In Winterskälte und Hungersnöten;
Wir haben vergebens gehofft und geharrt,
Er hat uns geäfft und gefoppt und genarrt—
    Wir weben, wir weben!

Ein Fluch dem König, dem König der Reichen,
Den unser Elend nicht konnte erweichen,
Der den letzten Groschen von uns erpresst
Und uns wie Hunde erschiessen lässt—
    Wir weben, wir weben!

Ein Fluch dem falschen Vaterlande,
Wo nur gedeihen Schmach und Schande,
Wo jede Blume früh geknickt,
Wo Fäulnis und Moder den Wurm erquickt—
    Wir weben, wir weben!

Das Schiffchen fliegt, der Webstuhl kracht,
Wir weben emsig Tag und Nacht—
Altdeutschland, wir weben dein Leichentuch,
Wir weben hinein den dreifachen Fluch,
    Wir weben, wir weben!

The Silesian Weavers

In gloomy eyes there wells no tear.
Grinding their teeth, they are sitting here:
Germany, your shroud's on our loom;
And in it we weave the threefold doom.
  We're weaving; we're weaving.

Doomed be the God who was deaf to our prayer
In winter's cold and hunger's despair.
All in vain we hoped and bided;
He only mocked us, hoaxed, derided—
  We're weaving; we're weaving.

Doomed be the king, the rich man's king,
Who would not be moved by our suffering,
Who tore the last coin out of our hands,
And let us be shot by his bloodthirsty bands—
  We're weaving; we're weaving.

Doomed be the fatherland, false name,
Where nothing thrives but disgrace and shame,
Where flowers are crushed before they unfold,
Where the worm is quickened by rot and mold—
  We're weaving; we're weaving.

The loom is creaking, the shuttle flies;
Nor night nor day do we close our eyes.
Old Germany, your shroud's on our loom,
And in it we weave the threefold doom;
  We're weaving; we're weaving.

        Translated by Aaron Kramer

Hymnus

Ich bin das Schwert, ich bin die Flamme.
Ich habe euch erleuchtet in der Dunkelheit, und als die Schlacht
begann, focht ich voran, in der ersten Reihe.
Rund um mich her liegen die Leichen meiner Freunde, aber wir
haben gesiegt. Wir haben gesiegt, aber rund umher liegen die
Leichen meiner Freunde. In die jauchzenden Triumph gesänge tö-
nen die Choräle der Totenfeier. Wir haben aber weder Zeit zur
Freude noch zur Trauer. Aufs neue erklingen die Drommeten, es
gilt neuen Kampf—
Ich bin das Schwert, ich bin die Flamme.

Karl I.

Im Wald, in der Köhlerhütte, sitzt
Trübsinnig allein der König;
Er sitzt an der Wiege des Köhlerkinds
Und wiegt und singt eintönig:

Eiapopeia, was raschelt im Stroh?
Es blöken im Stalle die Schafe—
Du trägst das Zeichen an der Stirn
Und lächelst so furchtbar im Schlafe.

Eiapopeia, das Kätzchen ist tot—
Du trägst auf der Stirne das Zeichen—
Du wirst ein Mann und schwingst das Beil,
Schon zittern im Walde die Eichen.

Der alte Köhlerglaube verschwand,
Es glauben die Köhlerkinder—
Eiapopeia—nicht mehr an Gott,
Und an den König noch minder.

Hymn

I am the sword, I am the flame.

I've lighted your way in the darkness, and when the fight began, battled ahead in the front lines.

Here round about me lie the bodies of my friends, but the victory was ours. The victory was ours, but here round about lie the bodies of my friends. Amid the wild paeans of triumph sound the chants of the funeral rites. But we have time neither for grief nor for rejoicing. The trumpets sound anew, fresh battles must be fought—

I am the sword, I am the flame.

Translated by Aaron Kramer

Charles I

In the woods, in a charcoal-burner's hut,
The King sits sad and alone;
He rocks the charcoal-burner's child,
And sings in a monotone:

Lullaby-lulla, what stirs in the straw?
I hear the bleat of the sheep—
You bear an omen upon your brow
And dreadfully smile in your sleep.

Lullaby-lulla, the pussycat's dead—
An omen's upon your brow—
You'll be a man and swing the axe;
The oaks are shuddering now!

The charcoal-burner's faith is gone;
No more do his children cling—
Lullaby-lulla—to trust in God,
And even less in the King.

Das Kätzchen ist tot, die Mäuschen sind froh—
Wir müssen zuschanden werden—
Eiapopeia—im Himmel der Gott
Und ich, der König auf Erden.

Mein Mut erlischt, mein Herz ist krank,
Und täglich wird es kränker—
Eiapopeia—du Köhlerkind,
Ich weiss es, du bist mein Henker.

Mein Todesgesang ist dein Wiegenlied—
Eiapopeia—die greisen
Haarlocken schneidest du ab zuvor—
Im Nacken klirrt mir das Eisen.

Eiapopeia, was raschelt im Stroh?
Du hast das Reich erworben,
Und schlägst mir das Haupt vom Rumpf herab—
Das Kätzchen ist gestorben.

Eiapopeia, was raschelt im Stroh?
Es blöken im Stalle die Schafe.
Das Kätzchen ist tot, die Mäuschen sind froh—
Schlafe, mein Henkerchen, schlafe!

Maria Antoinette

Wie heiter im Tuilerienschloss
Blinken die Spiegelfenster,
Und dennoch dort am hellen Tag
Gehn um die alten Gespenster.

Es spukt im Pavillon de Flor'
Maria Antoinette;
Sie hält dort morgens ihr Lever
Mit strenger Etikette.

The pussycat's dead, the mice rejoice—
What shall our names be worth—
Lullaby-lulla—great God on high,
And I, the lord of earth?

My courage dies, my heart is sick,
Each day I've deeper pain—
Lullaby-lulla—I know it, child,
At your hands I'll be slain.

My death song is your cradle song—
Lullaby-lulla—the old
Locks of my hair you'll cut off first;
At my throat the iron rings cold.

Lullaby-lulla, what stirs in the straw?
You shall not be denied.
You'll take the empire, and cut off my head—
The pussycat has died.

Lullaby-lulla, what stirs in the straw?
I hear the bleat of the sheep.
The pussycat's dead, the mice rejoice—
Sleep, little slayer, sleep!

Translated by Aaron Kramer

Marie Antoinette

How the windowpanes of the Tuileries
   In the merry sunshine glow!
And yet, by broad daylight within,
   The old ghosts come and go.

Flora's Pavilion is haunted still
   By Marie Antoinette;
She holds her morning levee there
   With strictest etiquette.

Geputzte Hofdamen. Die meisten stehn,
Auf Tabourets andre sitzen;
Die Kleider von Atlas und Goldbrokat,
Behängt mit Juwelen und Spitzen.

Die Taille ist schmal, der Reifrock bauscht,
Darunter lauschen die netten
Hochhackigen Füsschen so klug hervor—
Ach, wenn sie nur Köpfe hätten!

Sie haben alle keinen Kopf,
Der Königin selbst manquieret
Der Kopf, und Ihro Majestät
Ist deshalb nicht frisieret.

Ja, Sie, die mit turmhohem Toupet
So stolz sich konnte gebaren,
Die Tochter Maria Theresias,
Die Enkelin deutscher Cäsaren,

Sie muss jetzt spuken ohne Frisur
Und ohne Kopf, im Kreise
Von unfrisierten Edelfraun,
Die kopflos gleicherweise.

Das sind die Folgen der Revolution
Und ihrer fatalen Doktrine;
An allem ist schuld Jean Jacques Rousseau,
Voltaire und die Guillotine.

Doch sonderbar! es dünkt mich schier,
Als hätten die armen Geschöpfe
Gar nicht bemerkt, wie tot sie sind
Und dass sie verloren die Köpfe.

Ein leeres Gespreize, ganz wie sonst,
Ein abgeschmacktes Scherwenzen—
Possierlich sind und schauderhaft
Die kopflosen Reverenzen.

Court ladies in point and gold brocade
   And satins and jewels shine;
They stand or sit on their taborets,
   Bedizened and decked and fine.

How slim their waists! The petticoats
   Are hooped and amply spread;
The little high-heeled shoes peep out—
   If only they had their heads!

Not a single head can the company boast;
   Not even the Queen has one—
Which forces Her Gracious Majesty
   To go with her hair undone.

Yes, the Queen with her toupee like a tower,
   Who once so proudly smiled:
The descendant of German emperors,
   And Maria Theresa's child:

Sits headless now, with never a curl,
   Amid her maids of honor,
Who, headless too, with no hair to frizz,
   Stand round and wait upon her.

The French Revolution of course is to blame
   For the sad and pitiful scene:
Rousseau and Voltaire and their doctrines vile
   That led to the guillotine.

But the strange thing is, I am almost sure
   That not one of those ladies flaunting
Has any idea how dead she is,
   Or knows that her head is wanting.

Affectedly still they fawn and bow,
   And mince and strut as they go.
How horrid to watch the headless trunks
   As they dip and curtsy low!

Es knickst die erste Dame d'atour
Und bringt ein Hemd von Linnen;
Die zweite reicht es der Königin,
Und beide knicksen von hinnen.

Die dritte Dam und die vierte Dam
Knicksen und niederknien
Vor Ihrer Majestät, um Ihr
Die Strümpfe anzuziehen.

Ein Ehrenfräulein kommt und knickst
Und bringt das Morgenjäckchen;
Ein andres Fräulein knickst und bringt
Der Königin Unterröckchen.

Die Oberhofmeisterin steht dabei,
Sie fächert die Brust, die weisse,
Und in Ermanglung eines Kopfs
Lächelt sie mit dem Steisse.

Wohl durch die verhängten Fenster wirft
Die Sonne neugierige Blicke,
Doch wie sie gewahrt den alten Spuk,
Prallt sie erschrocken zurücke.

The first of the ladies brings a chemise
   Of linen without a flaw;
The second one hands the chemise to the queen,
   And, curtsying, both withdraw.

A third and a fourth advance in turn,
   When the first and the second are gone,
And, kneeling down at Her Majesty's feet,
   They pull her stockings on.

Then a maid of honor curtsying comes,
   And hands her her morning sacque;
Another one brings her her petticoat,
   And, bowing low, falls back.

The mistress of the robes stands by;
   Her bosom she fans the while,
And, her head being gone, with her other end
   She does her best to smile.

The sun peeps in with a curious glance
   To see what the curtains hide,
But recoils in terror as soon as he spies
   The poor old ghost inside.

Translated by Margaret Armour

Der Apollogott

1

Das Kloster ist hoch auf Felsen gebaut,
Der Rhein vorüberrauschet;
Wohl durch das Gitterfenster schaut
Die junge Nonne und lauschet.

Da fährt ein Schifflein, märchenhaft
Vom Abendrot beglänzet;
Es ist bewimpelt von buntem Taft,
Von Lorbeern und Blumen bekränzet.

Ein schöner blondgelockter Fant
Steht in des Schiffes Mitte;
Sein goldgesticktes Purpurgewand
Ist von antikem Schnitte.

Zu seinen Füssen liegen da
Neun marmorschöne Weiber;
Die hochgeschürzte Tunika
Umschliesst die schlanken Leiber.

Der Goldgelockte lieblich singt
Und spielt dazu die Leier;
Ins Herz der armen Nonne dringt
Das Lied und brennt wie Feuer.

Sie schlägt ein Kreuz, und noch einmal
Schlägt sie ein Kreuz, die Nonne;
Nicht scheucht das Kreuz die süsse Qual,
Nicht bannt es die bittre Wonne.

The God Apollo

1

The cloister towers atop the rocks;
The Rhine flows by and glistens;
Down from her lattice-window looks
The youthful nun, and listens.

A little boat goes sailing by
In the red of the sunset hours;
Around it streamers of taffeta fly;
It's crowned with laurel and flowers.

There stands in the vessel, fair to behold,
A gallant with curly blond hair;
His purple garment, embroidered in gold,
Is fashioned of ancient wear.

And at this godlike creature's feet
Nine lovely women lie;
Their slender bodies hide, discreet,
In tunics tucked up high.

Sweetly the golden-headed one
Sings, and plays the lyre;
And in the heart of the wretched nun
His ballad burns like fire.

She crosses herself again and again,
But nothing can suppress
Her luscious agony of pain,
Her bitter happiness.

2

Ich bin der Gott der Musika,
Verehrt in allen Landen;
Mein Tempel hat in Gräcia,
Auf Mont-Parnass gestanden.

Auf Mont-Parnass in Gräcia,
Da hab ich oft gesessen
Am holden Quell Kastalia,
Im Schatten der Zypressen.

Vokalisierend sassen da
Um mich herum die Töchter,
Das sang und klang la-la, la-la!
Geplauder und Gelächter.

Mitunter rief tra-ra, tra-ra!
Ein Waldhorn aus dem Holze;
Dort jagte Artemisia,
Mein Schwesterlein, die Stolze.

Ich weiss es nicht, wie mir geschah:
Ich brauchte nur zu nippen
Vom Wasser der Kastalia,
Da tönten meine Lippen.

Ich sang—und wie von selbst beinah
Die Leier klang, berauschend;
Mir war, als ob ich Daphne sah,
Aus Lorbeerbüschen lauschend.

Ich sang—und wie Ambrosia
Wohlrüche sich ergossen,
Es war von einer Gloria
Die ganze Welt umflossen.

2

I am the God of harmonies,
Revered in every land;
On Mount Parnassus' peak in Greece
My temple used to stand.

On Mount Parnassus' peak in Greece
I'd often find repose
Within the shade of cypress trees
Where bright Castalia flows.

The daughters sat around my knees,
And sang: La-la, la-la!
Their chatter and their revelries
Resounded near and far.

At times we'd hear among the trees
A bugle tooting loud;
The hunting call of Artemis,
My sister, swift and proud.

I never learned the cause of this—
I needed but to sip
Castalia's water—melodies
Would burn upon my lip.

I sang—with more than mortal ease
My spellbound lyre stirred;
As though behind those laurel trees
The peeping Daphne heard.

I sang—and at the melodies
Ambrosial fragrance poured;
The whole world lay in ecstasies
Beneath a glory-chord.

Wohl tausend Jahr aus Gräcia
Bin ich verbannt, vertrieben—
Doch ist mein Herz in Gräcia,
In Gräcia geblieben.

3

In der Tracht der Beguinen,
In dem Mantel mit der Kappe
Von der gröbsten schwarzen Sersche,
Ist vermummt die junge Nonne.

Hastig längs des Rheines Ufern
Schreitet sie hinab die Landstrass,
Die nach Holland führt, und hastig
Fragt sie jeden, der vorbeikommt:

"Habt ihr nicht gesehn Apollo?
Einen roten Mantel trägt er,
Lieblich singt er, spielt die Leier,
Und er ist mein holder Abgott."

Keiner will ihr Rede stehen,
Mancher dreht ihr stumm den Rücken,
Mancher glotzt sie an und lächelt,
Mancher seufzet: Armes Kind!

Doch des Wegs herangetrottelt
Kommt ein schlottrig alter Mensch,
Fingert in der Luft, wie rechnend,
Näselnd singt er vor sich hin.

Einen schlappen Quersack trägt er,
Auch ein klein dreieckig Hütchen;
Und mit schmunzelnd klugen Äuglein
Hört er an den Spruch der Nonne:

Long, long have I been gone from Greece:
Been driven out, expelled—
And yet, through all the centuries
In Greece my heart has dwelled.

3

Soon the young nun wraps herself
In the habit of Beguines,
Hides her face behind her mantle
With its cape of coarse black serge.

Breathlessly the maiden hurries
Up the road that leads to Holland,
And she hurriedly questions
Everyone who comes along:

"Have you seen the God Apollo?
It's a scarlet cloak he wears;
Sweetly sings and plays the lyre—
And he is my lovely idol."

No one offers her an answer;
Many turn their backs in silence;
Many stare in cold amusement;
Many sigh: Unhappy child!

But a slovenly old fellow
Slowly trudges down the road;
In the air his fingers reckon;
Nasally he hums a tune.

On his back's a sloppy wallet,
On his head a little tricorne;
And his clever eyes keep laughing
As he listens to her story:

"Habt ihr nicht gesehn Apollo?
Einen roten Mantel tragt er,
Lieblich singt er, spielt die Leier,
Und er ist mein holder Abgott."

Jener aber gab zur Antwort,
Während er sein Köpfchen wiegte
Hin und her, und gar possierlich
Zupfte an dem spitzen Bärtchen:

Ob ich ihn gesehen habe?
Ja, ich habe ihn gesehen
Oft genug zu Amsterdam,
In der deutschen Synagoge.

Denn er war Vorsänger dorten,
Und da hiess er Rabbi Faibisch,
Was auf Hochdeutsch heisst Apollo—
Doch mein Abgott ist er nicht.

Roter Mantel? Auch den roten
Mantel kenn ich. Echter Scharlach,
Kostet acht Florin die Elle,
Und ist noch nicht ganz bezahlt.

Seinen Vater Moses Jitscher
Kenn ich gut. Vorhautabschneider
Ist er bei den Portugiesen.
Er beschnitt auch Souveräne.

Seine Mutter ist Cousine
Meines Schwagers, und sie handelt
Auf der Gracht mit sauern Gurken
Und mit abgelebten Hosen.

Haben kein Pläsier am Sohne.
Dieser spielt sehr gut die Leier,
Aber leider noch viel besser
Spielt er oft Tarock und L'hombre.

"Have you seen the god Apollo?
It's a scarlet cloak he wears;
Sweetly sings and plays the lyre—
And he is my lovely idol."

But the tattered fellow answers,
While he wags his little head
To and fro, and comically
Tugs his pointed little beard:

"If I've seen him? Sure I've seen him!
Not just once, but many times:
Back home up in Amsterdam,
At the German synagogue.

For he was the cantor there,
And his name was Rabbi Faibish,
In High German that means Phoebus—
But *my* idol he is not.

Scarlet cloak? I know that also;
It's a genuine piece of scarlet;
Every yard is worth eight florins,
And it hasn't all been paid for.

And I'm rather well acquainted
With his father, Moses Yitscher:
Circumcises Portuguese.
He has also clipped some sovereigns.

And his mother is a cousin
Of my brother-in-law; she sells
Sour pickles in the market,
And decrepit trousers, too.

They've no pleasure in their son.
He's a first-rate lyre player,
Yet, alas, he's even better
When he plays *taroc* and *l'ombre.*

Auch ein Freigeist ist er, ass
Schweinefleisch, verlor sein Amt,
Und er zog herum im Lande
Mit geschminkten Komödianten.

In den Buden, auf den Märkten,
Spielte er den Pickelhering,
Holofernes, König David,
Diesen mit dem besten Beifall.

Denn des Königs eigne Lieder
Sang er in des Königs eigner
Muttersprache, tremulierend
In des Nigens alter Weise.

Aus dem Amsterdamer Spielhuis
Zog er jüngst etwelche Dirnen,
Und mit diesen Musen zieht er
Jetzt herum als ein Apollo.

Eine dicke ist darunter,
Die vorzüglich quiekt und grünzelt;
Ob dem grossen Lorbeerkopfputz
Nennt man sie die grüne Sau.

Jetzt wohin?

Jetzt wohin? Der dumme Fuss
Will mich gern nach Deutschland tragen;
Doch es schüttelt klug das Haupt
Mein Verstand und scheint zu sagen:

Zwar beendigt ist der Krieg,
Doch die Kriegsgerichte blieben,
Und es heisst, du habest einst
Viel Erschiessliches geschrieben.

He has even turned freethinker,
Eaten swine, and lost his job;
Now he roams around the country
With a troupe of painted comics.

In the stalls, in marketplaces,
He performs as Merry Andrew,
Holofernes and King David;
In this last he's cheered the most.

For he sings the Songs of David
In that king's own mother tongue,
And he makes the music quaver
In the old style of the Nigen.

Recently he lured some wenches
From the Amsterdam Casino,
And he's touring with these 'Muses'
In the role of an Apollo.

There's a fat one, who surpasses
All the rest in squeaking, grunting;
For her giant laurel headdress
She's been nicknamed the Green Sow."

Translated by Aaron Kramer

Which Way Now?

Which way now? My stupid foot
Steers me toward Germany;
But my reason shakes its head,
Wisely seems to say to me:

True, the war has ended now,
But the war tribunals stay,
And you wrote some lines for which
You could be lined up, they say.

Das ist wahr, unangenehm
Wär mir das Erschossenwerden;
Bin kein Held, es fehlen mir
Die pathetischen Gebärden.

Gern würd ich nach England gehn,
Wären dort nicht Kohlendämpfe
Und Engländer—schon ihr Duft
Gibt Erbrechen mir und Krämpfe.

Manchmal kommt mir in den Sinn
Nach Amerika zu segeln,
Nach dem grossen Freiheitstall,
Der bewohnt von Gleichheitsflegeln—

Doch es ängstet mich ein Land,
Wo die Menschen Tabak käuen,
Wo sie ohne König kegeln,
Wo sie ohne Spucknapf speien.

Russland, dieses schöne Reich,
Würde mir vielleicht behagen,
Doch im Winter könnte ich
Dort die Knute nicht ertragen.

Traurig schau ich in die Höh,
Wo viel tausend Sterne nicken—
Aber meinen eignen Stern
Kann ich nirgends dort erblicken.

Hat im güldnen Labyrinth
Sich vielleicht verirrt am Himmel,
Wie ich selber mich verirrt
In dem irdischen Getümmel.

It would be discomforting,
To be sure, if I were shot.
I have no dramatic skill,
And a hero I am not.

I might go to England, but
Coal fumes make the air too thick;
And the English—just their smell
Gives me cramps and makes me sick.

There are times I'd like to think
That America's for me
(Freedom's stable filled with herds
Seeking mob equality),

But I'm fearful of a land
Where tobacco leaves they chew,
Where they bowl without a king,
Where without spittoon they spew.

For a pleasant land to live,
Russia may be the way out.
But I know in wintertime
I could not endure the knout.

Gloomily I lift my eyes—
Stars galore are greeting me,
Many thousands fill the skies
But my own star I can't see.

In that golden labyrinth
It perhaps has gone astray,
Just as in the turmoil here
On this earth I've lost my way.

Translated by Max Knight

Weltlauf

Hat man viel, so wird man bald
Noch viel mehr dazu bekommen.
Wer nur wenig hat, dem wird
Auch das wenige genommen.

Wenn du aber gar nichts hast,
Ach, so lasse dich begraben—
Denn ein Recht zum Leben, Lump,
Haben nur die etwas haben.

Rückschau

Ich habe gerochen alle Gerüche
In dieser holden Erdenküche;
Was man geniessen kann in der Welt,
Das hab ich genossen wie je ein Held!
Hab Kaffee getrunken, hab Kuchen gegessen,
Hab manche schöne Puppe besessen;
Trug seidne Westen, den feinsten Frack,
Mir klingelten auch Dukaten im Sack.
Wie Gellert ritt ich auf hohem Ross;
Ich hatte ein Haus, ich hatte ein Schloss.
Ich lag auf der grünen Wiese des Glücks,
Die Sonne grüsste goldigsten Blicks;
Ein Lorbeerkranz umschloss die Stirn,
Er duftete Träume mir ins Gehirn,
Träume von Rosen und ewigem Mai—
Es ward mir so selig zu Sinne dabei,
So dämmersüchtig, so sterbefaul—
Mir flogen gebratne Tauben ins Maul,
Und Englein kamen, und aus den Taschen
Sie zogen hervor Champagnerflaschen—
Das waren Visionen, Seifenblasen—

Course of the World

If a man's already rich,
More and more he will amass.
Who has little, will be robbed
Of the little that he has.

If you don't have anything,
Better dig yourself a ditch—
For the right to live, you scum,
Is restricted to the rich.

Translated by Max Knight

Retrospective

I've smelled all smellable odors and scents
Which this fair earthly kitchen presents;
Whatever is joyful both near and far,
I have enjoyed it, as ever a tsar!
I have drunk coffee, I've eaten cake,
Among beautiful women I was quite a rake;
I've worn silken vests, the finest jackets,
And ducats jingled in all my pockets.
Like Gellert, I rode on a noble steed,
I had a house, a castle indeed,
I was lying on fortune's greenest meadow,
The sun shone golden, there was no shadow;
A laurel wreath on my head like a crown,
Sent dreams of fragrant vapors down—
Dreams of roses, of eternal May,
I felt so wishlessly blissful and gay,
So twilight-happy, so lazy-blah,
I was in the land of Shangri-la!
And angels appeared from where they had lain,
And opened bottles of icy champagne . . .
But those were visions, soap bubbles, alas,

Sie platzten—Jetzt lieg ich auf feuchtem Rasen,
Die Glieder sind mir rheumatisch gelähmt,
Und meine Seele ist tief beschämt.
Ach, jede Lust, ach, jeden Genuss
Hab ich erkauft durch herben Verdruss;
Ich ward getränkt mit Bitternissen
Und grausam von den Wanzen gebissen;
Ich ward bedrängt von schwarzen Sorgen,
Ich musste lügen, ich musste borgen
Bei reichen Buben und alten Vetteln—
Ich glaube sogar, ich musste betteln.
Jetzt bin ich müd vom Rennen und Laufen,
Jetzt will ich mich im Grabe verschnaufen.
Lebt wohl! Dort oben, ihr christlichen Brüder,
Ja, das versteht sich, dort sehn wir uns wieder.

Der Abgekühlte

Und ist man tot, so muss man lang
Im Grabe liegen; ich bin bang,
Ja, ich bin bang, das Auferstehen
Wird nicht so schnell vonstatten gehen.

Noch einmal, eh mein Lebenslicht
Erlöschet, eh mein Herze bricht—
Noch einmal möcht ich vor dem Sterben
Um Frauenhuld beseligt werben.

Und eine Blonde müsst es sein,
Mit Augen sanft wie Mondenschein—
Denn schlecht bekommen mir am Ende
Die wild brünetten Sonnenbrände.

They burst—now I'm lying in a moist patch of grass,
My aching limbs rheumatically lame,
And my poor soul quite sick with shame.
Ach, every pleasure, each happiness,
I had to pay for with bitter distress;
I was stung and bitten by bedbugs and fleas,
My tribulations did never cease,
I was cast down by many a sorrow,
I had to lie, I had to borrow,
From young, rich knaves and at times an old hag,
I even believe I had to beg.
Now I am tired of running nonstop,
Now in my grave I want to rest up
Adieu, farewell, Christian friends, *mes chers frères,*
We'll meet again—who can doubt it—up there.

Translated by Felix Pollak

Cooling Off

Long must we lie, when we are dead,
In our graves; I am afraid
The resurrection will not be
Accomplished quite so easily.

Once more, ere darkness caps my light,
Before my heart concedes the fight,
I wish I could just once more vie
For a woman's love, before I die.

And let her be a blonde, with eyes
As mild as moonlit summer skies;
I am too old to be upset
By the sunny glare of a brunette.

Das junge Volk voll Lebenskraft
Will den Tumult der Leidenschaft,
Das ist ein Rasen, Schwören, Poltern
Und wechselseitges Seelenfoltern!

Unjung und nicht mehr ganz gesund,
Wie ich es bin zu dieser Stund,
Möcht ich noch einmal lieben, schwärmen
Und glücklich sein—doch ohne Lärmen.

Im Oktober 1849

Gelegt hat sich der starke Wind,
Und wieder stille wirds daheime;
Germania, das grosse Kind,
Erfreut sich wieder seiner Weihnachtsbäume.

Wir treiben jetzt Familienglück—
Was höher lockt, das ist vom Übel—
Die Friedensschwalbe kehrt zurück,
Die einst genistet in des Hauses Giebel.

Gemütlich ruhen Wald und Fluss,
Von sanftem Mondlicht übergossen;
Nur manchmal knallts—Ist das ein Schuss?—
Es ist vielleicht ein Freund, den man erschossen.

Vielleicht mit Waffen in der Hand
Hat man den Tollkopf angetroffen
(Nicht jeder hat so viel Verstand
Wie Flaccus, der so kühn davongeloffen).

Es knallt. Es ist ein Fest vielleicht,
Ein Feuerwerk zur Goethefeier!—
Die Sontag, die dem Grab entsteigt,
Begrüsst Raketenlärm—die alte Leier.

The young folks, full of vim and zest,
Like the tumult of passion best;
There's so much tearing, swearing, bussing
And mutually destructive fussing!

No longer young and well these days,
I may be somewhat out of place,
But yearning still for love, its joys,
Its happiness—but not its noise.

Translated by Felix Pollak

October 1849

The wind's asleep, that howled so wild;
At home it's quiet as could be;
Germania, the great big child,
Plays happily around his Christmas tree.

Domestic joy's our main concern;
Whatever tempts beyond, we label
Sin—the doves of peace return,
That used to make their nest within our gable.

The wood and stream rest cozily,
By gentle moonlight comforted;
But—on a sudden—can it be
A shot?—perhaps it is a friend, shot dead.

Perhaps, with weapon in his hand,
They came upon the harebrained one.
(Not every lad can understand
As well as Flaccus—when it's time to run.)

A shot. Is someone being fêted?
Fireworks lit to Goethe's glory?
—The risen Sontag's celebrated
By rockets sounding off—the same old story!

Auch Liszt taucht wieder auf, der Franz,
Er lebt, er liegt nicht blutgerötet
Auf einem Schlachtfeld Ungarlands;
Kein Russe, noch Kroat hat ihn getötet.

Es fiel der Freiheit letzte Schanz,
Und Ungarn blutet sich zu Tode—
Doch unversehrt blieb Ritter Franz,
Sein Säbel auch—er liegt in der Kommode.

Er lebt, der Franz, und wird als Greis
Vom Ungarkriege Wunderdinge
Erzählen in der Enkel Kreis—
"So lag ich und so führt ich meine Klinge!"

Wenn ich den Namen Ungarn hör,
Wird mir das deutsche Wams zu enge,
Es braust darunter wie ein Meer,
Mir ist als grüssten mich Trompetenklänge!

Es klirrt mir wieder im Gemüt
Die Heldensage, längst verklungen,
Das eisern wilde Kämpenlied—
Das Lied vom Untergang der Nibelungen.

Es ist dasselbe Heldenlos,
Es sind dieselben alten Mären,
Die Namen sind verändert bloss,
Doch sinds dieselben "Helden lobebären."

Es ist dasselbe Schicksal auch—
Wie stolz und frei die Fahnen fliegen,
Es muss der Held, nach altem Brauch,
Den tierisch rohen Mächten unterliegen.

Und diesmal hat der Ochse gar
Mit Bären einen Bund geschlossen—
Du fällst; doch tröste dich, Magyar,
Wir andre haben schlimmre Schmach genossen.

And Franz Liszt, too, pops up once more;
He lives, he does not lie bloodred
On a Hungarian field of war;
No Russian, no Croatian left him dead.

The final trench of freedom fell,
And Hungary is bleeding, dying—
But Franz, Sir Franz, remained quite well;
His saber, too—in his commode it's lying!

Franz is alive, and when he's old,
What tales of the Hungarian war
His children's children will be told!
"Thus stood I—and thus, thus my blade I bore!"

When someone speaks of Hungary
My German vest becomes too small;
A mighty tide wells up in me—
I hear the challenge of a bugle call.

That myth of heroes, hushed so long,
Once more goes crashing through my soul:
The iron-savage hero song
That tells us of the Nibelungen's fall.

The heroes' fate remains the same . . .
It is the very same old story;
There's only been a change in name,
Yet these are the same "heroes crowned in glory."

There's little difference in their lot.
Though proud and free the banners fly,
Conforming to the ancient plot
The bestial forces win; the heroes die.

This time the ox and bear combined
Their brutal, overwhelming powers.
You fall; but, Magyar, rest your mind!
—An ignominy even worse is ours.

Anständge Bestien sind es doch,
Die ganz honett dich überwunden;
Doch wir geraten in das Joch
Von Wölfen, Schweinen und gemeinen Hunden.

Das heult und bellt und grunzt—ich kann
Ertragen kaum den Duft der Sieger.
Doch still, Poet, das greift dich an—
Du bist so krank und schweigen wäre klüger.

Enfant perdu

Verlorner Posten in dem Freiheitskriege,
Hielt ich seit dreissig Jahren treulich aus.
Ich kämpfte ohne Hoffnung, dass ich siege,
Ich wusste, nie komm ich gesund nach Haus.

Ich wachte Tag und Nacht.—Ich konnt nicht schlafen,
Wie in dem Lagerzelt der Freunde Schar—
(Auch hielt das laute Schnarchen dieser Braven
Mich wach, wenn ich ein bisschen schlummrig war).

In jenen Nächten hat Langweil ergriffen
Mich oft, auch Furcht—(nur Narren fürchten nichts)—
Sie zu verscheuchen, hab ich dann gepfiffen
Die frechen Reime eines Spottgedichts.

Ja, wachsam stand ich, das Gewehr im Arme,
Und nahte irgendein verdächtger Gauch,
So schoss ich gut und jagt ihm eine warme,
Brühwarme Kugel in den schnöden Bauch.

Mitunter freilich mocht es sich ereignen,
Dass solch ein schlechter Gauch gleichfalls sehr gut
Zu schiessen wusste—ach, ich kanns nicht leugnen—
Die Wunden klaffen—es verströmt mein Blut.

For those were decent beasts, that broke
Your fortresses with manners fine;
While we are bowed beneath the yoke
Of heartless wolves, and common dogs, and swine.

They howl, and bark, and grunt—my nose
Can scarcely bear the victor's reek.
Poet, be still; your anguish grows—
You are so sick . . . it were wiser not to speak.

Translated by Aaron Kramer

Enfant Perdu

For more than thirty years I've been defending,
  In freedom's struggle, many a desperate post.
I knew the fight was hopeless, never-ending;
  But still I fought, wounded and battle-tossed.

Waking through nights and days, no peaceful slumbers
  Were mine while all the others slept their fill.
(The mighty snoring of these valiant numbers
  Kept me awake when I was tired or ill.)

In those long nights I have been often frightened,
  For only fools are not afraid of fear,
But I would whistle till the terror lightened,
  And sing my mocking rhymes to give me cheer.

Yes, I have stood, my musket primed and ready,
  On guard; and when some rascal raised his head
I took good aim, my arm was always steady,
  And let him have a bellyful of lead.

And yet those knaves—I may as well admit it—
  Could shoot quite well; the rascals often chose
A splendid mark, and, what is more, they hit it.
  My wounds are gaping, and the blood still flows.

Ein Posten ist vakant!—Die Wunden klaffen—
Der eine fällt, die andern rücken nach—
Doch fall ich unbesiegt, und meine Waffen
Sind nicht gebrochen—Nur mein Herze brach.

Das Sklavenschiff

1

Der Superkargo Mynher van Koek
Sitzt rechnend in seiner Kajüte;
Er kalkuliert der Ladung Betrag
Und die probabeln Profite.

"Der Gummi ist gut, der Pfeffer ist gut,
Dreihundert Säcke und Fässer;
Ich habe Goldstaub und Elfenbein—
Die schwarze Ware ist besser.

Sechshundert Neger tauschte ich ein
Spottwohlfeil am Senegalflusse.
Das Fleisch ist hart, die Sehnen sind stramm,
Wie Eisen vom besten Gusse.

Ich hab zum Tausche Branntewein,
Glasperlen und Stahlzeug gegeben;
Gewinne daran achthundert Prozent,
Bleibt mir die Hälfte am Leben.

Bleiben mir Neger dreihundert nur
Im Hafen von Rio-Janeiro,
Zahlt dort mir hundert Dukaten per Stück
Das Haus Gonzales Perreiro."

One post is vacant! As a bloody token
  I wear my wounds. Another takes my part.
But, though I fall, my sword is still unbroken;
  The only thing that's broken is my heart.

Translated by Louis Untermeyer

The Slave Ship

1

The supercargo Mynher van Koek
Sits in his cabin, counting;
He calculates his lading bills
And sees the profits mounting.

"The rubber's good, the pepper's good:
Three hundred barrels and sacks;
I've gold dust and rare ivory—
But best is my cargo of blacks.

I bought them on the Senegal,
Six hundred heads—all told.
Their flesh is hard, their sinews taut
As the finest iron mold.

Whiskey, beads, and trinkets of steel
Were all the fortune I spent—
Should half of my cargo stay alive
I'll make eight hundred percent.

Should only three hundred blacks remain
When I get to Rio Janeiro,
I'll make three hundred ducats apiece
From the house of Gonzales Perreiro."

Da plötzlich wird Mynher van Koek
Aus seinen Gedanken gerissen;
Der Schiffschirurgius tritt herein,
Der Doktor van der Smissen.

Das ist eine klapperdürre Figur,
Die Nase voll roter Warzen—
Nun, Wasserfeldscherer, ruft van Koek,
Wie gehts meinen lieben Schwarzen?

Der Doktor dankt der Nachfrage und spricht:
"Ich bin zu melden gekommen,
Dass heute nacht die Sterblichkeit
Bedeutend zugenommen.

Im Durchschnitt starben täglich zwei,
Doch heute starben sieben,
Vier Männer, drei Frauen—Ich hab den Verlust
Sogleich in die Kladde geschrieben.

Ich inspizierte die Leichen genau;
Denn diese Schelme stellen
Sich manchmal tot, damit man sie
Hinabwirft in die Wellen.

Ich nahm den Toten die Eisen ab;
Und wie ich gewöhnlich tue,
Ich liess die Leichen werfen ins Meer
Des Morgens in der Fruhe.

Es schossen alsbald hervor aus der Flut
Haifische, ganze Heere,
Sie lieben so sehr das Negerfleisch;
Das sind meine Pensionäre.

Sie folgten unseres Schiffes Spur,
Seit wir verlassen die Küste;
Die Bestien wittern den Leichengeruch,
Mit schnupperndem Frassgelüste.

But all at once Mynher van Koek
Was roused from his reflection;
The ship surgeon, van der Smissen by name,
Returned from his tour of inspection.

He's a skinny thing—red warts on his nose;
"Now tell me," the captain cries,
"Tell me, ship surgeon, how do you find
My dear black merchandise?"

The doctor nods his thanks, and says:
"That's what I've come to announce—
Tonight the rate of mortality
Significantly mounts.

A daily average of two have died,
But seven went today:
Four men, three women—I entered the loss
In the records right away.

I looked the corpses over well,
For many a time these knaves
Pretend to be dead, because they hope
We'll toss them out on the waves.

I took the irons off the dead,
And, as usual, gave an order
Early this morning, that every corpse
Should be cast out into the water.

Sharkfish, whole battalions of them,
Shot swiftly up from the brine;
They love the Negro meat so well!
They're pensioners of mine.

Since first our ship put out to sea
They've stubbornly pursued;
These monsters catch the corpses' scent
With a sniffing hunger for food.

Es ist possierlich anzusehn,
Wie sie nach den Toten schnappen!
Die fasst den Kopf, die fasst das Bein,
Die andern schlucken die Lappen.

Ist alles verschlungen, dann tummeln sie sich
Vergnügt um des Schiffes Planken
Und glotzen mich an, als wollten sie
Sich für das Frühstück bedanken."

Doch seufzend fällt ihm in die Red
Van Koek: Wie kann ich lindern
Das Übel? wie kann ich die Progression
Der Sterblichkeit verhindern?

Der Doktor erwidert: "Durch eigne Schuld
Sind viele Schwarze gestorben;
Ihr schlechter Odem hat die Luft
Im Schiffsraum so sehr verdorben.

Auch starben viele durch Melancholie,
Dieweil sie sich tödlich langweilen;
Durch etwas Luft, Musik und Tanz
Lässt sich die Krankheit heilen."

Da ruft van Koek: "Ein guter Rat!
Mein teurer Wasserfeldscherer
Ist klug wie Aristoteles,
Des Alexanders Lehrer.

Der Präsident der Sozietät
Der Tulpenveredlung im Delfte
Ist sehr gescheit, doch hat er nicht
Von Eurem Verstande die Hälfte.

Musik! Musik! Die Schwarzen solln
Hier auf dem Verdecke tanzen.
Und wer sich beim Hopsen nicht amüsiert,
Den soll die Peitsche kuranzen."

It's a comical thing to see the sharks
Go snapping after the dead!
One of them tears at the rags, and one
At the legs, and one at the head.

When everything's swallowed, they cheerfully stir
Around the vessel's planks,
And gape at me with sated eyes
As though to express their thanks."

But, sighing, the captain interrupts:
"How can I end this curse?
How can I keep the rate of death
From getting worse and worse?"

"Through their own fault," the surgeon sneers,
"Many succumb to death;
The air in the hold of the ship is foul
From their offensive breath.

And many die because they're sad,
For they're kept in a boredom that kills;
A bit of music, dancing, and air,
Will cure them of all their ills."

"Splendid advice!" the captain cries,
"My dear old van der Smissen's
More clever than Aristotle was,
Who gave Alexander lessons.

The Tulip Society's president
Has more than an average mind,
But when it comes to reasoning
You leave him far behind.

Music! Music! The blacks shall dance
Here on the deck of the ship;
And whomever the hopping can't amuse,
Let him be cured by the whip!"

2

Hoch aus dem blauen Himmelszelt
Viel tausend Sterne schauen,
Sehnsüchtig glänzend, gross und klug,
Wie Augen von schönen Frauen.

Sie blicken hinunter in das Meer,
Das weithin überzogen
Mit phosphorstrahlendem Purpurduft;
Wollüstig girren die Wogen.

Kein Segel flattert am Sklavenschiff,
Es liegt wie abgetakelt;
Doch schimmern Laternen auf dem Verdeck,
Wo Tanzmusik spektakelt.

Die Fiedel streicht der Steuermann,
Der Koch, der spielt die Flöte,
Ein Schiffsjung schlägt die Trommel dazu,
Der Doktor bläst die Trompete.

Wohl hundert Neger, Männer und Fraun,
Sie jauchzen und hopsen und kreisen
Wie toll herum; bei jedem Sprung
Taktmässig klirren die Eisen.

Sie stampfen den Boden mit tobender Lust.
Und manche schwarze Schöne
Umschlingt wollüstig den nackten Genoss—
Dazwischen ächzende Töne.

Der Büttel ist maître des plaisirs,
Und hat mit Peitschenhieben
Die lässigen Tänzer stimuliert,
Zum Frohsinn angetrieben.

2

Many thousands of stars look out
From the high blue tent of the skies:
Longingly radiant, large and bright,
Like lovely ladies' eyes.

They gaze down into the endless sea
With its phosphorous purple hue;
Soft in the night the sleepless waves
Voluptuously coo.

There's not a sail on the slave ship now;
It drifts unrigged and bare;
But lanterns glitter along the deck,
And music's in the air.

The helmsman plays a violin,
The doctor's trumpet sounds,
The cook plays flute, while a cabin boy
Stands at the drum, and pounds.

A hundred Negroes, women and men,
Are whirling around—insane—
Shouting and hopping; at every leap
A rhythmic clatter of chains.

They stamp the boards with blusterous joy,
And many a naked beau
Embraces his beautiful Negro lass—
Between them a sigh of woe.

The hangman is *maître des plaisirs:*
And, swinging left and right,
He's whipped the sluggish dancers on,
Driven them to delight.

Und Dideldumdei und Schnedderedeng!
Der Lärm lockt aus den Tiefen
Die Ungetüme der Wasserwelt,
Die dort blödsinnig schliefen.

Schlaftrunken kommen geschwommen heran
Haifische, viele hundert;
Sie glotzen nach dem Schiff hinauf,
Sie sind verdutzt, verwundert.

Sie merken, dass die Frühstückstund
Noch nicht gekommen, und gähnen,
Aufsperrend den Rachen; die Kiefer sind
Bepflanzt mit Sägezähnen.

Und Dideldumdei und Schnedderedeng—
Es nehmen kein Ende die Tänze.
Die Haifische beissen vor Ungeduld
Sich selber in die Schwänze.

Ich glaube, sie lieben nicht die Musik,
Wie viele von ihrem Gelichter.
Trau keiner Bestie, die nicht liebt
Musik! sagt Albions grosser Dichter.

Und Schnedderedeng und Dideldumdei—
Die Tänze nehmen kein Ende.
Am Fockmast steht Mynher van Koek
Und faltet betend die Hände:

"Um Christi willen verschone, o Herr,
Das Leben der schwarzen Sünder!
Erzürnten sie dich, so weisst du ja,
Sie sind so dumm wie die Rinder.

Verschone ihr Leben um Christi willn,
Der für uns alle gestorben!
Denn bleiben mir nicht dreihundert Stück,
So ist mein Geschäft verdorben."

And diddle-dum-dee and shnedderedeng!
The noise allures from the deep
The monsters of the water world
That were lying sound asleep.

Many hundreds of sharks come close
With sleepy, half-shut eyes;
They stare up at the reveling ship
In wonder and surprise.

They know it's not their breakfast time,
And open wide their jaws—
Revealing rows of shiny teeth
As huge and sharp as saws.

And diddle-dum-dee and shnedderedeng—
No end to the exultations.
The sharkfish bite themselves in the tail—
So great is their impatience.

I think they don't like music much,
Like many of their gang.
"Trust no music-hating beast!"
Albion's bard once sang.

And shnedderedeng diddle-dum-dee—
There's never an end to the dance!
Mynher van Koek, at the bow of the ship,
Prayerfully folds his hands:

"Take pity, O Lord, in the name of Christ,
And let these sinners live!
You know they're stupid as cows, O Lord,
And if they enrage you—forgive!

Spare their lives in the name of Christ
Who died for us all on the cross!
For unless three hundred heads remain
I'll suffer a terrible loss."

Translated by Aaron Kramer

Lass die heilgen Parabolen,
Lass die frommen Hypothesen—
Suche die verdammten Fragen
Ohne Umschweif uns zu lösen.

Warum schleppt sich blutend, elend,
Unter Kreuzlast der Gerechte,
Während glücklich als ein Sieger
Trabt auf hohem Ross der Schlechte?

Woran liegt die Schuld? Ist etwa
Unser Herr nicht ganz allmächtig?
Oder treibt er selbst den Unfug?
Ach, das wäre niederträchtig.

Also fragen wir beständig,
Bis man uns mit einer Handvoll
Erde endlich stopft die Mäuler—
Aber ist das eine Antwort?

Wie langsam kriechet sie dahin,
Die Zeit, die schauderhafte Schnecke!
Ich aber, ganz bewegungslos
Blieb ich hier auf demselben Flecke.

In meine dunkle Zelle dringt
Kein Sonnenstrahl, kein Hoffnungsschimmer,
Ich weiss, nur mit der Kirchhofsgruft
Vertausch ich dies fatale Zimmer.

Vielleicht bin ich gestorben längst;
Es sind vielleicht nur Spukgestalten
Die Phantasien, die des Nachts
Im Hirn den bunten Umzug halten.

Forget the holy parables,
Forget pious hypotheses—
And try to answer the damn questions
Minus those evasions, please.

Why must the good one always suffer
Thorns and cross and brutal force,
While the villain rides victorious
Through the streets on his high horse?

Who's to blame? Might the almighty
Not be almighty, after all?
Or himself the mischief maker?
That, I say, would show some gall.

Thus we ask and keep on asking
Till a handful of black earth for
Good and ever seals our kissers.
But is that indeed an answer?

Translated by Felix Pollak

How slow is time, that dreadful snail!
I wonder—does it move or not?
I, to be sure, quite motionless,
Am stuck here at the selfsame spot.

No ray of sun does ever enter,
No ray of hope, this cell of gloom;
I know, only a graveyard crypt
Will follow this my fatal room.

Perhaps I died some time ago,
Perhaps it's just that spooks are prancing,
Phantasmagorias of the night,
Through my poor brain, gyrating, dancing.

Es mögen wohl Gespenster sein,
Altheidnisch göttlichen Gelichters;
Sie wählen gern zum Tummelplatz
Den Schädel eines toten Dichters.—

Die schaurig süssen Orgia,
Das nächtlich tolle Geistertreiben,
Sucht des Poeten Leichenhand
Manchmal am Morgen aufzuschreiben.

Mich locken nicht die Himmelsauen
Im Paradies, im selgen Land;
Dort find ich keine schönre Frauen
Als ich bereits auf Erden fand.

Kein Engel mit den feinsten Schwingen
Könnt mir ersetzen dort mein Weib;
Auf Wolken sitzend Psalmen singen,
Wär auch nicht just mein Zeitvertreib.

O Herr! ich glaub, es wär das Beste,
Du liessest mich in dieser Welt;
Heil nur zuvor mein Leibgebreste,
Und sorge auch für etwas Geld.

Ich weiss, es ist voll Sünd und Laster
Die Welt; jedoch ich bin einmal
Gewöhnt, auf diesem Erdpechpflaster
Zu schlendern durch das Jammertal.

Genieren wird das Weltgetreibe
Mich nie, denn selten geh ich aus;
In Schlafrock und Pantoffeln bleibe
Ich gern bei meiner Frau zu Haus.

Most likely they're ghosts all right,
Heathenish gods, the old diehards,
Whose favorite playground seems to be
The skull of a departed bard.

Their shudderingly sweet orgiastics,
The way these nightly trolls cavort,
The poet's dead hand still endeavors
Sometimes, when day breaks, to record.

Translated by Felix Pollak

I'm not allured by a lofty field
In paradise, on holy ground.
No ladies there could be revealed
More fair than I've already found.

No angel with the daintiest wing
Could compensate me for my wife;
And on the clouds to sit and sing
The psalms, is not my way of life.

O Lord! It would be best to leave me
In *this* world; but I beg of you,
Heal the infirmities that grieve me,
And let me have some money, too.

I know what sinning and deceit
Are in the world; but many years
Upon this pavement trained my feet
To saunter through the vale of tears.

The world's events won't get me down,
For seldom do I leave the house;
In slippers and in dressing gown
I like to stay here with my spouse.

Lass mich bei ihr! Hör ich sie schwätzen,
Trinkt meine Seele die Musik
Der holden Stimme mit Ergötzen.
So treu und ehrlich ist ihr Blick!

Gesundheit nur und Geldzulage
Verlang ich, Herr! O lass mich froh
Hinleben noch viel schöne Tage
Bei meiner Frau im statu quo!

Erinnerung aus Krähwinkels Schreckenstagen

Wir Bürgermeister und Senat,
Wir haben folgendes Mandat
Stadtväterlichst an alle Klassen
Der treuen Bürgerschaft erlassen.

Ausländer, Fremde, sind es meist,
Die unter uns gesät den Geist
Der Rebellion. Dergleichen Sünder,
Gottlob! sind selten Landeskinder.

Auch Gottesleugner sind es meist;
Wer sich von seinem Gotte reisst,
Wird endlich auch abtrünnig werden
Von seinen irdischen Behörden.

Der Obrigkeit gehorchen, ist
Die erste Pflicht für Jud und Christ.
Es schliesse jeder seine Bude
Sobald es dunkelt, Christ und Jude.

Wo ihrer drei beisammen stehn,
Da soll man auseinander gehn.
Des Nachts soll niemand auf den Gassen
Sich ohne Leuchte sehen lassen.

Leave me with her! My soul rejoices
To hear her chattering. Like wine
I drink that loveliest of voices!
—Her eyes so truly answer mine.

Money and health are all I ask,
O Master! Let me live my life
In *statu quo,* and gaily bask
Here in the sunlight, with my wife!

Translated by Aaron Kramer

Remembering Krähwinkel's Reign of Terror

We, the senate and the mayor,
After intensive thought and prayer
For all the various creeds and classes,
Enjoin these laws upon the masses:

"Beware of aliens, for they sow
Seeds of revolt where'er they go;
Rebellious souls and other vermin
Are scarcely ever (praise God) German.

They're mostly blasphemers as well
Whose souls will be condemned to hell;
And furthermore an apostate
Will flout his local magistrate.

Obedience to their ruler's due
From Christian and (much more) from Jew;
And Jew and Christian, every one
Must close their shops when day is done.

No one shall walk abroad at night
Unless accompanied by a light.
If three shall walk in any street
They shall disperse—before they meet.

Es liefre seine Waffen aus
Ein jeder in dem Gildenhaus;
Auch Munition von jeder Sorte
Wird deponiert am selben Orte.

Wer auf der Strasse räsoniert,
Wird unverzüglich füsiliert;
Das Räsonieren durch Gebärden
Soll gleichfalls hart bestrafet werden.

Vertrauet Eurem Magistrat,
Der fromm und liebend schützt den Staat
Durch huldreich hochwohlweises Walten;
Euch ziemt es, stets das Maul zu halten.

Jammertal

Der Nachtwind durch die Luken pfeift,
Und auf dem Dachstublager
Zwei arme Seelen gebettet sind;
Sie schauen so blass und mager.

Die eine arme Seele spricht:
Umschling mich mit deinen Armen,
An meinen Mund drück fest deinen Mund,
Ich will an dir erwarmen.

Die andere arme Seele spricht:
Wenn ich dein Auge sehe,
Verschwindet mein Elend, der Hunger, der Frost
Und all mein Erdenwehe.

Sie küssten sich viel, sie weinten noch mehr,
Sie drückten sich seufzend die Hände,
Sie lachten manchmal und sangen sogar,
Und sie verstummten am Ende.

Discard your weapons, bring them all
Hastily to the City Hall;
Retain no sort of ammunition
Unless you long for quick perdition.

Who holds another point of view,
He shall be shot without ado;
And argument by gesture is
Even more dangerous than this.

Honor your mayor; it is he
Who guards the state and zealously
Decides what's best for old and young.
So listen well—and hold your tongue."

Translated by Louis Untermeyer

This Vale of Tears

The windows shake, the whistling gale
Tries panes loose and unleaded;
And in the attic, poor and pale,
Two freezing souls are bedded.

One speaks: "These are but vain alarms.
What though the world is stormy,
Your mouth on mine is sweet, your arms
Are all I need to warm me."

The other, whispering, replies:
"Such moments make us stronger;
For when I look into your eyes
There is no cold or hunger."

They laugh and hold each other fast,
Their kisses have no number;
They weep and sing, and then at last
Fall into wordless slumber.

Am Morgen kam der Kommissär,
Und mit ihm kam ein braver
Chirurgus, welcher konstatiert
Den Tod der beiden Kadaver.

Die strenge Wittrung, erklärte er,
Mit Magenleere vereinigt,
Hat beider Ableben verursacht, sie hat
Zum mindesten solches beschleunigt.

Wenn Fröste eintreten, setzt' er hinzu,
Sei höchst notwendig Verwahrung
Durch wollene Decken; er empfahl
Gleichfalls gesunde Nahrung.

Die Wanderratten

Es gibt zwei Sorten Ratten:
Die hungrigen und satten.
Die satten bleiben vergnügt zu Haus,
Die hungrigen aber wandern aus.

Sie wandern viel tausend Meilen,
Ganz ohne Rasten und Weilen,
Gradaus in ihrem grimmigen Lauf,
Nicht Wind noch Wetter hält sie auf.

Sie klimmen wohl über die Höhen,
Sie schwimmen wohl durch die Seen;
Gar manche ersäuft oder bricht das Genick,
Die lebenden lassen die toten zurück.

Es haben diese Käuze
Gar fürchterliche Schnäuze;
Sie tragen die Köpfe geschoren egal,
Ganz radikal, ganz rattenkahl.

Next day there came the coroner
And doctor, widely cherished;
And both of them agreed, 'twas clear
That the poor souls had perished.

"An empty stomach," they averred,
"Combined with bitter weather
Hastened the death that here occurred,
Or caused it altogether.

When cold sets in one must withstand
The weather; we've discovered
It's best to be well nourished and
To lie in bed well covered."

Translated by Louis Untermeyer

The Wander-Rats

There are two kinds of rat:
The hungry and the fat.
The fat ones are jolly and stay in place,
While the hungry ones become emigrés.

They move for miles abreast,
With neither a stop nor a rest;
They grimly proceed on their straight road,
They will not by wind or weather be slowed.

They climb over hills that are steep,
They swim through lakes that are deep;
Many drown, some break a neck or a head,
The living are leaving behind the dead.

They have, those down-and-outs,
Very mean and horrible snouts
On heads as bald as billiard balls,
More radical than most radicals.

Die radikale Rotte
Weiss nichts von einem Gotte.
Sie lassen nicht taufen ihre Brut,
Die Weiber sind Gemeindegut.

Der sinnliche Rattenhaufen,
Er will nur fressen und saufen,
Er denkt nicht, während er säuft und frisst,
Dass unsre Seele unsterblich ist.

So eine wilde Ratze,
Die fürchtet nicht Hölle, nicht Katze;
Sie hat kein Gut, sie hat kein Geld
Und wünscht aufs neue zu teilen die Welt.

Die Wanderratten, o wehe!
Sie sind schon in der Nähe.
Sie rücken heran, ich höre schon
Ihr Pfeifen—die Zahl ist Legion.

O wehe! wir sind verloren,
Sie sind schon vor den Toren!
Der Bürgermeister und Senat,
Sie schütteln die Köpfe, und keiner weiss Rat.

Die Bürgerschaft greift zu den Waffen,
Die Glocken läuten die Pfaffen.
Gefährdet ist das Palladium
Des sittlichen Staats, das Eigentum.

Nicht Glockengeläute, nicht Pfaffengebete,
Nicht hochwohlweise Senatsdekrete,
Auch nicht Kanonen, viel Hundertpfünder,
Sie helfen Euch heute, Ihr lieben Kinder!

Heut helfen Euch nicht die Wortgespinste
Der abgelebten Redekünste.
Man fängt nicht Ratten mit Syllogismen,
Sie springen über die feinsten Sophismen.

That radical mob knows not
A singular thing about God.
They never baptize their ugly broods,
The women are communal goods.

The sensual riffraff, indeed,
Wants only to guzzle and feed.
And while it eats and while it drinks,
Not once of the soul's immortality thinks.

Why, such a rotten rat
Fears neither hell nor cat;
Lacks property, lacks money too,
And wants to divide the world anew.

The wander-rats, oh, dear!
They are already near.
They're coming on, their whistling is mounting,
Their numbers are vast, too vast for counting.

Oh, my! We're lost. That roar
Means, the rabble is at the door!
The mayor, the senators, fearing a coup,
Are shaking their heads and don't know what to do.

The citizens pick up their arms,
The clerics start tolling alarms.
Endangered is our morality,
In another word, our property.

Not the knelling of bells, not priestly prayer,
Not learned decretals by senate and mayor,
Not even cannons that weigh many tons
Will help you today, my beloved sons!

Today, it's too late for verbal gimmicks,
Nor will you succeed as rhetorical mimics;
You won't catch rats with syllogisms,
They jump over your most brilliant sophisms.

Im hungrigen Magen Eingang finden
Nur Suppenlogik mit Knödelgründen,
Nur Argumente von Rinderbraten,
Begleitet mit Göttinger Wurst-Zitaten.

Ein schweigender Stockfisch, in Butter gesotten,
Behaget den radikalen Rotten
Viel besser als ein Mirabeau
Und alle Redner seit Cicero.

Das Hohelied

Des Weibes Leib ist ein Gedicht,
Das Gott der Herr geschrieben
Ins grosse Stammbuch der Natur,
Als ihn der Geist getrieben.

Ja, günstig war die Stunde ihm,
Der Gott war hochbegeistert;
Er hat den spröden, rebellischen Stoff
Ganz künstlerisch bemeistert.

Fürwahr, der Leib des Weibes ist
Das Hohelied der Lieder;
Gar wunderbare Strophen sind
Die schlanken, weissen Glieder.

O welche göttliche Idee
Ist dieser Hals, der blanke,
Worauf sich wiegt der kleine Kopf,
Der lockige Hauptgedanke!

Der Brüstchen Rosenknospen sind
Epigrammatisch gefeilet;
Unsäglich entzückend ist die Zäsur,
Die streng den Busen teilet.

The hungry belly will only receive
The logic of soup with a dumpling motif,
Or arguments based on steak delectations,
And bolstered by Göttingen sausage citations.

A silent well-buttered codfish accords
Far better with the tastes of these hordes
Than a truly great man, such as Mirabeau,
Or all rhetoricians since Cicero.

Translated by Felix Pollak

The Song of Songs

The woman's body is a song,
Written by God the Lord
In nature's giant diary,
When the spirit guided His word.

Ah yes, the hour favored Him,
The God was quite art-inspired;
He worked till the brittle rebellious stuff
Left nothing to be desired.

Indeed, the woman's body is
Of all songs the most sublime;
How marvelous its stanzas are,
And the white limbs' flawless rhyme.

Oh, it's divinely masterful
How this slim neck is wrought.
Upon which sits the little head,
The curly capital thought.

The little, young breasts, like rosebuds, are
Two epigrams turned to perfection,
While the lovely and strict caesura divides
The bosom in two equal sections.

Den plastischen Schöpfer offenbart
Der Hüften Parallele;
Der Zwischensatz mit dem Feigenblatt
Ist auch eine schöne Stelle.

Das ist kein abstraktes Begriffspoem!
Das Lied hat Fleisch und Rippen,
Hat Hand und Fuss; es lacht und küsst
Mit schöngereimten Lippen.

Hier atmet wahre Poesie!
Anmut in jeder Wendung!
Und auf der Stirne trägt das Lied
Den Stempel der Vollendung.

Lobsingen will ich dir, o Herr,
Und dich im Staub anbeten!
Wir sind nur Stümper gegen dich,
Den himmlischen Poeten.

Versenken will ich mich, o Herr,
In deines Liedes Prächten;
Ich widme seinem Studium
Den Tag mitsamt den Nächten.

Ja, Tag und Nacht studier ich dran,
Will keine Zeit verlieren;
Die Beine werden mir so dünn—
Das kommt vom vielen Studieren.

The accomplished sculptor is revealed
By the hips, their parallel grace;
The interval with the fig leaf on top
Is also a pretty place.

This is no abstract, conceptual poem!
This song has flesh and ribs,
Has hand and foot; it kisses and laughs
With perfectly rhymed lips.

Each breath here is true poetry!
Each turn a delectation!
And proudly bears this song the mark
Of ultimate consummation.

Your praises will I sing, O Lord!
Can I be humble enough?
What duffers we are, compared to You,
The heavenly poet above.

I will immerse me in this song,
Its glories will I view,
And study them devotedly
All days, and all nights too.

Yes, day and night I study it,
Time will so quickly pass;
My legs are getting thin. The cause?
My studious life, alas!

Translated by Felix Pollak

Ich habe verlacht, bei Tag und bei Nacht,
So Männer wie Frauenzimmer,
Ich habe grosse Dummheiten gemacht—
Die Klugheit bekam mir noch schlimmer.

Die Magd ward schwanger und gebar—
Wozu das viele Gewimmer?
Wer nie im Leben töricht war,
Ein Weiser war er nimmer.

Lotosblume

Wahrhaftig, wir beide bilden
Ein kurioses Paar,
Die Liebste ist schwach auf den Beinen,
Der Liebhaber lahm sogar.

Sie ist ein leidendes Kätzchen,
Und er ist krank wie ein Hund,
Ich glaube, im Kopfe sind beide
Nicht sonderlich gesund.

Vertraut sind ihre Seelen,
Doch jedem von beiden bleibt fremd
Was bei dem andern befindlich
Wohl zwischen Seel und Hemd.

Sie sei eine Lotosblume,
Bildet die Liebste sich ein;
Doch er, der blasse Geselle,
Vermeint der Mond zu sein.

Die Lotosblume erschliesset
Ihr Kelchlein im Mondenlicht,
Doch statt des befruchtenden Lebens
Empfängt sie nur ein Gedicht.

I have laughed by day, I have laughed by night,
   With maid and with man been jolly,
I've sometimes done wrong and sometimes right,
   And right was the greater folly.

The maid was a mother before a wife—
   Why all the lamenting after?
If you've never been foolish at all in your life,
   Your wisdom's a thing for laughter.

Translated by Charles Godfrey Leland

Lotus Blossom

Truly, the two of us warrant
A certain comical fame,
The loved one's legs are shaky,
The lover is actually lame.

She is an ailing kitten,
He's sick as a dog all around;
In the head, I believe, neither one is
Particularly sound.

Their souls are closely united,
Yet neither of them could know less
What between their souls and their shirts they
Might otherwise possess.

She thinks she's a lotus blossom,
Whose petals will open soon,
While he, her pale companion,
Fancies himself the moon.

The lotus shyly bares her
Cup to the moonlight above,
But instead of the seed of life, she
Receives a poem of love.

Translated by Felix Pollak

Part Two

NARRATIVE
PROSE

The Harz Journey

Nothing is as lasting as change; nothing as constant as death. Every beat of the heart wounds us, and life would be an eternal bleeding to death if there were no poetry. Poetry grants us what nature denies: a golden age that is never tarnished, a springtime that never ceases to bloom, cloudless joy and eternal youth.

Börne

Black their coats, of silk their stockings,
White their frilly cuffs, and smart,
Smooth their talk and their embraces—
If they only had a heart!

If they had some heart, and loving,
Loving, and a heart that glows—
Ah, it kills me when I listen
To their lies of lovelorn woes.

I will climb the lofty mountains,
Where the humble cabins stand,
Where a man can breathe in freedom
And free air blows through the land.

I will climb the lofty mountains,
Where dark fir trees tower high,
Where the brooks rush, and the birds sing,
And the clouds sail proudly by.

Polished floors! And polished ladies!
Polished gentlemen! Adieu!
I will climb the lofty mountains,
Laughing I'll look down on you.

The town of Göttingen, renowned for its sausages and university, belongs to the King of Hanover and contains 999 fireplaces, sundry churches, a maternity hospital, an observatory, a university house of detention, a library, and a rathskeller where the beer is very good. The brook that flows by is called the Leine and is used for bathing in summer; the water is very cold and in some spots so broad that Lüder really had to get a good running start when he jumped over it. The town itself is pretty and is most pleasing when viewed by one's back. It must have existed for a very long time, for I recall that when I matriculated there five years ago and was soon thereafter expelled, it already had that same hoary, pretentious appearance and was already completely provided with rattles, poodles, dissertations, tea dances, laundresses, compendia, roast pigeons, Guelfic orders, graduation carriages, pipe heads, court councilors, councilors of justice, dismissal councilors, professional buffoons, and other buffoons. Some even maintain that the town was built in the period of the Germanic migrations, that every German tribe left behind at that time an unbound copy of its members and from these descended all the Vandals, Frisians, Swabians, Teutons, Saxons, Thuringians, etc., who even now, distinguished by the colors of their caps and pipe tassels, roam in hordes over Weende Street in Göttingen, fight eternally with each other on the bloody battlefields of the Rasenmühle, the Ritschenkrug, and Bovden, continue to observe the manners and customs of the age of the migrations, and are governed partly by their *duces,* who are known as chief cocks, partly by their ancient law book, which is entitled *The Code* and merits a place among the *legibus barbarorum.*

In general, the inhabitants of Göttingen are divided into students, professors, philistines, and cattle—four classes, however, that are anything but rigorously kept apart. The cattle class is the most important. It would take too long to recount here the names of all students and of all regular and irregular professors; besides, at present I do not remember all the students' names, while among the professors there are many who as yet have no name whatever. The number of Göttingen philistines must be very large, like sand or, to put it better, like mud by the sea; indeed, when I saw them in the morning, planted with their dirty faces and clean accounts in front of the gates of the academic court, I could scarcely comprehend how God could have created such a pack of rascals.

Further details concerning the town of Göttingen can be very conveniently found in the description of the town by K. F. H. Marx. Although I am bound by the most sacred obligations to the author, who was my physician and was extremely kind to me, I nonetheless cannot recommend his work without reservation, and I must reproach him for not strongly enough contradicting the incorrect opinion that the feet of the women of Göttingen are much too large. Indeed I have long occupied myself with an earnest refutation of this opinion; for this purpose I have heard lectures on comparative anatomy, excerpted the rarest works in the library, studied for hours the feet of the ladies passing through Weende Street, and in the learned treatise that is to contain the results of these studies I shall speak of (1) feet in general, (2) the feet of the ancients, (3) the feet of elephants, and (4) the feet of the ladies of Göttingen; (5) I shall collect everything that has already been said about these feet in Ullrich's Garden; (6) I shall consider these feet in their context and shall extend my observations at this point to calves, knees, etc.; (7) and finally, if I can only get hold of paper large enough, I shall add some copperplates with facsimiles of the feet of Göttingen ladies.

It was still very early when I left Göttingen, and the learned —— was surely still lying in bed and dreaming, as usual, that he was wandering about in a beautiful garden in whose beds were growing nothing but white bits of paper covered with quotations that glowed pleasingly in the sunlight and of which he picks several here and there and laboriously transplants them into a new bed while the nightingales regale his old heart with their sweetest sounds.

In front of the Weende Gate I came across two small local schoolboys, one of whom was saying to the other, "I don't want to have anything more to do with Theodore; he is a worthless scamp, because yesterday he didn't even know what the genitive of *mensa* is."As insignificant as these words sound, I must nevertheless repeat them; as a matter of fact, I would like to have them inscribed right away as a town motto on the gate, because "like father, like son," those words characterize perfectly the narrow, dry love of pedantry of the highly learned Georgia Augusta.

On the highway a brisk morning breeze was blowing, the birds were singing quite merrily, and I, too, gradually began to feel brisk and merry. Such refreshment was necessary. For some time I had not escaped from the pandect stall; Roman casuists had covered my mind as with a gray cobweb; my heart was as if wedged in between the iron paragraphs of self-centered legal systems; the sounds of "Tribonian, Justinian, Hermogenian, and Block-headian" rang ceaselessly in my ears, and I even mistook a tender pair of lovers sitting under a tree for an edition of the *corpus juris* with hands entwined. Signs of life began to appear on the road. Milkmaids went past, also donkey drivers with their gray charges. Beyond Weende I encountered Schäfer and Doris. This is not the idyllic pair of whom Gessner sings; rather, they are duly installed university proctors who must attentively watch out to see that no students duel in Bovden and that no new ideas, which must still remain in quarantine outside Göttingen for several decades, are smuggled in by a speculating instructor. Schäfer greeted me colle-gially, for he is likewise an author and has often mentioned me in his semiannual writings; just as he has also often cited me and, when he did not find me at home, was always so kind as to write the citation in chalk on the door to my room. Now and then a one-horse carriage rolled past, well packed with students going away for the vacation, or forever. In such a university town there is a constant arriving and departing; every three years there is a new generation of students; it is an eternal human stream in which one semester wave crowds out the other, and only the old profes-sors remain in this general movement, immovably firm like the pyramids of Egypt, except that no wisdom is hidden in these uni-versity pyramids.

Out of the myrtle bowers near Rauschenwasser I saw two hope-ful youths riding forth. A wench who plies her horizontal trade there accompanied them up to the road, clapped the lean shanks of the horses with practiced hand, laughed aloud when one of the riders delivered some gallantries with his whip on her broad spon-taneity, and then pushed off in the direction of Bovden. The youths, however, raced toward Nörten, yodeling very cleverly and singing most delightfully Rossini's song: "Drink beer, dear, dear Liese!" I heard these sounds far in the distance, but I soon completely lost sight of the sweet singers themselves, since they mercilessly whipped and spurred forward their horses, which basically seemed to have a sluggish German character. Nowhere is there greater mistreatment of horses than in Göttingen, and often when I saw how such a sweat-dripping, lame old plug was being tortured for his bit of fodder by our knights of Rauschenwasser or was even being forced to pull a whole wagonful of students, I thought to myself, "Oh, you poor animal, surely your ancestors ate forbidden oats in Eden!"

At the inn at Nörten I met the two youths again. One of them was devouring a herring salad, and the other was conversing with the sallow, leather-faced maid, Fusia Canina, also called Wagtail. He paid her some compliments, and in the end they came to close quarters. To lighten my knapsack I again took out my blue trousers, which are very strange from a historical standpoint, and presented them to the little waiter, who is known as Hummingbird. In the meantime Bussenia, the old landlady, brought me a slice of bread and butter and complained because I now visit her so seldom; for she loves me very much.

Beyond Nörten the sun stood high and brilliant in the sky. It meant well toward me and so warmed my head that all unripe thoughts in it came to maturity. The nice Sun Inn in Nordheim is also not to be disdained; I stopped in here and found the midday meal ready. All the dishes were tastefully prepared and suited me better than the tasteless academic dishes, the saltless, leathery dried fish and old cabbage that were set before me in Göttingen.

After I had appeased my appetite somewhat, I noticed in the same public room a gentleman with two ladies who were on the verge of departing. This man was clad all in green; he even wore a pair of green spectacles that cast a gleam as of verdigris on his red copper nose, and he looked like King Nebuchadnezzar in his later years when, according to the legend, like a beast in the forest he ate nothing but salad. The green one wanted me to recommend to him a hotel in Göttingen, and I advised him to ask the first student he met for the Hotel de Brühbach. One of the ladies was the gentleman's wife, a large, expansive lady, her face a red square mile with dimples in the cheeks that looked like spittoons for gods of love; her long, fleshy double chin that hung down seemed to be a poor continuation of her face, and her bosom was stacked high and surrounded by stiff lace and many pointed, festooned collars like turrets and bastions. It resembled a fortress that certainly would as little resist an ass laden with gold as those other fortresses of which Philip of Macedonia speaks. The other lady, her sister, constituted the exact antithesis of the one just described. If the former descended from Pharaoh's fat cows, the latter must have descended from the lean ones. Her face merely a mouth between two ears, her breast disconsolately desolate like the Lüneburg Heath; her whole dried-out figure resembled a charity table for poor theologians. Both ladies asked me at the same time whether respectable people stay at the Hotel de Brühbach. I affirmed it in good conscience, and as the charming trio drove off, I waved to them once more from the window. The innkeeper of the Sun grinned wryly, for he doubtless knew very well that the university house of detention in Göttingen is called Hotel de Brühbach by the students.

Beyond Nordheim it is already hilly, and here and there beautiful knolls stand out. On the way I met mostly shopkeepers going to the Brunswick Fair, also a swarm of girls, each of whom was carrying on her back a large pack almost as high as a house and covered with white linen. In them were sitting all sorts of captive songbirds, which continually chirped and twittered while their bearers merrily hopped on and chattered. To me it seemed very silly to see one bird carrying another to market.

In pitch-dark night I arrived in Osterode. Having no appetite for supper, I went to bed right away. I was as tired as a dog and slept like a god. In my dream I returned to Göttingen again, in fact to the library there. I stood in a corner of the Hall of Law, rummaged through old dissertations, became absorbed in reading, and when I stopped, noticed to my surprise that it was night and that low-hanging crystal lamps illumined the hall. The nearby church clock was just striking twelve, the hall door opened slowly, and in stepped a proud, gigantic woman, respectfully accompanied by the members and disciples of the law faculty. The giant woman, though already advanced in years, bore nevertheless in her countenance the traces of a stern beauty; each of her glances revealed the high Titaness, the powerful Themis. She carelessly held sword and scales in one hand; in the other she held a parchment roll, while two young *doctores juris* carried the train of her faded gray garment; at her right side the lean Court Councilor Rusticus, the Lycurgus of Hanover, hopped about airily here and there, declaiming from his new draft of a bill; at her left side hobbled, quite gallantly and cheerfully, her *cavaliere servente,* the Privy Councilor of Justice Cujacius, constantly cracking legal jokes and himself laughing so heartily over them that even the grave goddess smilingly bent down to him several times, patted him on the shoulder with her large parchment roll, and whispered in a friendly fashion, "You naughty little rascal who wants to prune the trees starting at the top!" Each of the other gentlemen now likewise approached with something to say or a smile, perhaps a newly concocted little system or petty hypothesis or similar miscarriage of his own little head. Through the open door to the hall several more unfamiliar gentlemen entered, giving themselves out to be other great men of illustrious order. Most of them were angular, sharp-eyed fellows who, with extreme complacency, straightaway fired off their definitions, made their fine distinctions, and disputed about every subheading of a pandect title. New figures kept coming in, ancient doctors of law in out-of-date costumes with white, full-bottomed wigs and long-forgotten faces and very much astonished that they, the very famous scholars of the past century, were not especially esteemed. In their own way the latter now joined in the general chattering and yelling and shouting, which, like the ocean surf, ever more confused and louder, roared about the mighty goddess until, losing her patience, she suddenly cried out in a tone of the most terrible gigantic pain, "Silence! Silence! I hear the voice of dear Prometheus; scornful power and brute force keep the innocent one chained to the martyr's rock, and all your chattering and squabbling cannot cool his wounds or break his fetters!" Thus cried the goddess, and streams of tears poured from her eyes; the whole assemblage howled as if seized by mortal fear; the ceiling of the hall cracked, the books tumbled down from their shelves; in vain old Münchhausen came out of his frame to restore order; the storming and screaming grew even wilder—and I escaped from this distressing madhouse commotion into the Hall of History, into that merciful place where the sacred statues of the Belvedere Apollo and the Medicean Venus stand side by side, and

I fell at the feet of the Goddess of Beauty; at the sight of her I forgot all the wild activity I had run from, my eyes ecstatically drank in the symmetry and the eternal loveliness of her most blessed form, Grecian calm passed through my soul, and over my head Phœbus Apollo poured, like a heavenly benediction, the sweetest sounds of his lyre.

On awaking I still heard a friendly ringing. The herds were going to pasture and their tiny bells were sounding. The lovely, golden sun shone through the window and illuminated the paintings on the walls of the room. They were pictures of the Wars of Liberation faithfully representing us all as heroes. There were also execution scenes from the period of the Revolution, Louis XVI on the guillotine and similar beheadings, which one simply cannot look at without thanking God that one is lying quietly in bed, drinking fine coffee and still has one's head sitting quite comfortably on one's shoulders.

After I had drunk coffee, dressed, read the inscriptions on the windowpanes, and paid up everything at the inn, I left Osterode.

This town has so-and-so many houses and various inhabitants, among whom there are even several souls, as one can read more precisely in Gottschalk's *Handbook for Harz Travelers*. Before striking out on the road, I climbed the ruins of the ancient castle of Osterode. They now consist only of half of a large, thick-walled tower that seems to have been gnawed by cankers. The road to Klaustal led me again uphill, and from one of the first heights I once more glanced down into the valley where Osterode with its red roofs peeps out of the green fir forests like a moss rose. The sun gave off a most kindly childlike light. From the tower half still standing it is possible to glimpse the imposing rear side.

There are many other castle ruins in this region. The most beautiful one is the Hardenberg in the vicinity of Nörten. Even if one has his heart on the left, on the liberal side, as is fitting, one cannot avoid a feeling of sadness at the sight of the rocky nests of those privileged birds of prey who handed down to their feeble progeny merely their enormous appetite. And that was the way I felt this morning. My heart gradually thawed out the farther I got from Göttingen; again, as usual, I began to have romantic thoughts, and as I hiked I composed the following song:

Rise anew, O vanished visions!
Open, gate before my heart!
Joys of singing, tears of sorrow
Forth in wondrous manner start.

Through the fir woods I'll go roaming,
Where the merry fountains spring,
Where the haughty stags go wandering,
Where the thrushes sweetly sing.

Up the mountains I'll go climbing,
Up the steep and rocky height,
Where the dingy castle ruins
Stand in early morning light.

There I'll sit in contemplation,
And remember times of old,
Ancient families in their splendor,
Glory sunk beneath the mold.

Grass bedecks the tourney place now,
Where the hero proudly fought,
Who the best in combat conquered,
Gained the victor's prize he sought.

Ivy clambers round the balcon,
And the pretty lady there
Overcame the haughty victor
With her radiant eyes so fair.

Ah! the victor and the victress
Death has conquered past recall—
Finally that withered scythe man
In the dust will stretch us all.

After I had walked some distance, I met up with a traveling
journeyman who had come from Brunswick and who told me
about a rumor current there: the young Duke had been captured

by the Turks on his way to the Promised Land and could only be freed in return for a huge ransom. The Duke's long trip may have prompted this tale. The common people still have the traditional fabulous train of thought that is so delightfully expressed in their *Duke Ernest*. The narrator of that piece of news was a journeyman tailor, a nice little young fellow so thin that the stars could shine through him as through Ossian's nebulous spirits and on the whole a popular baroque mixture of caprice and melancholy. This was expressed especially in the amusingly touching manner in which he sang the wonderful folksong, "A beetle sat upon the hedge; buzz, buzz!" That is what is nice about us Germans: none of us is so crazy that he cannot find someone still crazier who will understand him. Only a German can have a feeling for that song and laugh and weep himself to death on hearing it. I also observed here how deeply the words of Goethe have penetrated into the life of the people. For my thin companion likewise trilled to himself from time to time, "Sorrowful and joyful, thoughts are free!" Such a corruption of the text is quite usual among the common people. He also sang a song in which Lottchen mourns "at the grave of her Werther." The tailor dissolved with sentimentality at the words:

> All alone I weep beside the flowers,
> Where us oft the tardy moon espied!
> Sadly by the spring I pass the hours,
> Where of joy and happiness it sighed!

But shortly afterward he became playful and told me, "We have a Prussian in the inn at Cassel who makes such songs himself; he can't sew a blessed stitch; if he has one groschen in his pocket, he is sure to have a thirst worth two groschen; and when he is drunk, he thinks the sky is a blue camisole, weeps like a gutter spout, and sings a song with double poetry!" I wanted an explanation of this last expression, but my little tailor, with his Ziegenhain legs, hopped back and forth, crying out continually, "Double poetry is double poetry!" Finally I got it out of him that he meant poems containing double rhymes, namely stanzas. Meanwhile, as a result of his extra exertion and the adverse wind, the knight of the needle had become very tired. He made, to be sure, several great efforts to leave and boasted, "Now I'll get a move on!" But soon he complained that he had walked blisters on his feet and that the world was far too large; and finally he sank down softly at the tree trunk, wagged his delicate little head like a mournful lamb's tail, and smiling woefully, he cried, "Well, here I am, poor devil, all done in again!"

The hills became even steeper here, the fir woods billowed like a green sea below, and the white clouds sailed in the blue sky above. The wildness of the region was tamed by its unity and simplicity. Like a good poet, nature does not like abrupt transitions. The clouds, as bizarre as they sometimes appeared to be shaped, have a white or at least a soft tint that corresponds harmoniously with the blue sky and the green earth, so that all the colors of a region melt into one another like gentle music, and every view of nature has the effect of quieting pain and calming the spirit. (The late Hoffmann would have painted the clouds in mottled colors.) Just like a great poet, nature knows how to produce the greatest effects with the fewest means. It has only a sun, trees, flowers, water, and love. To be sure, if the last is lacking in the heart of the observer, the whole view will probably seem to be a poor one; the sun is then only so-and-so many miles in diameter, the trees are good for kindling, the flowers are classified by their stamens, and water is wet.

A small boy seeking brushwood in the forest for his sick uncle showed me the village of Lerbach, whose tiny huts with their gray roofs stretch out for more than half an hour through the valley. "There," said he, "live stupid people with goiters and white Moors." The Albinos are given this name by the common people. The youngster had his own special understanding with the trees; he greeted them as good acquaintances, and they seemed to acknowledge his greeting with their rustling. He whistled like a siskin, all around the other birds answered with their twittering, and before I was aware of it, he had sprung off into the thick woods with his bare feet and his bundle of brushwood. Children, I thought, are younger than we are; they can still remember when they were also trees or birds and are thus still in a position to understand them; we, however, are already old and have too many cares, jurisprudence, and bad verses in our heads. Those years when things were different quite vividly came back to my mind upon my entrance into Klaustal. I arrived in this nice little mountain village, which cannot be seen until one is standing right before it, just as the clock was striking twelve and the children were jubilantly getting out of school. The dear boys, nearly all of them red-cheeked, blue-eyed and flaxen-haired, jumped and shouted, arousing in me the wistfully happy memory of how once upon a time I myself as a small lad was not permitted to stand up during the whole blessed morning from my wooden bench in the gloomy Catholic cloister school in Düsseldorf and had to endure so much Latin, punishment, and geography, and then also shouted and rejoiced to excess when the old Franciscan clock finally struck twelve. The children saw from my knapsack that I was a stranger and greeted me most hospitably. One of the boys told me that they had just had instruction in religion, and he showed me the Royal Hanoverian Catechism used for instructing them in Christianity. This booklet was very badly printed, and I am afraid that the articles of faith consequently make an unpleasant blotting-paper impression on the minds of the children. It also displeased me enormously that the multiplication table, which as a matter of fact dangerously conflicts with the doctrine of the Holy Trinity, was printed in the catechism itself, and what is worse, on the last page; for children can thereby be led early to sinful doubtings. In Prussia we are much more sensible, and in our zeal to convert those people who are so good at making calculations we guard against having the multiplication table printed after the catechism.

I had dinner at the Crown in Klaustal. I was served spring-green parsley soup, violet-blue cabbage, a roast of veal as big as Chimborazo in miniature, as well as a kind of smoked herring called Bücking, named for its inventor, Wilhelm Bücking, who died in 1447, and who was so respected by Charles V for his invention that the latter traveled *anno* 1556 from Middelburg to Bievlied in Zeeland merely to visit there the grave of that great man. How glorious is the taste of such a dish if one knows the historical references to it while devouring it! Only the coffee following dinner was spoiled for me by a talkative young man who sat down next to me and bragged so terribly that the milk on the table turned sour. He was a young tradesman with twenty-five colored vests and just as many gold signets, rings, stick pins, etc. He looked like a monkey who has put on a red jacket and then says to himself, "Clothes make the man." He knew by heart a great number of charades as well as anecdotes, which he always brought in where they were least appropriate. He asked me what was new in Göttingen, and I told him that before my departure a decree of the Academic Senate had appeared, according to which it was forbidden, under penalty of a three-taler fine, to cut the tails off dogs, because mad dogs carry their tails between their legs during the dog days and can thus be distinguished from the non-mad dogs, which could not be done if they had no tails at all. After dinner I started out to visit the mines, the silver foundries, and the mint.

In the silver foundries I missed, as often in my life, the glimpse of silver. In the mint I had better luck and could see how money is made. I did not, to be sure, get any further with it. On such occasions I could only watch; and I believe, if talers ever rain down from heaven, I would get nothing but holes in my head, while the children of Israel would merrily gather in the silver manna. With a feeling in which reverence and emotion were most comically mixed, I observed the newborn shining talers, took one that had just come from the die into my hand and spoke to it: "Young taler! What a destiny awaits thee! How much good and how much evil thou wilt cause! How thou wilt shield vice and patch up virtue, how thou wilt be loved and then again be cursed! How thou wilt help in carousing, pandering, lying, and murdering! How thou wilt roam around restlessly, through clean and dirty hands for centuries until at last, guilt-ridden and weary of sin, thou art gathered unto thine own in the bosom of Abraham, who will melt thee down and refine and transform thee to a new and better being!"

I found the visit to the two best mines in Klaustal, the Dorothy and the Caroline, very interesting, and I must tell about it in detail.

A half hour before the town one comes upon two large blackish buildings. There one is immediately received by the miners. They wear dark, loose-fitting jackets, usually steel-blue, that hang down over their stomachs; trousers of a similar color; leather aprons tied in back; and small, completely brimless, green felt hats like truncated cones. The visitor is also fitted out in such clothes, only without the leather apron in back, and a mine foreman, having lighted his miner's lamp, leads him to a dark opening that looks like a chimney sweep's hole, descends to his chest, gives instructions on how to hold fast to the ladders and asks you to follow without fear. The thing itself is anything but dangerous, but one does not believe it at first if totally unfamiliar with mining. Even the necessity of undressing and putting on dark prison garb produces a strange enough sensation. And now it is necessary to climb down on all fours, and the dark hole is so dark, and God knows how long the ladder may be. One soon notices that there is not just one ladder extending down into black eternity, but that there are several with fifteen to twenty rungs, each of which leads to a small plank on which one can stand and in which a new hole leads again to a new ladder. I descended first into the Caroline. That is the dirtiest and most unpleasant Caroline I ever knew. The ladder rungs are wet with filth. And we make the descent from one ladder to another, with the foreman in front always giving assurances that it is not dangerous at all, it is merely necessary to hold onto the rungs tightly and not look at one's feet and not get dizzy, and for heaven's sake not step on the side plank, where the whizzing bucket rope is now going up and where two weeks ago a careless person fell and unfortunately broke his neck. Down below, there is a confused rustling and humming; one constantly bumps against moving beams and ropes that haul up the buckets containing broken ore or the water that has trickled out. At times one arrives at hewn-out passages called galleries where one can see the ore growing and where the lonely miner sits all day long laboriously breaking the pieces of ore out of the wall with his hammer. I did not go down to the lowest depths where, as some assert, one can hear the people in America crying, "Hurrah, Lafayette!" Confidentially, the point I reached seemed already deep enough—continuous roaring and buzzing, mysterious movements of machines, subterranean murmuring of springs, water dripping down on all sides, earth vapors ascending smokily, and the miner's lamp glimmering ever paler into the lonely night. It was truly stupefying; I found it hard to breathe, and I had difficulty holding onto the slippery ladder rungs. I had no attack of so-called anxiety but, strangely enough, down there in the depths I recalled that in the preceding year at about the same time I had experienced a storm on the North Sea, and I thought now that it was really very cozy and pleasant when the ship rocked back and forth, the winds let loose with their trumpetings, the lusty shouts of the sailors resounded in the intervals, and everything was newly flooded over with God's blessed, fresh air. Yes, air! Panting for air, I again climbed up several dozen ladders, and my foreman led me to the Dorothy mine through a long and narrow passage cut into the hillside. Here it is airier and fresher, and the ladders are cleaner but also longer and steeper than in the Caroline. Here I began to feel better, especially since I again perceived traces of living beings. In the depths wandering gleams became visible; miners with their miners' lamps gradually came up with the greeting "Good luck!" and with the same greeting on our part they ascended past us; mysteriously illumined by the mine lamp, the profoundly clear expressions, the piously serious, somewhat pale faces of these old and young men who had worked the whole day in their dark, lonely mine shafts and now yearned to come up to the blessed light of day and to the eyes of wife and child struck me like a familiarly peaceful and yet at the same time tormentingly puzzling, memory.

My cicerone himself had a thoroughly honest, poodle-German nature. With inward joy he showed me the very gallery where the Duke of Cambridge had eaten when he went through the mine with his entire retinue and where the long, wooden dining table still stands as well as the great chair of ore on which the Duke sat. The good miner said it was to remain as an eternal memorial, and he spiritedly related how many festivities had taken place then, how the whole gallery had been decorated with lights, flowers, and foliage, how a miner had played the zither and sung, how the dear, fat, delighted Duke had drunk many toasts, and how many of the miners—and most especially he himself—would gladly let themselves be killed for the dear, fat Duke and the entire House of Hanover. I am deeply touched every time I see how this feeling of fealty is so simply and naturally expressed. It is such a beautiful feeling! And it is such a truly German feeling! Other peoples may be cleverer, wittier, and more amusing, but none are so loyal as the loyal German people. If I did not know that loyalty is as old as the world, I would believe that a German heart had invented it. German loyalty! It is no modern flowery phrase. At your courts, O German princes, should be sung and sung again the lay of the faithful Eckart and the evil Burgundian who had his dear children slain and nonetheless still considered him loyal. You have the most loyal people and are wrong in thinking that the old, sensible, loyal dog has suddenly gone mad and is snapping at your sacred calves.

Like German loyalty, the tiny miner's lamp without much flickering had now guided us quietly and surely through the labyrinth of shafts and galleries; we climbed up out of the damp night of the mines, the sunlight was shining—good luck!

Most of the miners live in Klaustal and in Zellerfeld, the small mountain village connected with it. I visited several of these stalwart people, saw their scanty domestic furnishings, heard some of their songs, which they accompany very prettily on the zither, their favorite instrument, had them tell me old mining tales and also recite the prayers that they hold together before they descend into the dark shaft, and many a good prayer I prayed with them. An old foreman even suggested that I stay with them and become a miner. When I, nevertheless, took leave, he gave me a message for his brother who lives in the vicinity of Goslar, and many kisses for his dear niece.

Although the life of these people seems so quiet and calm, it is nevertheless an authentic, lively existence. The aged, trembling woman sitting behind the stove opposite the large cupboard may well have been sitting there for a quarter of a century, and her thinking and feeling have certainly become intimately entwined with all the corners of this stove and all the carvings of this cupboard. And cupboard and stove live because a human being has imparted some of his soul to them.

Only through such a profound life of observation, only through immediacy, did the German fairy tale come into being, the peculiarity of which consists in the fact that not only animals and plants but also seemingly inanimate objects speak and act. To pensive, harmless people in the quiet, peaceful seclusion of their low mountain or forest huts was revealed the inner life of such objects. These acquired an inevitability and consistency of character, a sweet mixture of fanciful caprice and purely human disposition; and thus we see in the fairy tale, wondrously and yet as if it were a matter of course: needle and pin come from the tailors' lodgings and get lost in the dark; blade of straw and piece of coal set out over the brook and have an accident; shovel and broom stand on the stairway quarreling and fighting; the mirror, when questioned, shows the picture of the most beautiful woman; even the drops of blood begin to speak anxious, dark words of the deepest compassion. For the same reason, our life in childhood is so infinitely impor-

tant; in that period everything seems to us equally important; we
hear everything, we see everything; in all impressions there is uni-
formity, whereas later we become more purposeful, occupy ourselves more exclusively with details, laboriously exchange the clear
gold of observation for the paper money of book definitions, and
gain in breadth of life what we lose in depth of life. Now we are
grown-up, refined people; we often move into new homes; the
maid tidies up every day and alters as she pleases the position of
the furniture; that interests us very little since it is either new or
belongs to Jack today, to Isaac tomorrow; even our clothes remain unfamiliar to us; we scarcely know how many buttons are
on the coat we are wearing at this very moment; indeed, we change
our garments as often as possible; none of them remain in a relationship to our inner and outer history—we can hardly remember
the appearance of that brown vest that once made us the object
of so much mockery and on whose broad stripes nevertheless the
sweet hand of our sweetheart so sweetly rested.

The old woman opposite the large cupboard behind the stove
wore a flowered dress of faded material, the wedding dress of her
late mother. Her great-grandson, a blond, keen-eyed boy dressed
as a miner, sat at her feet counting the flowers on her dress, and
she may well have told him many tales about this dress, many grave,
fine stories that the youngster will certainly not forget so soon,
and that will often hover before his mind's eye when soon, as a
grown man, he is working all alone in the nocturnal galleries of
the Caroline, and that he will perhaps retell when his dear grandmother has long been dead and he himself, a silver-haired, worn-
out old man is sitting, surrounded by his grandchildren, opposite
the large cupboard behind the stove.

I also spent the night in the Crown, where meanwhile the Court
Councilor B. from Göttingen had arrived. I had the pleasure of
paying my respect to the old gentleman. When I wrote my name
in the hotel register and leafed through the month of July, I discovered the dearly loved name of Adalbert von Chamisso, the
biographer of the immortal Schlemihl. The innkeeper told me that
this gentleman had arrived in indescribably bad weather and had
left in weather just as bad.

The next morning I had to lighten my knapsack once more. I
threw overboard the pair of boots packed in it, picked up my feet,

and went to Goslar. I arrived there without knowing how. I can recall only so much: I sauntered once more uphill, downhill; looked down into many a pretty meadow vale; silvery waters splashed, sweet forest birds twittered, the herd bells tinkled, the numerous green trees were showered in gold by the blessed sun, and the blue silk canopy of the sky was so transparent that one could gaze far into it, even into the Holy of Holies where the angels sit at the feet of God, studying *basso continuo* in the features of His countenance. But I was still living in the dream of the preceding night, which I could not banish from my soul. It was the old tale of the knight who descends into a deep well, down to where the most beautiful princess lies under the curse of a benumbing, magical sleep. I myself was the knight, and the well was the dark Klaustal mine; and suddenly many lights appeared, the watchful dwarfs lunged out of all the side holes, made angry faces, lashed at me with their short swords, and blew shrilly into their horns, so that more and more dwarfs rushed in, their broad heads shaking frightfully. Only when I struck at them and the blood flowed did I realize that they were the red-blooming, long-bearded thistle heads that I had cut off the day before on the road. They were all immediately frightened off too, and I arrived in a bright, splendid hall; in the middle, veiled in white and like a statue fixed and motionless, stood my heart's beloved. I kissed her mouth and, by the living God, I felt the inspiring breath of her soul and the sweet trembling of her lovely lips! It seemed to me that I heard God crying out, "Let there be light." A dazzling ray of the eternal light shot down, but in the same moment it was night again and everything ran chaotically together into a wild, desolate sea. A wild, desolate sea! The spirits of the dead raced anxiously over the foaming waters, their white shrouds fluttering in the wind, while a motley harlequin ran behind them, driving them on by cracking his whip, and that was I myself—and suddenly from out of the dark waves the sea monsters stretched their misshapen heads and reached for me with outspread claws, and I awoke from fright.

How the most beautiful fairy tales are sometimes spoiled! Actually, when the knight has found the sleeping princess, he is supposed to cut a piece out of her precious veil; and when the spell of her magical sleep is broken by his boldness, and she is again sitting on her golden throne in her palace, the knight must approach her and say, "My most beautiful princess, do you know me?" And then she answers, "My bravest of knights, I do not know you." Then he shows her the piece cut out of her veil, which fits perfectly into it, and they embrace each other tenderly, the trumpeters blow, and the wedding is celebrated.

It is really my own peculiar misfortune that my dreams of love rarely come to such a beautiful conclusion.

The name Goslar has such a pleasant ring, and so many ancient memories of emperors are connected with it that I expected a stately, imposing town. But so it goes when celebrities are seen from close up. I found a decayed and moldy nest with mostly narrow and crooked, labyrinthine streets, through the middle of which flows a small bit of water, probably the Gose, and a pavement as bumpy as Berlin hexameters. Only the ancient buildings in the setting—that is, remains of walls, towers, and battlements—impart something piquant to the town. One of these towers, called the Zwinger, has such thick walls that whole rooms are hewn out in it. The space in front of the town where the renowned open shooting match is held is a beautiful, large meadow surrounded by high mountains. The marketplace is small; in the center there is a fountain whose waters flow into a large metal basin. When there is a fire, it is struck several times and produces a sound that carries a great distance. Nothing is known of the origin of this basin. Some say the devil once put it there on the marketplace at night. In those days the people were still stupid, the devil was also stupid, and they exchanged presents.

The Town Hall in Goslar is a guardroom painted white. The guild house standing next to it has a better appearance. At about an equal distance from the earth and the roof are the smokily black, partly gilded statues of German emperors, holding in one hand the scepter, in the other the globe; they look like roasted university proctors. One of these emperors holds a sword instead of a scepter. I could not guess what this difference was supposed to mean. It must have meant something, for the Germans have the strange custom of associating a meaning with everything they do.

In Gottschalk's *Handbook* I had read a great deal about the ancient cathedral and the famous emperor's throne at Goslar. But when I wanted to see both of them, I was told that the cathedral had been torn down and that the emperor's throne had been taken to Berlin. And so one day the traveler will come to Europe and ask in vain for Germany. Our lance-skilled friends will have put it in their pockets and dragged it away under their high saddles. We live in portentous times: cathedrals a thousand years old are razed, and the thrones of emperors are thrown into the dustbin.

Some of the curiosities of the late cathedral are now on display in the Church of Saint Stephan. Paintings on glass, which are wonderfully beautiful, some bad paintings, among which is reputedly a Lucas Cranach, also a wooden Christ on the Cross, and a pagan sacrificial altar of unknown metal; it has the shape of a longish four-cornered chest and is borne by four caryatids who, in bent-over position, hold their hands supportingly over their heads and make unpleasantly ugly faces. Still more unpleasant, however, is the just-mentioned large wooden cross standing near it. This head of Christ with natural hair and thorns and blood-smeared face shows most masterfully, to be sure, the death of a man but not of a divine savior. Only material suffering is carved into this face, not the poetry of pain. Such a statue sooner belongs in an anatomy lecture hall than in a house of God. The art-loving sexton's wife, who took me around, showed me also, as a quite special rarity, a many-cornered, well-planed, black piece of wood covered with white numbers, which hangs like a lamp in the center of the church. Oh how brilliantly the inventive spirit is revealed in the Protestant church! For who would have thought of it! The numbers on that piece of wood are the psalm numbers, which are usually written with chalk on a blackboard and have a somewhat sobering effect on the aesthetic senses; but now, by means of the above-mentioned invention, they actually serve as an ornament for the church and are a sufficient substitute for Raphael's paintings, so often missed in it. Such progress gives me infinite pleasure since I, who am a Protestant and a Lutheran as well, have always been profoundly distressed whenever Catholic opponents were able to mock the empty, God-forsaken appearance of Protestant churches.

I stayed at an inn near the marketplace where the dinner would have tasted much better if my host, with his long, superfluous face and his boring questions, had not sat down beside me; fortunately, I was soon rescued by the arrival of another traveler who had to endure the same questions in the same order: *Quis? Quid? Ubi? Quibus auxiliis? Cur? Quomodo? Quando?* This stranger was a worn-out, tired old man who, as became evident from his talk, had journeyed through the whole world, had lived especially long in Batavia, had made a great deal of money and lost it again, and now, after an absence of thirty years, was returning to Quedlinburg, his home town, "For," he added, "our family has its burial plot there." My host made the very enlightened remark that it was really a matter of indifference to the soul where one's body is buried. "Do you have it in writing?" replied the stranger, while uncanny, sly rings formed about his pitiful lips and faded little eyes. "But," he added in an anxious endeavor to please, "it was not my intention to say anything malicious about others' graves; the Turks bury their dead far more beautifully than we do, their cemeteries are truly gardens, and they sit there on their white, beturbaned gravestones under the shadow of a cypress and stroke their serious beards and calmly smoke their Turkish tobacco in their long Turkish pipes; and as for the Chinese, it is a genuine pleasure to see them capering about politely on the resting places of their dead and praying and drinking tea and playing the violin and to see how well they know how to adorn their beloved graves very prettily with all sorts of gilded latticework, porcelain figures, scraps of colorful silk material, artificial flowers, and colored lanterns—everything very pretty—how far do I have to Quedlinburg?"

The graveyard in Goslar did not appeal to me very much. All the more, however, did that beautiful curly-haired countenance that smilingly looked out of a rather high ground-floor window as I arrived in town. After dinner I sought the dear window again, but now only a tumbler of water containing bluebells stood there. I climbed up, took the pretty little flowers from the glass, stuck them calmly in my cap, and concerned myself very little with the wide-open mouths, petrified noses, and goggle eyes with which the people on the street, especially the old women, watched this qualified theft. When I passed the same house an hour later, the lovely one was standing at the window, and when she noticed the bluebells on my cap, she blushed and withdrew. I had now seen the fair face even more clearly; it was a sweet, transparent embodiment of the breath of a summer evening, moonlight, the song of the nightingale, and the fragrance of roses. Later, when it had gotten quite dark, she stepped in front of her door. I came—I approached—she retreats slowly into the dark hall—I take her by the hand and say, "I am a lover of pretty flowers and kisses, and steal whatever is not voluntarily given"—and I kiss her quickly—and just as she is on the point of fleeing, I whisper soothingly, "Tomorrow I'm going away and I'll probably never return"—and I feel the secret response of her lovely lips and small hands—and I hurry away laughing. Yes, I have to laugh when I consider that I had unconsciously uttered the magic formula with which, more often than by their moustached charm, our redcoats and bluecoats conquer the hearts of the ladies: "Tomorrow I'm going away and I'll probably never return!"

My lodgings offered a glorious view of the Rammelsberg. It was a beautiful evening. The night raced on its black steed, its long mane fluttering in the wind. I stood at the window and looked at the moon. Is there really a man in the moon? The Slavs say he is called Chlotar and that he causes the waxing of the moon by pouring water on it. When I was still young, I had heard that the moon was a fruit that, after it had become ripe, was plucked by God and placed, along with the other full moons, in the huge cupboard at the end of the world where it is nailed up with boards. When I grew older, I noticed that the world is not so narrowly limited and that the human spirit broke through its wooden barriers and, with the idea of immortality, opened up all seven heavens with a gigantic Saint Peter's key. Immortality! Beautiful thought! Who first thought you up? Was it a Nuremberg philistine who, with white nightcap on his head and white clay pipe in his mouth, sat in front of his house on a warm summer evening and quite comfortably reflected that it would be really nice if he could continue to vegetate just like this, without his pipe and his little breath of life going out, into blessed eternity? Or was it a young lover who thought that thought of immortality in the arms of his beloved, and thought it because he felt it, and because he could not feel and think otherwise? Love! Immortality! My breast suddenly became so hot that I thought the geographers had shifted the equator and that it was now running straight through my heart. And from my heart poured the feelings of love, poured forth yearningly into the broad night. The flowers in the garden under my window gave off a stronger scent. Scents are the feelings of flowers, and just as the human heart feels stronger in the night when it believes itself alone and unwatched, so too the flowers, pensively shamefaced, seem only to await the cover of darkness in order to give themselves over wholly to their feelings and to breathe them out in sweet scents. Pour forth, ye scents of my heart, and seek behind those mountains the beloved of my dreams! She is lying asleep now; angels kneel at her feet, and when she smiles in her sleep, that is a prayer the angels repeat; in her breast lies heaven with all its delights, and when she breathes, my heart trembles in the distance; the sun has set behind the silken lashes of her eyes and when she opens her eyes again, then it is day and the birds are singing, the herd bells are tinkling, the hills are shimmering in their emerald garments, and I bind up my knapsack and go on my way.

During these philosophical observations and private feelings I was surprised by a visit from the Court Councilor B., who had likewise recently arrived in Goslar. I could have never before felt so deeply the benevolent good nature of this man. I esteem him greatly for his remarkable and successful astuteness, and even more for his modesty. I found him unusually cheerful, fresh, and vigorous. This last quality he proved recently in his new book *The Religion of Reason,* a work that delighted the rationalists so much, annoyed the mystics, and caused quite a stir in the general public. Of course I myself am at present a mystic, for reasons of health; I am following my doctor's orders to avoid all stimulants to thought. Still, I do not fail to appreciate the inestimable value of the rationalist endeavors of a Paulus, a Gurlitt, a Krug, an Eichhorn, a Bouterwek, a Wegscheider, etc. It is coincidentally to my own great benefit that these people have cleared away so much obsolete rubbish, especially the old clerical refuse in which there are so many snakes and stenches. The air in Germany is too dense and sultry, and I often fear that I will be smothered by my dear fellow mystics in their heat of love. Therefore, I am anything but angry with the good rationalists, even if they do thin out and cool the air a little too much. After all, nature herself has set limits to rationalism; a human being cannot survive under an air pump or on the North Pole.

During the night I spent in Goslar, the most extraordinary thing happened to me. Even now, I cannot think back on it without fear. I am not timid by nature, but I am almost as afraid of ghosts as the *Austrian Observer*. What is fear? Does it spring from the mind or from the emotions? I debated this question often with Dr. Saul Ascher whenever we met by chance at the Café Royal in Berlin, where for a long time I ate my midday meal. He always maintained that we fear something because we recognize it as fearful through the processes of reasoning. Only reason is a force, he said, not the emotions. While I was eating and drinking well, he continued to demonstrate to me the merits of reason. Toward the end of his demonstration he used to glance at his watch and he always concluded with: "Reason is the highest principle!" Reason! Whenever I hear this word now, I can still see Dr. Saul Ascher, with his abstract legs, his narrow, transcendentally gray coat, and his hard, freezingly cold face that could serve as a copperplate in a textbook of geometry. This man, well into his fifties, was a personified straight line. In his strivings for the positive, the poor fellow had philosophized everything glorious out of life, all sunbeams, all faith, and all flowers, and nothing remained for him but the cold, positive grave. He had a special malice toward the Belvedere Apollo and Christianity. Against the latter, he even wrote a brochure in which he proved its unreasonableness and untenability. He wrote, indeed, a great many books, in which reason always boasts of its own excellence. The poor doctor certainly had serious intentions and accordingly deserved all respect. The joke of it, however, was that he made such a gravely silly face when he could not comprehend what every child comprehends simply because it is a child. Several times I visited the doctor of reason in his own house, where I found pretty girls staying with him; for reason does not forbid sensuality. Once when I went to see him, his servant told me that the doctor had just died. I did not feel anything much more than if he had said that the doctor had moved away.

But back to Goslar. "The highest principle is reason!" I said soothingly to myself as I climbed into bed. But it did not help. In Varnhagen von Ense's *German Tales*, which I had brought along from Klaustal, I had just been reading that horrible story about how a son, whose own father intended to murder him, is warned at night by the ghost of his dead mother. The remarkable portrayal in this story caused an inner horror to chill through me while I was reading. Ghost stories arouse an even greater feeling of terror when one reads them on a trip, especially at night in a town, in a house, in a room where one has never been before. "What awful things may already have taken place on the very spot where you are lying?" one thinks involuntarily. Moreover, the moon was now shining so ambiguously into my room; on the wall all sorts of unbidden shadows were stirring and when I sat up in bed to look at them, I glimpsed . . .

There is nothing more uncanny than when one chances to see one's own face in the mirror by the light of the moon. At the same moment a ponderous, yawning clock struck for such a long time and so slowly that I was sure, after the twelfth stroke, that a full twelve hours had meanwhile passed and that it would have to begin again from the beginning to strike twelve. Between the next-to-the-last and the last stroke, another clock struck very quickly, almost peevishly shrill, perhaps vexed at the slowness of its good neighbor. When both iron tongues fell silent and deep, deathly silence prevailed in the whole house, I suddenly seemed to hear something shuffling and clattering along on the corridor outside my room, like the uncertain gait of an old man. Finally the door opened and slowly the deceased Dr. Saul Ascher entered. A cold chill trickled through marrow and bone, and I trembled like an aspen leaf, scarcely daring to glance at the ghost. He looked quite as usual, the same transcendentally gray coat, the same abstract legs and the same mathematical face. But his face was somewhat sallower than usual, and his lips, which ordinarily formed two angles of twenty-two and a half degrees, were pressed closely together, and his eye sockets had a greater radius. Tottering and, as usual, leaning on his Spanish cane, he approached me, speaking pleasantly in his customary lazy-lipped dialect: "Don't be afraid, and don't imagine that I am a ghost. It is a delusion of your imagination if you believe that you are seeing me as a ghost. What is a ghost? Can you give me a definition? Deduce for me the conditions of the possibility of a ghost. What reasonable connection could such an appearance have with reason? Reason, I say reason . . ." And now the ghost proceeded to an analysis of reason, cited Kant's *Critique of Pure Reason*, Part 2, Division 1, Book 2, Section 3, the difference between phenomena and noumena, constructed thereupon the problematical belief in ghosts, added one syllogism to another and concluded with the logical proof that there is absolutely no such thing as a ghost. Meanwhile, cold sweat was running down my back, my teeth rattled like castanets, in mortal fear I nodded unconditional agreement at every sentence with which the spooky doctor proved the absurdity of all fear of ghosts and gesticulated so eagerly that once in his absentmindedness, he took, instead of a gold watch, a handful of worms out of his watch pocket and, noting his error, stuck them in again with comically nervous haste. "Reason is the highest—" Then the clock struck one and the ghost vanished.

Next morning I went on from Goslar, half at random, half with the intention of seeking out the brother of the Klaustal miner. Beautiful, delightful Sunday weather again. I climbed hills and mountains, saw how the sun was trying to banish the fog, wandered happily through the shuddering woods, while the bluebells of Goslar tinkled around my dreaming head. The mountains stood in their white nightgowns, the firs shook the sleep out of their limbs, the fresh morning breeze trimmed their flowing green hair, the little birds held their hour of prayer, the meadow vale flashed like a diamond-strewn canopy of gold, and the shepherd strode over it with his tinkling herd. No doubt I had gone astray. One always strikes out on side roads and footpaths, thinking one will come nearer the goal. As in life in general, so it goes with us in the Harz. But there are always good souls to bring us on the right path again; they are glad to do so and are especially pleased whenever they can point out to us with self-satisfied mien and benevolently loud voice what great detours we have made, into what abysses and marshes we could have sunk, and what good fortune we had meeting people so familiar with the area just in time. I found such a corrector not far from the Harz Castle. He was a well-fed citizen of Goslar with a shiningly bloated, stupidly clever face; he looked as though he had invented hoof-and-mouth disease. We walked a short distance together, and he told me all sorts of ghost stories, which would have sounded nice if they had not all ended in the statement that it was not a real ghost but that the white figure was a poacher and the whimpering sounds came from the newborn young of a wild sow (female hog), and that the noise on the ground came from the house cat. Only when a person is ill, he added, does he believe he is seeing ghosts; as for his own small self, well, he was rarely ill; only occasionally did he suffer from skin diseases, and then he cured himself each time with plain saliva. He also called my attention to the purposefulness and utility in nature. The trees are green, because green is good for the eyes. I agreed with him, adding that God had created cattle because meat broth strengthens people, that He had created asses so they could serve men for comparisons, and that He had created man himself so he might consume meat broth and not be an ass. My companion was delighted to have found someone of like mind, his countenance beamed even more happily, and at parting he was moved.

As long as he walked beside me, all of nature almost lost its magic, but as soon as he was gone, the trees began to speak again, the sunbeams sang, the meadow flowers danced, and the blue sky embraced the green earth. Yes, I know better: God created man to marvel at the glory of the world. Every author, however great he may be, wants his works to be praised. And in the Bible, the memoirs of God, it is expressly stated that He created mankind for His praise and fame.

After a long wandering back and forth I reached the dwelling of the brother of my Klaustal friend, spent the night there, and experienced the following pretty poem:

1

On the mountain stands a cabin,
Wherein lives a mountaineer;
All the evergreens are rustling
And the moon turns golden here.

In the cabin there's an armchair
Curiously carved and high.
He who sits in it is lucky;
And that lucky man am I.

On the footstool there's a maiden,
In my lap her arms repose;
Eyes like two blue stars that sparkle,
And her mouth's a crimson rose.

And the stars so blue and lovely,
Wide as heaven, gaze at me;
And she puts her lily finger
On the rose coquettishly.

No, the mother does not see us,
For she spins and spins away;
And the father plays the zither,
Singing some forgotten lay.

And the maiden whispers softly,
Softly, almost breathlessly;
While a host of weighty secrets
Gravely she confides to me.

"But since Auntie died," she tells me,
"We can never hope to go
To the picnic grounds at Goslar;
That's the loveliest place I know.

On the mountains here it's lonely;
Colder far than down below;
And in winter we are almost
Lost and buried in the snow.

Though I'm quite a girl, I tremble
Like a child that's seized with fright,
At the evil mountain spirits
And the things they do by night."

Suddenly she stops as though her
Own words chill and terrorize;
And she raises both hands quickly,
Quickly covering her eyes.

In the trees the rustling's louder,
Faster still the wheel is stirred,
And above the tinkling zither
Something of the song is heard:

"Do not fear, my child, my darling,
Fear no spirit's evil might!
Overhead, my child, my darling,
Angels guard thee day and night!"

2

Now the fir tree's long, green fingers
Tap against the windowpane,
And the moon, that quiet listener,
Sheds a flood of golden rain.

Father, mother, sleeping soundly,
Snore for hours without a break;
But we two, with lively chatter,
Keep each other wide awake.

"That you spend much time in praying
I've my doubts; for always there
Is a sneer about your features
That was never taught by prayer.

Oh, that sneer, so cold and cruel,
Makes me shiver, though I know
You are kind. Your eyes are gentle,
And they have a tender glow.

Yet I doubt that you believe in
The inspired faith of most.
Do you worship God the Father,
And the Son and Holy Ghost?"

"Ah, my child, while still a youngster,
While at mother's knee I stood,
I believed in God the Father,
He whose rule is great ánd good.

He who made the earth we dwell on,
And the people here below;
He who made sun, moon, and planets,
Teaching them the way to go.

Then, my child, as I grew older,
My belief had but begun,
And I mastered with my reason,
And I worshiped God the Son;

The Belovèd Son, who, loving,
Gave us love to bless and guide;
And for his reward, as always,
Was condemned and crucified.

Now that I've matured and learned much,
Read and roamed from coast to coast,
Now my heart, with deep conviction,
Bows before the Holy Ghost.

He has worked the greatest wonders,
And he works them still; he broke,
Once for all, the tyrant's power,
And he burst the bondman's yoke.

All the ancient scars have vanished,
Justice takes its rightful place;
Now all men are free and equal
In a pure and noble race.

Mists and every evil fancy
That had filled each night and day,
Cares that crowded out our gladness—
These have all been swept away!

And a thousand armored champions
He has sanctified and sent
To fulfill his sacred mission,
Fired with their high intent.

Now their splendid swords are shining
And their unfurled flags are bright!
What, my child, you long to look on
Such a proud and holy knight?

Well, my darling, come and kiss me;
Look at me and you can boast
You have known just such a stalwart
Champion of the Holy Ghost."

3

Still the bashful moon is hiding
Close behind the evergreen;
And the lamp upon the table
Flickers and is scarcely seen.

But those two blue stars are shining
O'er the heaven of her cheeks;
And the crimson rose is glowing,
And the lovely girl still speaks.

"Tiny goblins, impish fairies,
Clean our little cupboard bare;
It is full of food at evening,
But at daylight—nothing's there!

And the thieving Little People
Skim our cream, our very best;
Then they leave the pans uncovered
And the cat licks up the rest.

And that cat's a witch, I know it;
For she slinks off every night
To the old and ruined castle
On the haunted mountain height.

Once a mighty castle stood there,
Full of armor and romance;
Shining knights and lovely ladies
Laughed in many a torchlight dance.

Then an old enchantress cursed it,
Cursed each stone and winding stair.
Now there's nothing left but ruins;
And the owls are nesting there.

But my dear old aunt once told me
If one speaks the Word of Might
At the proper, magic moment,
And the hour and place be right,

Then the castle shall be lifted
From the ruined stones—and then
All the vanished knights and ladies
Will arise and dance again.

And who speaks that Word of Magic,
Knights and ladies, wall and tower,
All are his; while drums and trumpets
Hail his new and happy power."

Thus the fairy legends blossom
From her mouth, that rose in bloom,
While her eyes are pouring starlight
In the still and darkened room.

Round my hands she winds her golden
Tresses, binding me at will;
Gives my fingers pretty nicknames;
Kisses, laughs—and then grows still.

And the hushed room edges closer,
Watching with a friendly light . . .
Table, chest—it seems I must have
Seen them all before tonight.

Amiably the old clock gossips,
And the zither, scarcely heard,
Plays itself with airy fingers;
And, as in a dream, I'm stirred.

This must be the proper hour;
Yes, the time and place are right.
And I think I feel it gliding
From my lips—that Word of Might.

Do you see, my child, how quickly
Midnight trembles now and breaks!
Brooks and pine trees murmur louder,
And the ancient mountain wakes.

Clang of zither, elfin voices
Rise from glens and fairy bowers,
And a wild, fantastic springtime
Brings a forest full of flowers.

Flowers, wondrous and audacious,
Flowers, strangely broad and tall,
Fling their eager scents and colors
As though passion swayed them all.

Roses, red as flame, and burning
From the brilliant tumult, rise;
Lilies, like great crystal columns,
Tower straight into the skies.

And the stars, with fiery longing,
Great as suns, look down and blaze,
Till the lilies' hearts are flooded
With those bold, transforming rays.

But ourselves, my child, are altered
More than all of these—for see!
Gleaming torches, silks and jewels
Shimmer 'round us radiantly!

You, you have become a princess,
And this hut's a castle tall;
Knights and ladies dance rejoicing;
And there's magic over all.

Ah, but I have won the castle,
Knights and ladies, wall and tower;
Even you—as drums and trumpets
Hail my new and happy power!

The sun rose. The mists fled like ghosts at the third cockcrow.
I climbed again uphill and downhill, while the beautiful sun hovered before me, illuminating ever new things of beauty. The spirit of the mountains was quite evidently favoring me, doubtless knowing that such a poet-person can retell many lovely things, and this morning let me see the Harz as surely few have seen it. But the Harz also saw me as only few have seen me; in my eyelashes glittered pearls just as precious as in the grasses of the valley. Love's morning dew moistened my cheeks, the rustling firs understood me, their branches opened wide, moving up and down like mute people who show their joy with their hands, and in the distance there was a wonderfully mysterious sound like the pealing of the bells of a lost woodland church. It is said they are the herd bells that in the Harz are tuned so sweetly, clear and pure.

According to the position of the sun, it was noon when I came upon such a herd, and the shepherd, a friendly blond young man, said that the great mountain at the foot of which I was standing was the old, world-famous Brocken. For many hours round about there is no house, and I was glad enough when the young man invited me to eat with him. We sat down to a *déjeuner dînatoire* consisting of cheese and bread; the lambs snatched up the crumbs; the dear, shiny little cows cavorted around us, ringing their small bells roguishly and laughing at us with their large, cheerful eyes. We dined quite royally; my host, indeed, seemed to me to be a genuine king and, because he is the only royal personage who until now has given me bread, I am going to sing of him royally.

He's a king, this happy herd boy,
And his throne's the grassy down,
While the sun above his forehead
Is his great and golden crown.

At his feet the sheep are lying,
Flattering courtiers, soft and sly;
And his cavaliers are cattle,
Pompously parading by.

And the kids are his court players,
Birds that flute before they drowse
Make a rustic chamber music
With the gentle bells of cows.

And they ring and sing so sweetly,
And the soothing murmurs creep
From the waterfall and forest,
That the young king falls asleep.

Like a minister, his watch dog,
Governs with an open ear;
And his loud, suspicious barking
Makes the very echos fear.

Sleepily the young king murmurs:
"Ah, to rule is hard and mean.
How I wish that I were home now
With my cozy little queen!

On her dear and queenly bosom
Soft my regal head would lie;
And I'd find my ancient kingdom
Shining in each love-lit eye."

Our parting was a friendly one and I merrily ascended the mountain. Soon a forest of sky-high firs, for which I have in every regard the greatest respect, received me. Growing has not been made so very easy for these trees, and they had a rough time of it in their youth. The mountain is strewn here with many great blocks of granite, so most of the trees had to encircle or burst these stones with their roots and laboriously seek soil in quest of nourishment. Here and there the stones lie piled up, forming as it were a gate, and on top of them stand the trees, stretching out their bare roots over that stone gate and touching the soil only at its base, so that they seem to be growing in mid-air. And yet they have risen to that splendid height and, as if grown together with the stones they are clasping, they stand more firmly than their comfortable colleagues in the cultivated soil of the flat land. So, too, in life stand those great men who have really strengthened and established themselves by overcoming early obstacles and hindrances. Squirrels clambered on the branches of the firs, while under them stalked yellow stags. Whenever I see such a lovely, noble animal, I cannot comprehend how educated people can find pleasure in pursuing and slaying it. Such an animal was more merciful than people, for it nursed the holy Genevieve's languishing Schmerzenreich.

Golden sunbeams shot most sweetly through the thick green of the firs. The roots of the trees formed a natural stairway. Everywhere swelling banks of moss; for the stones are overgrown with a foot of the most beautiful species of moss, as if with bright green velvet cushions. Delightful coolness and dreamy murmuring of springs. Here and there one sees how the water trickles silverbright under the stones, rippling over the trees' bare roots and fibers. Bending down to all these doings, one overhears as it were the secret cultural history of the plants and the mountain's heartbeat. In many places the water bubbles more forcefully from the stones and roots and forms small cascades. It is pleasant to sit there. There is such a wonderful murmuring and rustling, the birds sing fragmentary songs of yearning, the trees whisper as if with a thousand girlish tongues; as if with a thousand girlish eyes the unusual mountain flowers gaze on us, stretching out toward us their wonderfully broad, drolly pointed leaves; the merry sunbeams playfully flicker to and fro, the pensive little plants tell each other green fairy tales, everything is as if enchanted, everything becomes more and more mysterious, an ancient dream comes to life, my beloved appears—alas, she vanishes again so quickly!

The higher one climbs up the mountain, the shorter, more

dwarflike the firs become; they seem to shrink up more and more until only bilberry and raspberry bushes remain. It is also perceptibly colder there. The strange groups of granite blocks are clearly visible here; they are often of astonishing size. Perhaps they are the balls that the evil spirits throw to each other during Walpurgis Night when the witches come riding up on broomsticks and dung forks and the fantastically infamous pleasure begins, as the credulous nursemaid tells it and as one can see on the charming Faust pictures by Master Retzsch. In fact, a young poet who rode by the Brocken on a trip from Berlin to Göttingen during the first night of May even noticed how some belletristic ladies were holding their aesthetic tea party on a corner of the mountain, cheerily reading to each other the *Evening Times,* praising as universal geniuses their poetic billygoats, which skipped bleating about the tea table, and pronouncing their final judgment on all publications in German literature; but, when they got to *Ratcliff* and *Almansor* and denied all piety and Christianity to the author, the hair of the young man stood on end, horror seized him—I gave my horse the spurs and raced past.

In fact, if one climbs the upper half of the Brocken, one cannot resist thinking of the delightful legends about the Blocksberg, and especially of the great, mystical, German national tragedy of Doctor Faust. I had the constant feeling that the cloven hoof was clambering up beside me and that someone was comically panting. And I believe that even Mephisto has difficulty catching his breath when he climbs his favorite mountain; it is an extremely exhausting path, and I was happy when I finally caught sight of the long-awaited Brocken House.

This house, which, as is known from the many pictures of it, consists only of a ground floor and is situated on the summit of the mountain, was constructed in 1800 by Count Stolberg-Wernigerode, who is also responsible for having it serve as an inn. The walls are amazingly thick because of the wind and the cold in winter; in the center of the low roof rises a towerlike lookout, and near the house are two small annexes, one of which served in earlier times as a shelter for visitors to the Brocken.

The entrance into the Brocken House aroused in me a rather unusual, fantastic sensation. After climbing around alone for a long time through firs and cliffs, one is suddenly placed in a cloud house;

towns, mountains, and woods remain below, and above one finds an oddly composed company of strangers by whom one is received, as is natural in such places, almost like an expected comrade, half inquisitively and half indifferently. I found the house full of guests and, as befits a clever man, I began to think of the night, of the discomfort of a straw bed; with a dying voice, I asked for tea right away, and the Brocken innkeeper was sensible enough to realize that I, sick man that I was, must have a decent bed for the night. He procured it for me in a narrow little room where a young merchant, a nauseating figure in a brown overcoat, had already established himself.

In the public room of the inn, I find plenty of life and movement. There are students from various universities. Some arrived a short time ago and are refreshing themselves, others are preparing for departure, binding up their knapsacks, writing their names in the guest book, receiving Brocken bouquets from the servant girls; there is a pinching of cheeks, there is singing, jumping, yodeling, questions and answers—good weather, luck on your way, to your health, good-bye. Some of those leaving are also a little tipsy and experience a double pleasure in the beautiful view, since a drunk person sees everything double.

After I had refreshed myself somewhat, I climbed the tower lookout, where I found a short gentleman with two ladies, one young and one elderly. The young lady was very beautiful: a glorious figure, on her curly head a helmetlike, black satin hat with whose white plumes the wind was playing; her slender limbs so tightly enclosed by a black silk coat that her noble shape was apparent; and her free, large eyes looked calmly out into the great, free world.

When I was still a boy, I thought of nothing but tales of magic and miracles, and I took every beautiful lady with ostrich feathers on her head for a queen of the elves, and if I happened to notice that the train of her dress was wet, I took her for a water sprite. Now I think differently, since I know from natural history that those symbolic feathers come from the most stupid bird and that the train of a lady's dress can get wet in the most natural way. Had I seen with those boyish eyes the already-mentioned young beauty on the Brocken in the already-mentioned position, I would surely have thought, "That is the fairy of the mountain, and she has just uttered the magic formula that makes everything down below seem so wonderful." Yes, everything seems very wonderful to us when we first look down from the Brocken, all aspects of our mind receive new impressions, and these, mostly various, even contradicting each other, unite in our soul to become a great, yet confused, uncomprehended feeling. If we succeed in grasping this feeling in its essence, we recognize the character of the mountain. This character is wholly German both in regard to its failings as well as its merits. The Brocken is a German. With German thoroughness it shows us clearly and plainly, like a giant panorama, the many hundreds of towns, villages, and hamlets, which mostly lie to the north, surrounded by all the mountains, forests, rivers, and plains into the infinite distance. But precisely because of this, everything seems like a sharply delineated, clearly illumined local map; nowhere is the eye delighted by really beautiful landscapes, just as it always happens that we German compilers, because of the honest exactitude with which we wish to represent all and everything, are never able to think of portraying the particular in a beautiful manner. The mountain also has something so quietly German, sensible, tolerant about it, simply because it can survey things so clearly and at such a great distance. And when such a mountain opens its giant eyes, it may well see rather more than we dwarfs who clamber around on it with our weak little eyes. Many even want to assert that the Brocken is very philistine, and Claudius sang, "The Blocksberg is the tall Philistine!" But that is wrong. With its bald head, which it occasionally covers with a white cap of fog, it admittedly gives itself a coating of philistinism; but as with so many other great Germans, that happens out of pure irony. It is even notorious that the Brocken has its hearty, fantastic periods, e.g., the first night of May. Then it jubilantly throws its cap of fog into the air and becomes, just as the rest of us, quite crazy in an authentically German and romantic sense.

I attempted at once to engage the beautiful lady in conversation, for the beauties of nature can be properly enjoyed when one can talk about them on the spot. She was not witty but attentively contemplative. She had really distinguished manners. I do not mean the usual stiff, negative air of distinction, which knows exactly what must not be said or done; but that rarer, free, positive elegance that tells us exactly what we may do and, with its total lack of affectation, gives us the greatest social assurance. To my own astonishment, I expounded on much geographical knowledge, mentioned to the inquisitive beauty the names of all the towns surrounding us, sought and showed them to her on my map, which, with a true professorial air, I spread out over the stone table standing in the middle of the tower platform. Many a town I could not find, perhaps because I was searching more with my fingers than with my eyes, which were meanwhile oriented toward the face of the lovely lady and discovered there more beautiful regions than Schierke and Elend. Her face was one of those that never charm, seldom delight, and always please. I love such faces, because they smile my sorely agitated heart to peace.

I could not determine just what relationship the short gentleman had to the ladies he was accompanying. He was a thin, strange character—a small head, sparsely covered with gray hair that extended down over the short forehead to his greenish, dragonfly eyes; his round, protruding nose; his mouth and chin, on the other hand, drawing back timidly toward the ears. This small face seemed to consist of a delicate, yellowish clay from which sculptors mold their first models; and when his narrow lips pressed together, some thousand semicircular, fine little folds appeared on his cheeks. The small man said nothing, and only now and then, when the older lady whispered something pleasant to him, did he smile like a pug dog with a cold.

The older lady was the mother of the younger and also had the most distinguished manners. Her eyes betrayed a morbidly extravagant melancholy, while her mouth was surrounded by severe piety, although it seemed to me as if it had once been very beautiful and had laughed much and received many kisses and given many in return. Her face resembled a *codex palimpsetus* on which the half-obliterated verses of an ancient Greek love poet peeped forth from under the monk's fresh black writing of a patristic text. Both ladies had been in Italy this year with their companion and told me all kinds of beautiful things about Rome, Florence, and Venice. The mother spoke a great deal about the Raphael paintings in Saint Peter's Church; the daughter spoke more about the opera in the Fenice Theater.

While we were talking, it began to grow dark: it became even colder, the sun sank lower, and the tower platform filled up with students, traveling journeymen, and some respectable burghers along with their wives and daughters, all wanting to see the sunset. It is a sublime sight that tunes the soul to prayer. For perhaps a quarter of an hour, everyone stood gravely silent and saw how the beautiful ball of fire gradually sank into the west; faces were lit up by the evening glow, hands folded involuntarily; it was as if we were standing, a silent congregation, in the nave of a gigantic cathedral, while the priest raised the Host of the Lord and from the organ came the tones of Palestrina's eternal chorale.

While standing sunk in devotion, I heard someone call out beside me, "How beautiful nature is in general!" These words came from the emotional breast of my roommate, the young merchant. Through them I returned to my workaday mood, and was now in a position to say many nice things to the ladies about the sunset, and to lead them quietly, as if nothing had happened, back to their room. They permitted me to entertain them for another hour. Like the earth itself, our conversation turned about the sun. The mother declared that the sun, as it sank into the fog, had looked like a glowing rose cast down by the gallant heaven into the outspread, white bridal veil of its beloved earth. The daughter smiled and said that the too-frequent sight of such natural phenomena weakened their impression. The mother corrected this erroneous opinion with a passage from Goethe's travel correspondence and asked me whether I had read *Werther*. I think we also spoke of Angora cats, Etruscan vases, Turkish shawls, macaroni, and Lord Byron, from whose poems the older lady recited some sunset passages, lisping and sighing very prettily. To the younger lady, who knew no English and wanted to read those poems, I recommended the translations by my beautiful, witty countrywoman, the Baroness Elise von Hohenhausen. On this occasion, as I usually do in the presence of young ladies, I did not hesitate to rail against Byron's godlessness, unkindness, pessimism, and heaven knows what else.

After this affair I continued walking on the Brocken, for it never becomes entirely dark there. The fog was not thick, and I observed the outlines of the two hills called the Witches' Altar and the Devil's Pulpit. I shot off my pistols, but there was no echo. Suddenly, however, I hear familiar voices and feel myself embraced and kissed. It was my compatriots who had left Göttingen four days after me and were greatly surprised to find me again all alone on the Blocksberg. With conversation, expressions of surprise, making plans, laughing, and reminiscing, what a joyful reunion.

The evening meal was eaten in the large room; a long table with two rows of hungry students. At first the usual university talk: duels, duels, and more duels. The company consisted mostly of students from Halle, so Halle was the main topic of conversation. The windowpanes of Court Councilor Schütz were exegetically illuminated. Then they related that the last court of the King of Cyprus had been very brilliant, that he had chosen a natural son, that he had contracted a morganatic marriage with a princess of Lichtenstein, that he had dismissed the mistress of state, and that the whole ministry, being much affected, had wept according to instructions. I probably do not need to mention that all this refers to cronies in Halle. The discussion then turned to the two Chinese who could have been seen in Berlin two years ago and who were now being trained in Halle as instructors in Chinese aesthetics. Then jokes were cracked. A conjecture was made: that a German was to be exhibited in China for money, and for this purpose an advertisement was prepared in which the mandarins Ching-Chang-Chung and Hi-Ha-Ho certified that it was a genuine German; in which, furthermore, his accomplishments, consisting mainly of philosophizing, tobacco smoking, and patience, were listed; and in which, finally, it was stated that no dogs could be brought along at twelve o'clock, which was his feeding hour, because they usually snatch away the best crumbs from the poor German.

A young member of the national students' club, who had recently been in Berlin for purification, talked a great deal about this city, although very one-sidedly. He had visited Wisotzki and the theater; both he judged wrongly. "Youth is quick to judge, etc." He spoke of expenditures for costumes, scandals involving actors and actresses, etc. The young man did not know that, since in Berlin the greatest importance is placed on appearance, as the popular phrase "just pretend" adequately suggests, this pretense must flourish all the more on stage, and that the management therefore must make absolutely certain about the "color of the beard in which a role is played," and the accuracy of the costumes, which are designed by certified historians and stitched by scientifically trained tailors. And that is necessary. For if Mary

Stuart were to wear a skirt from the age of Queen Anne, the banker
Christian Gumpel would surely and quite rightly complain that all
illusion was lacking; and if Lord Burleigh were to put on the trousers of Henry IV by mistake, the wife of the Councilor of War,
von Steinzopf, née Lilientau, would not have lost sight of this
anachronism the whole evening. Such attention to deception on
the part of the general management extends, however, not only to
skirts and trousers but also to the persons wrapped in them. Thus
from now on Othello is to be played by an actual Moor, for whom
Professor Lichtenstein, with this purpose in mind, has already
written to Africa; in *Misanthropy and Repentance* Eulalia is to be
played in the future by an actual wayward wench, Peter by an
actual stupid youth, and the Unknown by an actual Privy Cuck-
old, all three of whom need not be ordered from Africa. If the
young man mentioned above has poorly understood conditions in
the Berlin theater, he realized even less that the Spontinian janis-
sary opera, with its drums, elephants, trumpets, and tomtoms, is
a heroic means of strengthening our enervated people to martial
deeds, a means already recommended with cunning statecraft by
Plato and Cicero. Least of all did the young man comprehend the
diplomatic significance of the ballet. With difficulty I showed him
how there is more politics in Hoguet's feet than in Buchholz' head,
how each of his dance steps indicates diplomatic negotiations, how
each of his movements has a political context, so that, for example, he means our cabinet when, bent forward yearningly, he extends his hands far; that he means the Bundestag when he spins
around a hundred times on one foot without stirring from the
spot; that he has the small princes in mind when he skips around
as if his legs were hobbled; that he is characterizing the European
balance of power when he totters back and forth like a drunkard;
that he is suggesting a congress when he entwines his bent arms
into each other like a coil; and finally, that he is representing our
all-too-great friend in the East when he gradually lifts himself up
on high, rests in this position a long time, and then suddenly breaks
out into the most terrible leaps. The young man's eyes were opened,
and he now realized why dancers receive higher fees than great
poets, why the ballet is an inexhaustible subject of conversation in
the diplomatic corps, and why a beautiful female dancer is often
entertained privately by the minister, who surely tries day and night

to make her receptive to his political system. By Apis! how large is the number of exoteric theater-goers and how small the number of esoteric! The silly people stand there and gape and admire leaps and turns and study anatomy in the positions of la Lemière and applaud the entrechats of Röhnisch and chatter about grace, harmony, and hips—and no one notices that in these danced codes he has the fate of the German fatherland before his eyes.

While such talk flew back and forth, utilitarian matters were not lost sight of, and the great dishes, honestly filled with meat, potatoes, etc., were industriously addressed. However, the meal was bad. I mentioned this casually to my neighbor, who replied very impolitely with an accent, by which I recognized that he was a Swiss, that we Germans were just as ignorant of true contentedness as of true freedom. I shrugged my shoulders and remarked that the real mercenaries and confectioners were everywhere Swiss and were preferably designated accordingly, and that anyway the present Swiss heroes of liberty who so loudly boast about their bold political deeds always seem to me like braggarts who shoot off their pistols at public fairs, astonish all the children and farmers by their boldness, but are braggarts nevertheless.

The son of the Alps had certainly not meant to be so malicious; "He was a fat man, consequently a good man," says Cervantes. But my neighbor on the other side, a Greifswalder, was greatly piqued by the utterance; he protested that German energy and simplicity were not yet extinguished, slapped his breast resoundingly, and emptied an enormous schooner of pale beer. The Swiss said, "Now, now!" But the more appeasingly he said this, the more zealously did the Greifswalder take up the cudgels. The latter was a man from the era when the lice had good times and the barbers were afraid of starving. He wore his long hair hanging down, a knightly beret, a black old German coat, a dirty shirt that also served as a vest, and under it a medallion with a tuft of hair from Blücher's white horse. He looked like a lifesized fool. I like to cause a little excitement at dinner and therefore allowed myself to be engaged by him in a patriotic dispute. He was of the opinion that Germany ought to be divided into thirty-three districts. I maintained, on the other hand, that it ought to be forty-eight, because one could then write a more systematic handbook about Germany and it was really obligatory to combine life with science.

My Greifswald friend was also a German bard who, as he confided to me, was working on a national heroic epic in honor of Hermann and the battle of the Teutoburg Forest. I gave him many useful hints for the preparation of this epic. I called his attention to the fact that he could suggest the marshes and log roads of the Teutoburg Forest very onomatopoetically by means of watery and uneven verse, and that it would be a patriotic refinement if he would have Varus and the other Romans speak sheer nonsense. I hope that this trick will work for him as well as it has for other Berlin poets, resulting in the most dubious illusion.

At our table the conversation became even louder and more familiar, wine displaced beer, the punch bowls steamed, there was drinking, toasting, and singing. The old "Father of His Country" and glorious songs by W. Müller, Rückert, Uhland, etc., rang out; beautiful Methfessel melodies. Best of all resounded the German words of our own Arndt: "The God who permitted iron to grow, He wanted no slaves!" And outside it raged as if the old mountain were singing with us, and some tottering friends even claimed that it was joyfully shaking its bald head, thus causing our room to move to and fro. Bottles became emptier and heads fuller. One bellowed, another sang falsetto, a third declaimed from *Guilt,* a fourth spoke Latin, a fifth preached on moderation, and a sixth stood up on his chair and lectured: "Gentlemen! The earth is a round cylinder, humans are individual pegs on it, apparently scattered at random; but the cylinder turns, the pegs strike here and there and sound, some often, the others rarely; this produces a wonderful, complicated music, and this is called world history. We shall, therefore, speak first about music, then about the world, and finally about history; the last, however, we shall divide into the positive and Spanish flies . . ." And so it went on with sense and nonsense.

A jolly Mecklenburger who had his nose in the punch bowl and, smiling blissfully, sniffed the vapors, made the remark that he felt as though he were again standing before the theater bar in Schwerin! Another held his wine glass like a telescope in front of his eyes and seemed to be attentively observing us while the red wine ran down his cheeks into his protruding mouth. The Greifswalder, suddenly inspired, threw himself on my breast and shouted, "Oh, if you could understand me, I am in love, I am a happy man, I am loved in return, and, by heaven, she is an educated girl, for she has a full bosom and wears a white dress and plays the piano." But the Swiss wept and tenderly kissed my hand and whimpered constantly, "O Bäbeli! O Bäbeli!"

In this confused turmoil in which the plates learned to dance and the glasses learned to fly, there sat two youths opposite me, fair and pale as marble statues, the one more like Adonis, the other resembling Apollo. Scarcely noticeable was the light rosy hue that the wine cast over their cheeks. With endless love they gazed at each other as though one could read in the eyes of the other, and these eyes radiated as if some drops of light had fallen into them from that bowl full of flaming love borne by a pious angel up above from one star to another. They spoke softly, their voices trembling with longing, and told sad tales, which emanated a wondrously painful tone. "Now Lore is dead too!" said one and sighed, and after a pause he told of a girl from Halle who was in love with a student and, when he left Halle, no longer spoke with anyone, ate little, wept day and night, and constantly looked at the canary that her sweetheart had once given her. "The bird died, and soon thereafter Lore died too!" So ended the tale, and both youths fell silent again and sighed as though their hearts would break. Finally the other spoke: "My soul is sad! Come with me out into the dark night! I want to inhale the breath of the clouds and the rays of the moon. Comrade of my woe! I love thee, thy words sound like whispering reeds, like gliding streams, they find an echo in my breast, but my soul is sad!"

Now the two youths stood up, one flung his arm around the neck of the other, and they left the tumultuous room. I followed them and saw how they stepped into a dark chamber, how one of them opened a large clothes closet instead of the window, how both of them, with longingly outstretched arms, remained standing before it and took turns speaking. "Ye breezes of the oncoming night," cried the first, "how refreshingly ye cool my cheeks! How delightfully ye play with my fluttering locks! I stand upon the cloudy summit of the mountain, beneath me lie the sleeping towns of men, and the blue waters gleam. Hark! There below in the valley rustle the firs! There over the hills, in misty shapes, pass the spirits of our fathers. Oh, could I race with you on my cloud steed through the stormy night, over the rolling sea, up to the stars! But alas! I am laden with grief, and my soul is sad!" The other youth had likewise extended his arms longingly toward the clothes closet; tears fell from his eyes, and he spoke with a mournful voice to a pair of yellow leather trousers, which he took for the moon: "Fair art thou, daughter of heaven! Gracious is the calm of thy countenance. Thou wanderest in loveliness! The stars follow thy blue paths in the east. The clouds rejoice at the sight of thee, and their dark shapes brighten. Who is like thee in heaven, daughter of the night? The stars are ashamed before thee and turn away their green sparkling eyes. Whither, when in the morning thy countenance pales, dost thou flee from thy course? Hast thou like me thy Halle? Dost thou dwell in the shadow of woe? Are thy sisters fallen from heaven? They, who roamed through the night with thee, are they no more? Yea, they are fallen down, oh, beautiful light, and thou hidest thyself often to bemoan them. But the night will come when thou, thou too art gone and hast abandoned thy blue course up there above. Then the stars, whom once thy presence put to shame, will raise their green heads; they will rejoice. But now thou art clad in thy radiant glory and gazest down from the gates of heaven. Rend the cloud, O winds, that the daughter of the night may shine forth, the shaggy mountains may brighten, and the ocean roll its foaming waves in light!"

A well-known, not very thin friend, who had drunk more than he had eaten, even though this evening he had as usual consumed a portion of beef that would have filled up six lieutenants of the guard and an innocent child, came running by in all too good a mood, i.e., quite like a pig, pushed the two elegiac friends somewhat ungently into the closet, stumbled toward the house door, and behaved most dreadfully outside. The noise in the room grew increasingly confused and muffled. The two youths in the closet lamented and whimpered that they were lying crushed at the foot of the mountain; out of their throats streamed the noble red wine, they inundated each other by turns, and the one spoke to the other, "Farewell! I feel that I am bleeding to death. Why dost thou wake me, breeze of spring? Thou wooest and sayest, 'I bedew thee with drops of heaven.' But the time of my fading is nigh, nigh is the blast that will scatter my leaves! Tomorrow the traveler will come, he who saw me in my beauty will come, his eye will seek me out in the field and will not find me." But everything was drowned out by the familiar bass voice that with curses and shouts blasphemously complained outside before the door that not a single lantern was burning on the whole Weende Street and it was not even possible to see whose windowpanes had been smashed in.

I can stand a great deal—modesty does not permit me to name the number of bottles—and I reached my bedroom in tolerably good condition. The young merchant, with his chalk-white nightcap and saffron-yellow jacket of hygienic flannel, was already in bed. He was not yet asleep and tried to start a conversation with me. He was from Frankfurt-on-the-Main and consequently spoke at once of the Jews, who had lost all feeling for what is beautiful and noble and sold English wares 25 percent below the factory price. I got the urge to mystify him somewhat, so I told him that I was a somnambulist and would have to beg his pardon in advance in case I should disturb him in his sleep. The poor fellow, therefore, as he confessed to me the next day, did not sleep the entire night, because he was afraid that in my state of somnambulism I might cause trouble with my pistols, which were lying in front of my bed. As a matter of fact, I did not fare much better than he; for I slept badly. Wild, alarming creations of the imagination. A piano selection from Dante's *Inferno*. At last I even dreamed that I was seeing a production of a juristic opera entitled *Falcidia*, traditional libretto by Gans and music by Spontini. A crazy dream. The Roman Forum shone brilliantly; Serv. Asinius Göschenus as praetor on his throne, tossing his toga in proud folds, vented himself in thundering recitatives; Marcus Tullius Elversus, as *prima donna legataria*, revealing all his lovely femininity, sang the love-melting bravura aria *quicunque civis romanus;* junior barristers, rouged brick-red, bellowed as a chorus of minors; instructors, clad as genii in flesh-colored tights, danced an ante-Justinian ballet and wreathed the twelve tables with flowers; the insulted spirit of Roman legislation rose from the earth in thunder and lightning followed by trumpets, tomtoms, a rain of fire, *cum omni causa.*

The Brocken innkeeper drew me away from this noise by waking me to see the sunrise. On the tower I found some people already waiting, rubbing their freezing hands; others, with sleep still in their eyes, were staggering up. Finally the quiet congregation from yesterday evening was again assembled, and in silence we saw how the small crimson ball rose on the horizon, a wintry pale illumination spread forth, the mountains swam as in a white-foaming sea, and only their tips projected visibly, so we thought we were standing on a small hill in the midst of an inundated plain where only here and there a dry clod appeared. In order to capture in words what I had seen and felt, I wrote down the following poem:

> Comes a spark, the sun's first glimmer;
> And the eastern sky's in motion.
> Far and faint the mountain summits
> Float upon a misty ocean.
>
> Had I seven-league boots, I'd hasten
> With the wind, as fast as telling;
> Running on the tops of mountains
> Till I reach my dear one's dwelling.
>
> I would draw the curtains softly
> From her bed, where she lies dreaming;
> Softly I would kiss her forehead
> And her lips, twin rubies gleaming.
>
> And still softer I would whisper
> In her frail and lily ear, "Love,
> Dream we've never lost each other,
> Dream we're lovers still, my dear love."

Meanwhile, my longing for breakfast was just as great and, after addressing a few polite remarks to my ladies, I hurried down to drink coffee in the warm public room. I needed it; in my stomach it was as empty as the Church of Saint Stephan in Goslar. But with the Arabian drink the warm Orient trickled through my limbs as well, roses of the East surrounded me with their scents, sweet nightingale songs rang out, the students were transformed into camels, the girls of the Brocken House, with their Congreve-rocket glances, turned into houris, the philistine noses became minarets, etc.

The book lying before me, however, was not the Koran. It contained, to be sure, plenty of nonsense. It was the so-called Brocken Book, in which all travelers who have climbed the mountain write their names; and most add some thoughts, or in the absence of thoughts, jot down their feelings. Many even express themselves in verse. In this book can be seen what horrors arise when the great tribe of Philistines on ordinary occasions, such as here on the Brocken, has endeavored to be poetic. The palace of the Prince of Pallagonia contains no such grievous tastelessness as this book. Particularly striking are the excise-tax collectors' moldy sentiments, the counter clerks' pathetic outbursts of the soul, the gymnastic banalities of the Old German dilettantes of the revolution, the Berlin schoolteachers' unfortunate phrases of rapture, etc. Mr. Johannes Hagel also wants to prove himself as a writer. Here the majestic splendor of the sunrise is described; elsewhere there are complaints about the weather, about disappointed expectations, about fog that obstructs the view. "Fogged coming up and fogged going down!" is a standing joke repeated by hundreds here.

The whole book smells of cheese, beer, and tobacco, making it seem like reading a novel by Clauren.

While I was drinking coffee, as I have said, and leafing through the Brocken Book, the Swiss with the deep red cheeks entered, and full of enthusiasm, he told of the sublime view he had enjoyed up in the tower when the pure, calm light of the sun, symbol of truth, struggled with the nocturnal masses of fog. He said it had looked like a battle of ghosts in which angry giants thrust out their long swords, armored knights race around on prancing steeds, battle chariots, fluttering banners, strange forms of animal emerge from the wildest confusion, until finally everything becomes entangled in the most insane distortions, grows paler and paler as it melts away and vanishes without a trace. I had missed this demagogic phenomenon of nature and, if it comes to an investigation, I can swear an oath that I know nothing except the taste of the good brown coffee. Alas, it was in fact to blame for my having forgotten my beautiful lady, and she was now standing in front of the door with mother and companion on the verge of climbing into the coach. I scarcely still had time to rush up to her and assure her that it was cold. She seemed annoyed that I had not come sooner, but I soon smoothed the petulant folds of her beautiful brow by presenting her with a remarkable flower that I had plucked from a steep wall of rock the day before at the risk of breaking my neck. Her mother wanted to know the name of the flower, just as if she found it improper for her daughter to pin a strange, unknown flower on her breast—for truly, the flower did receive this enviable place, although it certainly could never have imagined such a thing yesterday on its lonely height. Her taciturn companion now opened his mouth all of a sudden, counted the stamens of the flower, and said quite dryly, "It belongs to the eighth class."

It annoys me every time I see that God's dear flowers have been divided into castes, just as we have been, and on the basis of similar appearances—namely, according to differences in stamens. If a division has to be made, then it would be preferable to follow the proposal of Theophrastus, who wanted to divide the flowers more by their spirit, that is, by their smell. As far as I am concerned, I have my own system in natural science: I divide everything into what can be eaten and what cannot be eaten.

Yet the mysterious nature of flowers was anything but hidden from the older lady, and involuntarily she stated that she was very well pleased with flowers while they were still growing in the garden or in a vase, but, on the other hand, that a slight feeling of pain, vaguely troubling, quivered through her breast when she saw a plucked flower—since such a flower was really a corpse and such a broken, tender flower-corpse lets its withered little head hang quite sadly like a dead child. The lady was almost shocked at the mournful effect of her remark, and it was my duty to dispel it with some verses from Voltaire. How a few French words can restore us immediately to the proper conversational state of mind! We laughed, hands were kissed, there were gracious smiles, the horses whinnied, and the coach hobbled slowly and arduously down the mountain.

Now the students also made preparations for departure. Knapsacks were tied; bills, which were cheaper than all expectations, were settled; the receptive housemaids, on their faces the traces of happy love, brought, as is customary, the Brocken bouquets, helped us to fasten them on our caps, were paid for their trouble with several kisses or groschen, and so we all descended the mountain; while some, among whom were the Swiss and the Greifswalder,

headed toward Schierke, the others, about twenty persons includ-
ing my countrymen and myself, led by a guide, went down through
the so-called snow holes toward Ilsenburg.

We went helter-skelter. Students of Halle march faster than the
Austrian militia. Before I was aware of it, the barren part of the
mountain with its scattered groups of stones was behind us, and
we came through a fir forest that I had seen the day before. The
sun poured down its most festive rays, lighting up the amusingly
colorfully clad youth who charged so cheerfully through the thicket,
disappeared here, came into view again there, ran over the tree
trunks laid across swampy places, clambered up steep gorges on
climbing roots, yodeled in the most delightful tones, and received
just as merry an answer from the twittering forest birds, from the
rustling firs, from the unseen rippling springs, and from the resounding echo. When happy youth and beautiful nature come together, they rejoice mutually.

The farther we descended, the more sweetly the subterranean
waters murmured, only here and there under rocks and under-
brush did they gleam forth and seem secretly to peek out to see if
they dared come out into the light, and finally a tiny wave came
leaping out determinedly. Now the usual phenomenon appears: a
bold one goes first, then the great tribe of hesitant ones is suddenly, to its own astonishment, seized with courage, and hurries
to unite with the first. Many other springs now hopped hurriedly
out of their hiding places, and soon they joined together to form
a sizable brooklet that rushes down into the mountain valley in
countless waterfalls and in remarkable meanderings. That, now, is
the lovely, sweet Ilse. It passes through the blessed Ilse Valley, on
both sides of which the mountains gradually rise higher, and these
are mostly overgrown down to their foot with beeches, oaks, and
ordinary deciduous undergrowth, no longer with firs and other
coniferous trees. For that kind of deciduous tree is predominant in
the "Lower Harz," as the eastern side of the Brocken is called in
contrast to its western side, which is known as the "Upper Harz"
and is actually much higher and therefore more suitable for the
thriving of conifers.

It is indescribable with what joy, naïveté, and grace the Ilse
rushes down over the strangely formed pieces of rock that it finds
in its course, so that the water hisses up wildly here or overflows

in foam, pours out there in pure arches from all sorts of clefts in the rocks as if out of frantic watering cans, and below skips again over the small stones like a merry little girl. Yes, the legend is true, the Ilse is a princess who runs laughing and blooming down the mountain. How her white garment of foam gleams in the sunshine! How her silver ribbons flutter in the wind! How her diamonds flash and sparkle. The tall beeches stand like serious fathers gazing with secret smiles at the mischievousness of the dear child; the white birches rustle like happy aunts, yet at the same time seem anxious about the daring leaps; the proud oak tree looks on like a vexed uncle who is expected to pay for the beautiful weather; the birds in the air shout their applause; the flowers on the bank whisper tenderly, "Oh, take us along, take us along, dear little sister!" But the merry girl springs ceaselessly onward and suddenly she grasps the dreaming poet, and a flowery rain of sounding rays and radiant sounds streams down upon me, and from sheer glory I lose my senses, and I hear nothing but the voice as sweet as a flute:

> I am the Princess Ilse
> And I dwell at Ilsenstein.
> Come with me to my castle,
> Thou shalt be blest, and mine.
>
> There I shall bathe thy forehead
> With waters clear and glad,
> Until thy pain shall vanish,
> Thou sick and sorrowing lad.
>
> With my white arms about thee,
> Upon my breast thou'lt be;
> And thou shalt lie there dreaming
> Of fairy legendry.
>
> And I shall kiss and hold thee
> As I would kiss and hold
> My lover, dear King Heinrich,
> Who now lies dead and cold.

The dead stay dead forever,
Only the living live,
My laughing heart is leaping;
I've youth and joy to give.

Then come down to my castle,
Come to my crystal halls;
The knights and maidens are dancing,
Happy are all my thralls.

There's rustling of silk and clatter
Of spurs, and the bright air hums;
The nimble dwarfs are playing
On fiddles and horns and drums.

But always my arms shall enfold thee
And I shall keep thee enthralled;
As I stopped the ears of King Heinrich
When the brazen trumpets called.

Infinitely blissful is the feeling when the world of appearances
blends with our world of emotions, and green trees, thoughts, the
song of birds, wistfulness, the blue of the heavens, memories, and
the fragrance of plants entwine in sweet arabesques. Women know
this feeling best, and it is perhaps for this reason that such a sweet,
incredulous smile hovers on their lips when we boast with scho-
lastic pride of our logical deeds, how we have divided everything
so nicely into objective and subjective, how we have arranged our
heads like an apothecary shop with a thousand compartments in
one of which is reason, in the second understanding, in the third
wit, in the fourth bad wit, and in the fifth nothing at all—that is,
an idea.

As if wandering on in a dream, I had almost failed to notice
that we had left the depths of the Ilse Valley and were again
climbing uphill. The path was very steep and strenuous, and many
of us became short of breath. But like our late cousin who lies
buried in Mölln, we thought in advance of the descent and were all
the more pleased. Finally we reached the Ilse Rock.

This is an enormous granite cliff rising boldly from the depths.

High, forest-covered mountains surround it on three sides; but the fourth, the north side, is open, and from here one sees the Ilsenburg lying below and the Ilse flowing far down into the lowlands. On the towerlike tip of the rock stands a great iron cross and, if need be, there is additional space for four human feet.

Just as nature has adorned the Ilse Rock with the fantastic charms of its position and form, so legend has also poured out its rosy glow over it. Gottschalk reports, "It is said that a cursed castle stood here in which the rich, beautiful Princess Ilse lived and that she still bathes every morning in the Ilse; and whoever is fortunate enough to strike upon the right moment is led by her into the cliff, where her castle is situated, and royally rewarded." Others tell of Miss Ilse's love for the knight of Westenberg, a pretty tale that one of our best-known poets has romantically rendered in the *Evening Times*. Still others give a different account: it is said to have been the Old Saxon Emperor Henry who enjoyed the most imperial hours with Ilse, the beautiful water nixie, in her enchanted castle in the cliff. A more recent author, Mr. Niemann, Esq.—who wrote a Harz travel guide in which with laudable diligence and precise figures he has indicated the heights of the mountains, the variations of the magnetic needle, the debts of the towns, and other such things—asserts on the contrary, "What is told about the beautiful Princess Ilse belongs to the realm of fable." So say all these people to whom such a princess has never appeared; we, however, who have been especially favored by fair ladies, know better. Emperor Henry also knew it. Not without reason did the Old Saxon emperors cling so fast to their native Harz. Let anyone merely leaf through the pretty *Lüneburg Chronicle,* where the good old fellows are pictured in remarkably faithful woodcuts, well armored, high upon their war steeds clad in chain mail, the holy imperial crown on their precious heads, scepter and sword in firm hands; and from their dear, moustached faces one can clearly read how often they have yearned for the sweet hearts of their Harz princesses and the familiar rustling of the Harz woods when they were staying in foreign lands, even in Italy, which is so rich in lemons and poison, where they and their successors were so often lured by the desire to be called Roman emperors—a truly German mania for titles, because of which emperor and empire perished.

But I advise anyone standing on the summit of the Ilse Rock not to think about emperor and empire, or about the beautiful Ilse, but only about his own feet. For as I was standing there, lost in thought, I suddenly heard the subterranean music of the magic castle, and I saw how the mountains round about stood on their heads, the red-brick roofs in Ilsenburg began to dance, and the green trees flew around in the blue air so that everything turned blue and green before my eyes, and seized by a fit of dizziness, I would surely have fallen into the abyss if I had not held fast in my mortal need to the iron cross. Certainly no one will blame me for doing this in such a precarious situation.

"The Harz Journey" is and remains a fragment, and the many-colored threads so prettily woven into it for the purpose of twining them harmoniously into a whole are suddenly cut off as if by the scissors of the inexorable goddess of fate. Perhaps I shall continue to weave them together in future songs, and what is now stingily left untold will then be said in full. In the end it comes to one and the same thing, when and where something has been said, if only it has actually been said once. The individual works may remain fragments if only they form a whole when brought together. Through such a union omissions may be filled in, rough places smoothed out, and what is all too harsh may be softened. This would perhaps have been the case with the first pages of "The Harz Journey," and they might have produced a less sour impression if it were elsewhere discovered that the indignation I harbor in general for Göttingen, although it is even greater than I expressed it, is far from being as great as the respect I feel for certain individuals there. And why should I conceal it? I mean here especially that very dear man who in earlier days took such a friendly interest in me, inspired in me at that time an ardent love for history, later strengthened me in my zeal for it, and in that manner led me on to quieter paths, steered my energies in more wholesome directions, and in general prepared for me those consolations of history without which I could never endure the tormenting phenomena of daily life. I am speaking of George Sartorius, the great historian and human being, whose eye is a bright star in our dark period and whose hospitable heart stands open to all the sorrows and joys of others, to the cares of beggars and kings, and to the last sighs of perishing peoples and their gods.

I must not fail to mention here that the Upper Harz, that part of the Harz that I have described up to the beginning of the Ilse Valley, does not by any means offer such delightful views as the romantically picturesque Lower Harz and contrasts greatly with the latter in its wild, rugged, and fir-dark beauty; just as similarly the three valleys of the Lower Harz formed by the Ilse, the Bode, and the Selke charmingly contrast with one another if one knows how to personify the character of each valley. They are three female figures, and one cannot so easily determine which is the fairest.

Of the dear, sweet Ilse, and how sweetly and charmingly she received me, I have already spoken and sung. The somber beauty, the Bode, did not receive me so graciously, and when I first glimpsed her in foundry-dark Rübeland, she seemed very sullen and hid herself in a silvery gray veil of rain. But with quick love she cast it off when I had reached the summit of the Horse's Hoof-print; her countenance shone toward me in sunniest glory, from all her features breathed a colossal tenderness, and out of the conquered breast of the cliff poured sounds like sighs of yearning and melting tones of sadness. Less tenderly but more joyfully the beauteous Selke showed herself to me, that fair and amiable lady whose noble simplicity and serene calm keeps all sentimental familiarity at a distance; but whose propensity for teasing is betrayed by a half-concealed smile; and I would blame this for all sorts of little troubles that afflicted me in the Selke Valley: that in trying to leap over the water, I plumped down right in the middle; that later, after I had exchanged my shoes for slippers, one of them slipped out of my hand—or rather slipped away from my foot; that a gust of wind carried off my cap, that the forest thorns scratched my legs to pieces, and, unfortunately, so forth. But I forgive the fair lady for all these troubles, for she is beautiful. And now she stands before my fantasy with all her quiet grace and seems to say, "Even though I laugh, I still mean well toward you, and I ask you please to sing about me!" The glorious Bode likewise comes forward in my memory, and her dark eyes say, "You are like me in your pride and your pain, and I want you to love me." The beautiful Ilse comes springing along also, tender and bewitching in mien, form, and movement; she is just like the charming creature that blesses my dreams, and just like her she looks at me with irresistible indifference, and yet, at the same time, she is so ardently, so eternally, so transparently true. Now I am Paris, the three goddesses stand before me, and I give the apple to the beautiful Ilse.

Today is the first of May; like a sea of life the springtime overflows the earth; the white foam of blossoms remains hanging on the trees; a wide, warm, misty luster spreads out everywhere; in the town the windowpanes of the houses glow joyously; on the roofs the sparrows are again building their little nests; people are walking on the street and marveling that the air is so invigorating and that they themselves feel so strange; the colorfully dressed women of Vierland carry bouquets of violets; the orphans with their blue jackets and their dear, illegitimate faces run along Maiden Lane and rejoice as much as if they were going to find a father again today; the beggar on the bridge looks as pleased as if he had won the grand prize in the lottery; even the black, still unhanged jobber running along there with his rascally shop-goods face is shone upon by the sun with its most tolerant rays. I am going to wander out in front of the town gate.

It is the first of May, and I am thinking of you, beautiful Ilse— or should I call you "Agnes," because you like this name best?—I am thinking of you, and I would like to watch you running radiantly down the mountain. But best of all I would like to stand down below in the valley and catch you in my arms. It is a beautiful day! Everywhere I see green, the color of hope. Everywhere, like lovely wonders, flowers bloom forth and my heart, too, wants to bloom again. This heart is a flower too, a very remarkable one. It is no modest violet, no laughing rose, no pure lily or other such flower that delights girlish hearts with its pleasant charms and can be prettily pinned on a pretty bosom, withering today and blooming again tomorrow. This heart resembles more that heavy, fantastic flower from the woods of Brazil, which, according to legend, only blooms once every century. I remember seeing such a flower when I was a boy. In the night we heard a shot as from a pistol, and on the next day the neighbor's children told me that it was their aloe that had suddenly bloomed with such a thundering crack. They led me into their garden, and there I saw, to my astonishment, that the low, hard growth with its foolishly broad, sharply pointed leaves, on which one could easily injure oneself, had now shot up high and was bearing on top the most glorious blossom like a golden crown. We children could not even look up so high, and the old, grinning Christian, who was fond of us, built a wooden staircase around the flower, and we clambered up on it like cats and gazed curiously down into the open calix from which the yellow stamens and wildly strange scents emerged with un-heard-of splendor.

Yes, Agnes, this heart does not bloom often and easily; as well as I can remember, it has bloomed but a single time, and that may well have been long ago, certainly a hundred years ago. I believe, though, that however gloriously its blossom developed at that time, it would nonetheless have pined away miserably for lack of sun-shine and warmth if it had not been violently destroyed by a dark winter's storm. Now, however, there is stirring and movement again in my breast, and if you suddenly hear the shot, young lady, do not be afraid! I have not shot myself; but my love is bursting its bud and is shooting up in radiant songs, in eternal dithyrambs, in the happiest fullness of song.

But if this high love is too high for you, young lady, then make it easy for yourself by climbing the wooden staircase and looking down from it into my blooming heart.

It is still early in the day, the sun has scarcely covered half its course, and my heart is exhaling such strong fragrances that they are rising stupefyingly to my head, so that I no longer know where irony ceases and heaven begins, that I populate the air with my sighs, and that I myself would like to melt again into sweet atoms, into the uncreated deity. How is it going to be when night comes and the stars appear in the heavens, "those unfortunate stars that can tell you . . ."

It is the first of May, the most wretched shop boy has the right to be sentimental today, and would you deny that right to the poet?

Translated by Frederic T. Wood
and adapted by Robert C. Holub
and Martha Humphreys

Ideas: Book Le Grand

The race of the Örindur
Like pillars shall defend
Our throne; they shall endure
Though nature itself may end.
                              Müllner

Evelina
Accept these pages
as
a Token of the Author's
Friendship and Love

Chapter 1

"She was lovable, and he loved her. He, however, was not lovable, and she did not love him."   —Old Play

Madame, are you familiar with that old play? It is an altogether extraordinary performance, just a little too melancholy. I myself once played the leading part in it, as a result of which all the ladies wept except one, who did not shed so much as a single tear, and that was simply the whole point of the play, the real catastrophe.

Oh, that single tear! It still torments my thoughts. When the devil desires to ruin my soul, he hums into my ear a ballad of that tear that was never wept, a fatal song with an even more fatal tune. Ah! such a tune is only heard in hell! . . .

You can readily imagine, madame, what life is like in heaven—the more readily as you are married. There people amuse themselves altogether superbly, every sort of entertainment is provided, and people live in delight and pleasure, or, as the saying goes, "like the Lord in France." There people dine from morning to night, and the cooking is as good as at Jagor's; roast geese fly around with gravy boats in their bills and feel flattered if anyone eats them; tarts gleaming with butter grow wild like sunflowers; everywhere there are rivulets of bouillon and champagne, everywhere trees with napkins fluttering from them, and people dine and wipe their lips and eat again without getting indigestion; people sing psalms or flirt and joke with the dear, delicate, little angels or take a walk on the green Hallelujah Meadow, and the white, flowing garments fit very comfortably, and nothing disturbs the feeling of bliss—no pain, no discomfort; even when someone accidentally treads on someone else's corns and exclaims, "*Excusez!*" the latter smiles as if enraptured and insists, "Your foot, brother, did not hurt in the least, quite *au contraire*, it only causes a deeper thrill of heavenly rapture to shoot through my heart!"

But of hell, madame, you have not the faintest idea. Of all the devils in existence, you have probably made the acquaintance only of Amor, the nice little *croupier* of hell who is the smallest Beelzebub of them all. And you know him only from *Don Juan* and doubtless think that for such a betrayer of female innocence hell can never be made hot enough, though our praiseworthy theater directors shower down upon him a spectacle of as much flame, fiery rain, squibs, and colophonium as any good Christian in hell can demand.

However, things in hell look much worse than our theater directors know—otherwise they would not have so many bad plays performed—for in hell it is infernally hot, and when I was once there during the dog days I found it unbearable. Madame, you have no idea of hell! We get very few official reports from there. Still it is rank calumny to say that down there all the poor souls are compelled to read all day long all the bad sermons ever printed up here. It is not that bad in hell—Satan will never invent such refined tortures. On the other hand, Dante's description is too mild—on the whole, too poetic. Hell appeared to me like a large, bourgeois kitchen with an endlessly long stove on which were three rows of iron pots, and in these sat the damned and were fried. In one row sat Christian sinners, and incredible as it may seem, their number was anything but small, and the devils poked the fire up under them with special diligence. In the next row sat the Jews, who continually screamed and were occasionally mocked by the fiends, which sometimes seemed droll enough—as, for instance, when a fat, wheezy pawnbroker complained of the heat and a little devil poured several buckets of cold water on his head so he might realize that baptism was a refreshing benefit. In the third row sat the heathens, who, like the Jews, could not take part in bliss and had to burn forever. I heard one of these, as a heavyset devil put fresh coals under his kettle, cry out from his pot, "Spare me! I was Socrates, the wisest of mortals; I taught truth and justice and sacrificed my life for virtue." But the heavyset, stupid devil went on with his work and grumbled, "Oh, shut up there! All heathens must burn, and we can't make an exception for the sake of one lone person." I assure you, madame, the heat was terrible. There was screaming, sighing, groaning, quacking, growling, complaining; and all these terrible sounds were distinctly penetrated by that fatal melody of the song of the unwept tear.

Chapter 2

"She was lovable, and he loved her. He, however, was not lovable, and she did not love him." —Old Play

Madame, that old play is a tragedy, although the hero in it is neither killed nor commits suicide. The eyes of the heroine are beautiful, very beautiful—madame, do you smell the fragrance of violets?—very beautiful, and yet so piercing that they penetrated my heart like poniards of glass and surely came out through my back, and yet I was not killed by those treacherous eyes. The voice of the heroine is also beautiful—madame, did you not just hear a nightingale singing?—a beautiful, silken voice, a sweet web of the sunniest tones, and my soul became entangled in it and choked and tormented itself. I myself—it is the Count of Ganges who now speaks, and the story takes place in Venice—I myself had enough of those tortures and even in the first act thought of putting an end to the play and of shooting down the fool's cap, head and all, and I went to a fancy store in the Via Burstah where I saw on display a pair of beautiful pistols in a case—I still remember them well; near them stood many cheerful toys of mother-of-pearl and gold, iron hearts on gilt chains, porcelain cups with delicate mottos and snuffboxes with pretty pictures such as the divine history of Susannah, the Swan Song of Leda, the Rape of the Sabines, Lucretia, the fat, virtuous person with her bare bosom into which she subsequently sticks a dagger; the late Bethmann, *la belle Ferroniere,* all beguiling faces; but I nonetheless bought the pistols without much ado, and then I bought bullets, then powder, and then I went to the restaurant of Signor Immodest and ordered oysters and a glass of Rhine wine.

I could eat nothing, and I could drink still less. The warm tears fell into my glass, and in that glass I saw my dear homeland, the blue, holy Ganges, the ever-gleaming Himalayas, the giant banyan woods amid whose broad, leafy paths wise elephants and white pilgrims calmly wandered; strange, dreamy flowers gazed at me in furtive admonishment; wondrous, golden birds wildly rejoiced; glimmering sun rays and the sweetly silly chatter of laughing monkeys pleasantly teased me; from far pagodas sounded the pious prayers of priests, and intermittently the mellifluously plaintive voice of the Sultana of Delhi could be heard. She ran stormily back and forth in her carpeted chamber; she tore her silver veil; with her peacock fan she struck the black female slave to the ground; she wept, she raged, she cried, but I could not understand her—the restaurant of Signor Immodest is three thousand miles away from the harem of Delhi, and moreover the beautiful Sultana has already been dead for three thousand years—and I quickly drank up the wine, the clear, joyous wine, and nonetheless my soul grew darker and sadder. I was condemned to death. . . .

As I emerged from the restaurant, I heard the sound of the death knell; a crowd of people swept past me; I, however, placed myself at the corner of the *Strada San Giovanni* and recited the following monologue:

In ancient tales they tell of golden castles,
Where harps are sounding, lovely ladies dance,
And trim attendants scurry, and jasmine,
Myrtle, and roses spread their soft perfume.
And yet a single word of disenchantment
Sweeps all the glory of the scene to naught.
And there remain but ruins old and gray,
And screaming birds of night and foul morass.
E'en so have I with a short single word
Quite disenchanted nature's loveliness.
There lies she now, lifeless and cold and pale,
E'en like a monarch's corpse laid out in state,
The cheeks fresh stained with rouge,
And in her hand the regal scepter laid;
Yet still the lips are yellow and most changed,
For they forgot to paint them as they should,
And mice are jumping o'er the regal nose,
And impertinently mock the large golden scepter.

It is generally agreed, madame, that everyone should deliver a soliloquy before committing suicide. Most people on such occasions use Hamlet's "to be or not to be." It is an excellent passage, and I would gladly have quoted it, but charity begins at home, and if someone has, as I have, likewise written tragedies in which such farewell-to-life speeches occur—as, for instance, in my immortal *Almansor*—it is very natural that one should prefer one's own words even to Shakespeare's. In any case, the delivery of such speeches is a very useful custom, for thereby at least a little time is gained. And thus it came to pass that I remained standing a long time on the corner of the *Strada San Giovanni,* and as I stood there, a man condemned to death, I suddenly caught a glimpse of her!

She wore her blue silk dress and rose-red hat, and her eyes looked at me so gently, with such an expression of vanquishing death, of giving life. Madame, you will know from Roman history that when the vestals came upon a criminal being led off to execution, they had the right to pardon him, and the poor rogue remained alive. With a single glance she saved me from death, and I stood before her as if revived, as if dazzled by the sunny brilliance of her beauty, and she walked on past and let me live.

Chapter 3

And she let me live, and I live, and that is the main point.

Others may enjoy the good fortune of having their lady love adorn their graves with garlands and water them with tears of fidelity. O women! Hate me, laugh at me, jilt me, but let me live! Life is all too wondrously sweet, and the world is so beautifully bewildered; it is the dream of a god intoxicated by wine, who has taken French leave of the carousing multitude of immortals and has lain down to sleep on a solitary star, not knowing that he himself also creates everything he dreams of—and the dream images often form so motley and wildly, often so harmoniously and reasonably—the *Iliad,* Plato, the battle of Marathon, Moses, the Medician Venus, the Cathedral of Strasbourg, the French Revolution, Hegel, steamboats, etc., are single good thoughts in this divine dream of creation—but it will not last long before the god will awake and rub his sleepy eyes and smile, and our world melts into nothingness; in fact, it never existed.

No matter, I am alive! If I am but the shadowy image in a dream, still this is better than the cold, black, empty nothingness of death. Life is the greatest of blessings and death the worst of evils. Berlin lieutenants of the guard may sneer and call it cowardice that the Prince of Homburg shudders when he beholds his open grave—Heinrich Kleist nonetheless had as much courage as his high-breasted, straitlaced colleagues and has unfortunately proved it. But all strong men love life. Goethe's Egmont does not cheerfully take leave from "the cheerful wontedness of being and action." Immermann's Edwin clings to life "like a child at its mother's breast." And though he finds it hard to live by alien mercy, he still begs for mercy,

"For life and breath are still the greatest boon."

When Odysseus in the underworld sees Achilles as the leader of dead heroes and extols his renown among the living and his glory even among the dead, the latter replies:

No more discourse of death, consolingly,
    noble Odysseus!
Rather would I in the field as daily laborer
    be toiling,
Slave to the meanest of men, a pauper and
    lacking possessions,
Than 'mid the infinite host of long-vanished
    mortals be ruler.

Yes, when Major Düvent challenged the great Israel Lion to fight with pistols and said to him, "If you do not take a stand, Mr. Lion, you are a dog!" the latter replied, "I would rather be a live dog than a dead lion!" And he was right—I have fought often enough, madame, if you don't mind my saying so—God be praised, I am alive! Red life seethes in my veins, the earth yields beneath my feet, in the glow of love I embrace trees and marble statues, and they come alive in my embrace. Every woman is to me a gift of a world. I revel in the melody of her countenance, and with a single glance of my eye I can enjoy more than others with their every limb through all their lives. Every instant is to me an eternity: I do not measure time with the ell of Brabant or of Hamburg, and I need no priest to promise me a second life; for I can live enough in this life when I live backward in the lives of my ancestors and conquer for myself an eternity in the realm of the past.

And I am alive! The great pulsebeat of nature also beats in my breast; and when I exult aloud, I am answered by a thousandfold echo. I hear a thousand nightingales. Spring sent them to awaken earth from her morning slumber, and earth trembles with ecstasy; her flowers are hymns that she sings in rapture to the sun; the sun moves far too slowly; I would like to lash his fiery steeds that they might advance more rapidly. But when it sinks hissing into the sea, and the night rises with its great longing eyes, oh, then true pleasure really pulsates in me, the evening breezes lie like flattering maidens upon my impetuous heart, and the stars wink, and I rise and float above the petty earth and the petty thoughts of mankind.

Chapter 4

But the day will come when the fire of youth will be quenched in my veins, when winter will dwell in my breast, when its white snowflakes will sparsely flutter about my head and its mists will dim my eyes. My friends will lie in their weather-worn tombs, and I alone will remain like a solitary stalk forgotten by the reaper. A new generation with new desires and new thoughts will have sprung up; full of astonishment, I hear new names and new songs; the old names are forgotten, and I myself am forgotten, perhaps still honored by a few, scorned by many, and loved by none! And the rosy-cheeked boys will leap around me and place the old harp in my trembling hand and say, laughing, "You have been silent a long time, you lazy, gray-haired old man; sing us again songs of the dreams of your youth."

Then I will grasp the harp, and my old joys and sorrows will awake, the mists will vanish, tears will again gleam on my lifeless cheeks; spring will bloom once more in my breast; sweet tones of melancholy will tremble on the harp string; I will once more see the blue stream and the marble palaces and the beautiful faces of women and young girls, and I will sing a song of the flowers of the Brenta.

It will be my last song; the stars will gaze on me as in the nights of my youth; the loving moonlight will once more kiss my cheeks; the choruses of the spirits of dead nightingales will sound flutelike from afar; my eyes, intoxicated with sleep, will softly close; my soul will fade away like the sounds of my harp—the flowers of the Brenta are fragrant.

A tree will shade my grave. I would have liked a palm tree, but it will not grow in the North. Probably it will be a linden, and on summer evenings lovers will sit there caressing; the green finch, which listens rocking itself in the branches, will fall silent; and my linden will rustle protectingly over the heads of the happy ones, who will be so happy that they will not even have time to read what is written on the white tombstone. But when, later, the lover has lost his love, then he will come again to the well-known linden and sigh and weep and gaze long and often upon the stone and will read the inscription, "He loved the flowers of the Brenta."

Chapter 5

Madame, I have deceived you. I am not the Count of the Ganges. Never in my life did I see the holy stream or the lotus flowers mirrored in its sacred waves. Never did I lie dreaming under Indian palms or praying before the diamond deity Juggernaut, who might easily have aided me. I have no more been in Calcutta than the turkey that I ate yesterday afternoon. Yet my ancestors came from Hindustan, and I therefore feel so well in Valmiki's great forests of song. The heroic sorrows of the divine Rama move my heart like a familiar grief; from the flower lays of Kalidasa the sweetest memories bloom; and when a few years ago a gentle lady in Berlin showed me the beautiful pictures that her father, who had long been Governor General in India, had brought back, the delicately painted, holy, calm faces seemed as familiar to me as if I were gazing at my own family portraits.

Franz Bopp—madame, you have of course read his *Nalus* and his *System of Sanskrit Conjugations*—gave me much information about my ancestry, and I now know definitely that I am descended from Brahma's head and not from his corns. I even suspect that the entire *Mahabharata,* with its two hundred thousand verses, is merely an allegorical love letter written by my forefather to my older foremother. Oh, they loved each other dearly; their souls kissed, they kissed with their eyes, they were both but one single kiss . . .

An enchanted nightingale sits on a red coral bough in the Pacific Ocean and sings a song of the love of my ancestors; the pearls look out curiously from their shells; the wondrous water flowers tremble with sad longing; the cunning sea snails, bearing on their backs many-colored porcelain towers, come creeping forward; the ocean roses blush with shame; the yellow, sharp-pointed starfish and the thousand-hued, glassy jellyfish quiver and stretch, and everything is swarming and listening . . .

Unfortunately, madame, this nightingale song is far too long to be recounted here; it is as long as the world itself—even its dedication to Ananga, the god of love, is as long as all Sir Walter Scott's novels together, and there is a passage referring to it in Aristophanes, which in German reads thus:

Tiotio, tiotio, tiotinx,
Totototo, totototo, tototinx.
—Voss's translation

No, I was not born in India. I first beheld the light of the world on the shores of that beautiful stream where folly grows on green mountains and is plucked in autumn, laid away in cellars, poured into barrels, and exported to foreign lands. In fact, only yesterday I heard someone speaking a piece of folly that was enclosed in the year 1811 in a bunch of grapes that I myself saw growing on the Johannisberg. But much folly is also consumed at home, and people are the same there as everywhere; they are born, eat, drink, sleep, laugh, cry, slander each other, are anxiously concerned about the continuation of their race, try to seem what they are not and to do what they cannot, never shave until they have a beard, and often have beards before they are reasonable; and when they are reasonable, they intoxicate themselves again with white and red folly.

Mon dieu! If I had so much faith that I could move mountains, the Johannisberg would be just the mountain that I would want to follow me everywhere. But since my faith is not so strong, fantasy must aid me, and it at once takes me to the beautiful Rhine.

Oh, there is a beautiful country full of loveliness and sunshine. In its blue streams are mirrored the mountain shores with their castle ruins, and woods, and ancient towns. There on summer evenings the good people sit in front of their houses and drink out of large jugs and gossip confidingly: how the wine—the Lord be praised!—thrives, and how the law courts should be free from all secrecy, and how Marie Antoinette being guillotined is none of our business, and how tobacco is made expensive by the tobacco tax, and how all men are equal, and how Görres is a splendid fellow.

I have never troubled myself much with such conversation and greatly preferred sitting by the maidens in the arched window and laughing about their laughter and letting them strike me in the face with flowers and pretending to be angry until they told me their secrets or some other important story. Beautiful Gertrude was half wild with delight when I sat by her. She was a girl like a flaming rose, and once when she embraced me, I thought she would burn up and evaporate in my arms. Beautiful Katherine melted in sonorous softness when she talked with me, and her eyes were of that pure, heartfelt blue that I have never found in men and animals and only seldom in flowers; one gazed so gladly into them and could then imagine the sweetest things. But beautiful Hedwiga loved me, for when I came to her she bowed her head toward the earth so that her black locks fell down over her blushing face, and her gleaming eyes shone forth like stars from a dark heaven. Her bashful lips spoke not a word, and I, too, could say nothing to her. I coughed and she trembled. She often asked me through her sisters not to climb the cliffs so hastily and not to swim in the Rhine if I had been running or drinking. Once I overheard her pious prayer to the image of the Virgin Mary, which was adorned with gold leaf and illuminated by the flickering of a small lamp and which stood in a corner of the vestibule. I heard clearly how she asked the Mother of God to keep me from climbing, drinking, and swimming! I would certainly have fallen in love with her had she been indifferent toward me; but I was indifferent toward her, because I knew that she loved me. Madame, if anyone wishes to be loved by me, they must treat me *en canaille.*

Beautiful Johanna was the cousin of the three sisters, and I was glad to be with her. She knew the most beautiful old legends, and when she pointed her white hand out the window in the direction of the mountains where everything that she narrated had happened, I became absolutely enchanted; the old knights visibly rose from the castle ruins and hewed away at each other's iron clothing; the Lorelei again stood on the mountain summit singing down her sweet ruinous song; and the Rhine rippled so reasonably, calmingly, and at the same time teasingly and uncannily—and beautiful Johanna gazed at me so bewilderingly, so mysteriously, so enigmatically confidingly, as though she herself were part of the tale she was just narrating. She was a slender, pale girl, deathly ill and pensive; her eyes were as clear as truth itself, her lips piously arched; in her features lay a great story, but it was a sacred story— perhaps a legend of love. I do not know what it was and never had the courage to ask. When I looked at her for a long time, I became calm and cheerful; it was as if a tranquil Sunday were in my heart and the angels were holding church service there.

In such happy hours I told her stories from my childhood, and she listened earnestly to me, and curiously enough, when I could not recall the names, she reminded me of them. When I then asked her in astonishment where she knew the names from, she answered with a smile that she had learned them from the birds that were nesting on her windowsill—and she tried to make me believe that these were the same birds that I as a boy had once bought with my pocket money from a hard-hearted peasant boy and then let fly away. I, however, believed that she knew everything because she was so pale and actually died soon thereafter. She also knew when she would die and wanted me to leave Andernach the day before. In parting, she gave me both her hands—they were white, sweet hands, and pure as the Host—and she said, "You are very good, and when you are bad, then think of little, dead Veronica."

Did the chattering birds also disclose this name? At times when I indulged in recollections, I had often wearied my brain and was still unable to remember that dear name.

And now that I have it again, my earliest childhood wants to bloom into memory again; and I am again a child playing with other children in the palace courtyard at Düsseldorf on the Rhine.

Chapter 6

Yes, madame, there I was born, and I am particular in calling attention to this fact, lest after my death seven cities—Schilda, Krähwinkel, Polwitz, Bockum, Dülken, Göttingen, and Schöppenstadt—contend for the honor of being my birthplace. Düsseldorf is a city on the Rhine where about sixteen thousand people live and where, in addition, several hundred thousand are buried. And among them are many of whom my mother says it would be better if they were still alive—for example, my grandfather and my uncle, the old Herr v. Geldern and the young Herr v. Geldern, who were both such celebrated doctors and saved the lives of so many people and yet had to die themselves. And pious Ursula, who carried me as a child in her arms, also lies buried there, and a rosebush grows on her grave; she loved rose fragrance so much during her lifetime, and her heart was all rose fragrance and goodness. And the shrewd old canon also lies buried there. Lord, how miserable he looked when I last saw him! He consisted of nothing but spirit and bandages, and nonetheless he studied night and day as though he feared the worms might find a few ideas missing in his head. Little William also lies there, and that is my fault. We were schoolmates in the Franciscan cloister and were playing one day on that side of the building where the Düssel flows between stone embankments, and I said, "William, go get the kitten that has just fallen in!" and he cheerfully climbed out onto the board that lay across the brook, pulled the cat out of the water but fell in himself, and when they took him out, he was wet and dead. The kitten, though, lived to a good old age.

The city of Düsseldorf is very beautiful, and if anyone who happens to have been born there thinks of it while in a foreign country, he will be overcome by strange feelings. I was born there and feel as if I must go home immediately. And when I say go home, I mean the Bolkerstrasse and the house in which I was born. This house will someday be very noteworthy, and I have sent word to the old lady who owns it that she must not under any circumstances sell it. For the whole house she would now hardly get as much as the gratuity the green-veiled English ladies will give the servant girl for showing them the room where I first saw the light of day and the hen house where my father generally locked me up for stealing grapes, and also the brown door on which my mother taught me to write the alphabet with chalk. O Lord! Madame, if I become a famous author, it has cost my poor mother trouble enough.

But my renown still slumbers in the marble quarries of Carrara; the wastepaper wreath with which they have crowned my brow has not yet spread its fragrance through the wide world, and when the green-veiled ladies now visit Düsseldorf, they leave the celebrated house unvisited and go directly to the marketplace and there gaze on the colossal black equestrian statue standing in the middle of it. This represents the Prince Elector, Jan Wilhelm. He wears black armor and a long, full-bottomed wig. As a boy I was told that the artist who made this statue noticed with horror while it was being cast that he did not have enough metal to fill the mold, so all the citizens of the town came running with their silver spoons and threw them in to make up the deficiency—and I often stood before the statue for hours, wondering how many spoons were concealed in it and how many apple tarts the silver would buy. Apple tarts were then my passion—now it is love, truth, freedom, and crab soup—and at the theater corner not far from the statue of the Prince Elector there generally stood a curiously built, saber-legged fellow with a white apron, and around him was tied a basket full of lovely, steaming apple tarts that he well knew how to praise in an irresistible descant voice: "Here you are! Fresh apple tarts! Just from the oven—see how they steam—quite delicious!" Truly, whenever in my later years the tempter tried to get at me, he always spoke in just such an enticing descant voice, and I would not have remained twelve hours with Signora Guilietta if she had not started in with her sweet, steaming, apple-tart manner. And, in fact, apple tarts would never have tempted me so much if crooked Hermann had not covered them up so mysteriously with his white apron: and it is aprons, you know, which . . . but I am wandering from the subject. I was speaking of the equestrian statue that has so many silver spoons in its body and no soup and that represents the Prince Elector, Jan Wilhelm.

He is alleged to have been a brave gentlemen, a lover of art and very talented himself. He founded the picture gallery in Düsseldorf; and in the observatory there they show a very artistic piece of work consisting of one box within another that he himself had carved in his leisure hours—he had twenty-four of them every day.

In those days princes were not yet persecuted people as nowadays, and crowns grew firmly on their heads, and at night they drew their nightcaps over them and slept in peace, and their people slumbered calmly at their feet, and when they awoke in the morning, they said, "Good morning, father!" and he replied, "Good morning, dear children!"

But things suddenly changed; one morning when we awoke in Düsseldorf to say "Good morning, father!" the father had traveled away, and in the whole town there was nothing but dull anxiety. Everywhere there was a kind of funereal atmosphere, and people slipped silently toward the market and read the long paper posted on the door of the Town Hall. The weather was nasty, yet the lean tailor Kilian stood in his nankeen jacket, which he otherwise wore only at home, and his blue woolen stockings were hanging down in such a way that his little bare legs peeped out sadly, and his thin lips quivered as he murmured the handbill to himself. An old disabled veteran from the Palatinate read it in a somewhat louder tone, and at many words a transparent tear trickled down his white, honorable old moustache. I stood next to him and wept too, and asked why we were weeping. And he replied, "The Prince Elector expresses gratitude." And then he read further, and at the words "for the long-manifested fidelity of his subjects" and "hereby releases you from allegiance," he wept still more. It is a strange sight when such an old man, in faded uniform and with a scarred veteran's face, suddenly bursts into tears. While we were reading, the Electoral coat of arms was being taken down from the Town Hall, and everything began to appear as fearfully dreary as if an eclipse of the sun were expected. The town councilors went about so slowly and resignedly; even the omnipotent beadle looked as though he had no more commands to give, and stood peacefully indifferent, although the crazy Aloysius again stood upon one leg and with foolish grimaces chattered off the names of the French generals while the drunken cripple Gumpertz rolled around in the gutter singing *"Ça ira, ça ira!"*

I, however, went home and wept and wailed, "The Prince Elector expresses gratitude!" My mother had trouble enough to explain, but I would hear nothing. I knew what I knew and went to bed weeping, and during the night dreamed that the world had come to an end—that all the fair flower gardens and green meadows of the world were taken up and rolled together like carpets from the floor; that the beadle climbed up on a high ladder and took down the sun from the sky, and that the tailor Kilian stood by and said to himself, "I must go home and dress myself neatly, for I am dead and am supposed to be buried today." And it grew darker and darker; a few stars glimmered faintly on high, and even these at length fell down like yellow leaves in autumn; gradually the people vanished, and I, poor child, wandered about anxiously and finally stood in front of the willow fence of a deserted farmhouse, and there I saw a man digging up the earth with a spade and next to him an ugly, spiteful-looking woman who held something in her apron like a decapitated human head, and that was the moon, and she laid it anxiously into the open grave—and behind me stood the disabled Palatine veteran, sobbing, and read, letter by letter, "The Prince Elector expresses gratitude."

When I awoke, the sun shone again as usual through the win-

dow, drums sounded in the street, and as I entered the sitting room
and wished my father, who was sitting in his white dressing gown,
a good morning, I heard the light-footed barber narrate in detail
while coifing his hair that homage would be paid this morning to
the Archduke Joachim at the Town Hall, and that the new ruler
was from an excellent family and had married the sister of the
Emperor Napoleon and was really a very respectable man; and
that he wore his beautiful black hair in curls and would shortly
enter the town and would surely please all the ladies. Meanwhile
the drumming in the streets continued, and I stood before the house
door and looked at the French troops marching in, that joyful
people of fame who, singing and ringing, swept over the world,
the merry-serious faces of the grenadiers, the bearskin shakos, the
tricolored cockades, the glittering bayonets, the *voltigeurs* full of
vivacity and *point d'honneur* and the omnipotent, gigantic, silver-
embroidered tambour major who was able to toss his gold-tipped
baton as high as the second story and his eyes up to the third
where pretty girls were also sitting at the windows. I was so glad
that soldiers were to be quartered in our house—my mother was
not glad—and I hurried to the marketplace. There everything
looked entirely different; it was as though the world had been
freshly painted. A new coat of arms hung on the Town Hall; the
iron banisters on its balconies were draped in embroidered velvet;
French grenadiers stood as sentinels; the old town councilors had
put on new faces and wore their Sunday coats and looked at each
other Frenchily and said *bon jour;* ladies were looking out of every
window; inquisitive citizens and trim soldiers filled the square; and
I, with other boys, climbed on the great horse of the Prince Elector
and looked down at the colorful market commotion.

Neighbors Pitter and lanky Kurz nearly broke their necks on
this occasion, and that would have been good; for the one afterward ran away from his parents, enlisted as a soldier, deserted,
and was shot in Mainz; the other, however, made geographical
investigations of other people's pockets and became on this account an active member of a public workhouse. He broke the iron
bands that bound him to it and to his fatherland, arrived happily
on the other side of the water, and died in London from wearing
a much-too-tight tie that tightened on its own when a royal official removed a plank from beneath his feet.

Lanky Kurz told us that there was no school today because of the homage. We had to wait a long time until it began. Finally, the balcony of the Town Hall was filled with colorful gentlemen, flags and trumpets, and our mayor in his famous red coat delivered a speech that stretched out like India rubber or like a knitted nightcap into which a stone has been thrown—only not the philosopher's stone—and I could distinctly understand many of the phrases, for instance, that "they want to make us happy," and at the last words the trumpets were sounded and the flags were waved and the drums were rolled, and the people shouted *"Vivat!"* and while I myself shouted *"Vivat!"* I held fast to the old Prince Elector. And that was necessary, for I really became dizzy. It already seemed to me as if the people were standing on their heads, because the world whirled around; the Prince Elector with the full-bottomed wig nodded and whispered, "Hold fast to me!" and only as a result of the cannon fire that now started did I come to my senses and slowly climb down from the Prince Elector's horse.

When I went home, I saw again how the crazy Aloysius was dancing on one leg while rattling off the names of the French generals, and how the crippled Gumpertz rolled around in the gutter drunk and roared *"Ça ira, ça ira!"* and I said to my mother that they want to make us happy and for this reason there is no school today.

Chapter 7

The next day the world was again all in order, and school was open again, and things were again learned by heart—the Roman emperors, dates, the nouns in *im*, the *verba irregularia*, Greek, Hebrew, geography, German, arithmetic—Lord, my head is still dizzy from it!—everything had to be learned by heart. And much of it was eventually to my advantage. For had I not learned the Roman emperors by heart, I would later have been entirely indifferent as to whether Niebuhr had or had not proved that they never really existed. And if I did not know these dates, how could I ever in later years have found my way about in vast Berlin, where one house is as like another as drops of water or grenadiers and where it is impossible to find one's acquaintances unless one knows the house number by heart. At that time I associated every friend with some historical event whose date corresponded to his house number, so I was able to recall the one when I thought of the other, and for this reason a historical event always came to mind when I saw an acquaintance. Thus, for example, when I met my tailor, I immediately thought of the battle of Marathon; if I saw the well-dressed banker Christian Gumpel, I promptly remembered the destruction of Jerusalem; if I saw a Portuguese friend deeply in debt, I immediately thought of the flight of Mahomet; if I saw the university proctor, a man whose strict probity is well known, I immediately thought of the death of Haman; and as soon as I saw Wadzeck, I at once thought of Cleopatra—ah, dear heaven, the poor creature is now dead; the lachrymal sacks are dry, and one can say with Hamlet, "Take her for all and all, she was an old woman, we oft shall look upon her like again!" As I said, dates are altogether necessary. I know people who have nothing in their heads but a few dates, and thus know how to find the right houses in Berlin and are now already full professors. I, however, had trouble in school with the many dates and a still harder time with arithmetic. I understood subtraction best of all, and for this there is one very practical main rule: four from three won't work, so I must borrow one—but I advise anyone in such an instance always to borrow a few groschen extra, because you never can tell.

But as for the Latin, madame, you really have no idea how complicated that is. The Romans would never have had time left to conquer the world if they had first had to learn Latin. Those fortunate people already knew in the cradle which nouns end in *im* in the accusative. I, in contrast, had to learn them by heart by the sweat of my brow. But still it is good that I know them. For if, for example, I had publicly disputed in Latin in the university auditorium in Göttingen on the twentieth of July 1825—madame, it was worth the effort to hear it—and had said *sinapem* instead of *sinapim,* the freshmen present would have noticed it, and for me that would have meant endless shame. *Vis, buris, sitis, tussis, cucumis, amussis, cannabis, sinapis.* These words, which have attracted so much attention in the world, accomplished this by joining a certain class and yet remaining an exception; for this reason I value them greatly, and that I have them at hand if I should suddenly need them gives me much inner peace and comfort in life's many gloomy hours. But, madame, the *verba irregularia*— they are distinguished from the *verbis regularibus* by the fact that with them even more whippings are given—really are terribly difficult. In the musty, arched hallways in the Franciscan cloister near our schoolroom there hung a large crucified Christ of gray wood, a dismal image that even now at times marches through my dreams and looks at me sorrowfully with staring, bloodshot eyes. I often stood before this image and prayed, "Oh, thou poor, tormented God who was similarly tortured, if it is at all possible for you, see to it that I not forget the *verba irregularia!*"

I do not want to say anything about Greek, otherwise I would upset myself too much. The monks in the Middle Ages were not entirely incorrect in asserting that Greek was an invention of the devil. Lord knows what I suffered through it. It went better with Hebrew, for I always had a great predilection for the Jews, although to this hour they crucify my name. But I, nonetheless, never could get so far in Hebrew as my watch, which had much intimate association with pawnbrokers and consequently adopted many Jewish customs; for example, it did not work on Saturday, learned the holy language, and later internalized the grammar, as I later, to my amazement, often heard on sleepless nights as it clicked away, repeating *katal, katalta, katalti—kittel, kittalta, kittalti— pokat, pokadeti—pikat, pik, pik.*

Meanwhile, I understood much more of the German language, and it is by no means child's play. For we poor Germans, who have already been plagued enough with quartering soldiers, military service, poll taxes, and a thousand other exactions, have burdened ourselves on top of this with noblification and torment each other with the accusative and dative. I learned much German from old Rector Schallmeyer, a worthy clerical gentleman whose protégé I was from childhood. But I also learned something of the matter from Professor Schramm, a man who had written a book on eternal peace and in whose class my schoolmates fought most of all.

While I was continuing to write without interruption and was thinking of all manner of things in the process, without noticing it I have become caught up in old school stories, and I seize this opportunity to show you, madame, that it was not my fault if I learned so little of geography that later in life I did not know how to find my way in the world. For in those days the French had shifted all frontiers, the countries were recolored on the map every day; those that were once blue suddenly became green, many even became bloodred; the textbook population figures became so confused and confounded that no one could possibly have recognized them anymore. The products of the country also changed; chicory and beets now grew where only hares and junkers running after them were formerly seen; even the character of the peoples changed; the Germans became pliant; the French no longer paid compliments; the English no longer threw money out the window; and the Venetians were not sly enough; there were many promotions among princes, old kings received new uniforms, new kingdoms were baked and sold like fresh rolls; many potentates, on the other hand, were chased from house and home and had to find another way of earning their bread, while others soon took up a trade and manufactured, for instance, sealing wax, or—madame, this sentence finally has to end or I shall be out of breath— in short, in such times it is impossible to advance far in geography.

Things are better, though, in natural history, for there not so many changes can occur, and there are definite engravings of apes, kangaroos, zebras, rhinoceroses, etc. Because such pictures remained in my memory, it often happened as a consequence that at first sight many people appeared to me to be old acquaintances.

Things also went well in mythology. I took a real delight in the rabble of deities who ruled the world so jolly naked. I do not believe any schoolboy in ancient Rome memorized the main clause of his catechism—for example, the loves of Venus—better than I. To tell the truth, since we, after all, once had to learn all the ancient deities by heart, we should also have kept them; and we perhaps do not have much advantage with our new Roman trinidolatry or even with our Jewish monoidolatry. Perhaps that mythology was not in reality so immoral as has been decried; it is, for example, a very decent thought of Homer to have given the much-loved Venus a husband.

But I fared best of all in the French class of the Abbé d'Aulnoi, a French emigré who had written a vast number of grammars and wore a red wig and hopped about very perkily when he recited his *Art poétique* and his *Histoire allemande*. Still, French also has its difficulties, and to learn it there must be much quartering of troops, much drumming, much *apprendre par coeur,* and above all no one should be a *bête allemande.* As a consequence, there was many a cross word, and I can remember as though it happened only yesterday that I experienced much unpleasantness through *la réligion.* I was asked at least six times in succession, "Henri, what is the French for *faith?*" And six times, ever more weepily, I replied, "It is called *le crédit.*" And the seventh time, his face brownish red with rage, my furious examiner cried, "It is called *la réligion.*" And punishment showered down on me and all my schoolmates laughed. Madame, since that time I cannot hear the word "religion" without my back turning pale from terror and my cheeks turning red from shame. And in all honesty *le crédit* has served me better in life than *la réligion.* At this moment it occurs to me that I still owe the landlord of the Lion in Bologna five talers—and I truly pledge my word of honor that I would owe him five talers more if only I need never again in this life hear that deplorable word *la réligion.*

Parbleu, madame! I have succeeded well in French. I understand not only *patois* but even aristocratic governess French. Not long ago, in noble society I understood almost half the conversation of two German countesses, each of whom could count at least sixty-four years and as many ancestors. Yes, in the Café Royal I once heard Monsieur Hans Michel Martens talking French and understood every word, although there was no understanding in any of it. It is necessary to know the spirit of the language, and this is best learned by drumming. *Parbleu,* how much do I not owe to the French drummer who was quartered in my house so long, who looked like a devil and yet had the good heart of an angel and who drummed so excellently.

He was a small, agile character with a terrible black moustache beneath which his red lips defiantly protruded while his wild eyes shot fiery glances back and forth.

As a small boy I stuck to him like a burr and helped him polish his military buttons until they were shiny and helped pipe-clay his vest—for Monsieur Le Grand liked to please—and I followed him to the watch, to the roll call, to the parade. In those times there was nothing but the gleam of weapons and merriment—*les jours de fête sont passés!* Monsieur Le Grand knew only a little broken

German, only the main expressions—bread, kiss, honor—but he could make himself understood very well with his drum. For example, if I did not know what the word *liberté* meant, he drummed the "Marseillaise"—and I understood him. If I did not know the meaning of the word *egalité,* he drummed the march

> *Ça ira, ça ira,*
> *Les aristocrats à la lanterne!*

and I understood him. If I did not know what *bêtise* meant, he drummed the Dessauer march, which we Germans, as Goethe also reports, drummed in Champagne—and I understood him. He once wanted to explain to me the word *l'Allemagne* and he drummed that all-too-simple, primitive melody that is played on market days for dancing dogs—namely, dum, dum, dum—I was annoyed, but I did understand him.

In a similar manner he taught me modern history. I did not, of course, understand the words he spoke, but since he constantly drummed while speaking, I knew what he wanted to say. This is basically the best teaching method. The history of the storming of the Bastille, of the Tuileries, etc., cannot be correctly understood until we know how the drumming was done on such occasions. In our school compendiums of history it is merely stated: "Their excellencies the Baron and Count as well as their spouses were beheaded. . . . Their highnesses the Dukes and Princes as well as their spouses were beheaded. . . . His Majesty the King and his most sublime spouse, the Queen, were beheaded." But when one hears the red guillotine march being drummed, one truly understands it correctly and learns the how and why. Madame, that is really a singular march! A ghastly shudder went through marrow and bone when I first heard it, and I was glad that I forgot it. Such things are forgotten as one grows older, and nowadays a young man has so many other things in his head—whist, Boston, genealogical tables, parliamentary decrees, dramaturgy, liturgy, carving skills at the table—and yet, despite all manner of rubbing my forehead, for a long time I could not recall that powerful melody! And just think, madame, not long ago I was sitting at a table with a whole menagerie of counts, princes, princesses, chamberlains, ladies-in-waiting, court wine pourers, superior court mistresses, court keepers of the royal silverware, court hunting mistresses, and whatever else these elegant domestics are called, and their underdomestics ran about behind their chairs and shoved full plates in front of their traps; but I, who was passed by and overlooked, sat at leisure without the least occupation for my jaws and kneaded little bread balls and drummed my fingers from boredom; and, to my horror, I suddenly found myself drumming the long-forgotten red guillotine march.

"And what happened?" Madame, these people do not permit themselves to be disturbed while eating and do not know that other people, when they have nothing to eat, suddenly start drumming, and what is more, they even drum strange marches believed to have been long forgotten.

Is drumming an inborn talent, or did I develop it at an early age? In any case, it is rooted in my limbs, in my hands and feet, and often involuntarily manifests itself. In Berlin I once was sitting in the seminar of Privy Councilor Schmalz, a man who had saved the state with his book on the danger of red and black coats. You remember, madame, from Pausanias that once as the result of the braying of an ass an equally dangerous plot was discovered; and you also know from Livy or from Becker's world history that geese once saved the capitol; and you must certainly know from Sallust that it was by means of a loquacious *putain*, Lady Fulvia, that the terrible conspiracy of Catiline came to light. But to return to the old goat just mentioned, I listened to a lecture on international law in Herr Privy Councilor Schmalz's seminar, and it was a boring summer afternoon, and I sat on the bench and heard less and less—my head had gone to sleep—when all at once I was wakened by the noise of my own feet, which had remained awake and had probably heard that just the opposite of international law was being presented and that constitutional sympathy was being berated, and my feet with their little corns saw through the way of the world better than the Privy Councilor with his large Juno eyes—these poor mute feet, incapable of expressing their humble opinion in words, strove to make themselves understood by drumming, and they drummed so loudly that I consequently really got into trouble.

Damned unreflecting feet! They played me a similar trick when I once sat in on a lecture by Professor Saalfeld in Göttingen and he with his stiff agility hopped back and forth behind his lectern and exhausted himself in order to be able to revile thoroughly the Emperor Napoleon—no, my poor feet, I cannot find fault with you for drumming then—indeed, I would not even have blamed you if in your mute naiveté you had expressed yourself still more clearly by your footsteps. How can I, the student of Le Grand, hear the Emperor being slandered? The Emperor! The Emperor! The great Emperor!

When I think of the great Emperor, my memory again becomes summer-green and golden. A long avenue of lindens radiantly appears; on the leafy branches sit singing nightingales; the waterfall rustles; flowers are growing in full, round beds, dreamily nodding their beautiful heads—I stood among them in wondrous intimacy, the rouged tulips, proud as beggars, condescendingly greeted me, the neurotic lilies nodded with melancholy tenderness, the tipsy red roses laughed at me even from afar, the night violets sighed; with myrtle and laurel I at that time still had no acquaintance, for they did not entice with a glowing bloom; but I was particularly intimate with the mignonette with whom I am now on such bad terms. I am speaking of the court garden of Düsseldorf, where I often lay on the grass and piously listened when Monsieur Le Grand told me of the great Emperor's warlike feats, meanwhile beating the marches that were drummed during those deeds in such a manner that I saw and heard everything vividly. I saw the march across the Simplon—the Emperor in front and the brave grenadiers climbing along behind him, while the flock of frightened birds started to croak, and the glaciers thundered in the distance. I saw the Emperor with flag in hand on the bridge of Lodi. I saw the Emperor in his gray cloak at Marengo. I saw the Emperor on his horse in the battle at the pyramids—nothing but the smoke of gunpowder and Mamelukes. I saw the Emperor in the battle of Austerlitz—ha, how the bullets whistled over their slick, icy paths! I saw, I heard the battle of Jena—dum, dum, dum. I saw, I heard the battles of Eylau, of Wagram—no, I could hardly endure it! Monsieur Le Grand drummed in such a way that it nearly burst my eardrum!

Chapter 8

But what were my feelings when I, with my own highly blessed eyes, first saw him, hosannah, the Emperor!

It was right in the avenue of the court garden at Düsseldorf. As I pressed through the gaping crowd, thinking of the deeds and battles that Monsieur Le Grand had drummed to me, my heart beat the general march—yet at the same time I thought of the police regulation that no one is permitted, under penalty of five-talers fine, to ride down the middle of the avenue. And the Emperor with his cortège rode straight down the avenue. The shuddering trees bowed toward him as he passed, the sun's rays quivered fearfully and inquisitively through the green leaves, and floating visibly in the blue heaven above was a golden star. The Emperor wore his modest green uniform and the small world-renowned hat. He rode a white horse, and it stepped with such calm pride, so confidently, so superbly—had I then been Crown Prince of Prussia, I would have envied that small horse. The Emperor sat carelessly, almost lazily, holding the reins with one hand, good-naturedly patting the horse's neck with the other. It was a bright marble hand, a mighty hand—one of the pair of hands that had tamed the many-headed monster of anarchy and settled the international power struggle—and it good-naturedly patted the horse's neck. Even the face had that hue that we find in Greek and Roman marble busts; the features, too, were as nobly proportioned as those of antiquity, and on that face was written, "Thou shalt have no gods except me!" A smile that warmed and calmed every heart flitted about his lips, and yet everyone knew that those lips needed but to whistle *et la Prusse n'existait plus,* those lips needed but to whistle and the entire clergy was silenced, those lips needed but to whistle and the entire Holy Roman Empire danced. And those lips smiled, and his eyes smiled too—these eyes were as clear as the sky; they could read the hearts of men; they rapidly saw at a glance all the things in the world, while we others see them only in succession and only their colored shadows. The brow was not so clear, the phantoms of future battles nested on it; and occasionally a quiver flickered across this forehead, and this was from the creative thoughts, the large seven-mile-boot thoughts with which the spirit of the Emperor strode invisibly over the world—and I believe that each one of those thoughts would have provided a German author enough material for a lifetime of writing.

The Emperor rode calmly straight down the middle of the avenue; no policeman stopped him. His cortège, loaded with gold and ornaments on panting horses, rode proudly behind him; the trumpets were sounded; the drums rolled; beside me the crazy Aloysius spun round and snarled the names of his generals; not far off the drunken Gumpert roared, and the people cried with a thousand voices, "Long live the Emperor!"

Chapter 9

The Emperor is dead. His lonely grave is on a desolate island in the Indian Ocean, and he for whom the world was too small lies peacefully under a little hillock where five weeping willows sorrowfully hang their green heads, and a pious little brook ripples by, sadly grieving. There is no inscription on his tombstone; but Clio, with her impartial stylus, wrote on it invisible words that will resound like spirit melodies through the millennia.

Britannia, you own the sea! But the sea does not have water enough to wash away the shame bequeathed to you by the mighty deceased as he expired. Not your windy Sir Hudson—no, you yourself were the Sicilian myrmidon hired by conspiring kings for the purpose of secretly avenging on the man of the people what the people had once publicly inflicted on one of your kind. And he was your guest and had sat down at your hearth.

For ages the boys of France will sing and tell of the terrible hospitality of Bellerophon, and when these songs of mockery and tears resound across the Channel, there will be a blush on the cheeks of every honorable Briton. But someday this song will resound there, and Britannia will no longer exist—when the people of pride have been felled, when Westminster's tombs lie in ruins, forgotten is the royal dust that they enclosed. And Saint Helena is the holy grave to which peoples from the Orient and the Occident will make their pilgrimage in ships bearing flags of many colors to strengthen their hearts through profound memory of the deeds of the secular savior who suffered under Sir Hudson Lowe, as it is written in the gospels of Las Casas, O'Meara, and Antommarchi.

Strange! A terrible fate has already befallen the three greatest opponents of the Emperor. Londonderry has cut his throat, Louis XVIII has rotted away on his throne, and Professor Saalfeld is still teaching in Göttingen.

Chapter 10

It was a clear, frosty morning in autumn when a young man who looked like a student slowly wandered through the avenue of the Düsseldorf court garden, occasionally kicking up, as if from childish pleasure, the rustling leaves that covered the ground, at times also sorrowfully gazing toward the withered trees from which a few yellow leaves still hung. As he glanced up in this manner, he thought of the words of Glaucus:

> As is the generation of leaves, so is that of humanity. The wind scatters the leaves on the ground, but the live timber burgeons with leaves again in the season of spring returning. So one generation of men will grow while another dies.

In former days the young person looked up at these same trees with quite different thoughts, and at that time he was a boy and looked for birds' nests or summer beetles, which truly delighted him as they merrily hummed about and enjoyed the beautiful world, content with a juicy green leaf and a small drop of dew, a warm ray of the sun and the sweet fragrance of herbs. At that time the boy's heart was as joyful as the fluttering insects. But now his heart had grown older, its little sunbeams had been extinguished, all its flowers had died, even its beautiful dream of love had paled; in that poor heart was nothing but courage and grief and, to say the most painful thing of all, it was my heart.

I had returned that day to my old home town, but I did not want to stay in it overnight and longed for Godesberg in order to sit again at the feet of my lady friend and tell of little Veronica. I had visited the dear graves. Of all my living friends and relatives I had found only an uncle and an aunt. If I still found familiar faces on the street, no one any longer recognized me, and the town itself looked at me with strange eyes. Many houses had in the meantime been freshly painted, unfamiliar faces looked out of the windows, worn-out sparrows fluttered around the old chimneys; everything looked so dead and yet as fresh as salad growing in a graveyard. Where French was once spoken, I now heard Prussian; even a small Prussian court had settled there, and the people bore court titles. My mother's former hairdresser had now become the court hairdresser, and there were now court tailors, court shoemakers, court bedbug exterminators, court liquor shops—the whole city seemed to be a court hospital for court lunatics. Only the old Prince Elector recognized me; he still stood in the same place, but he seemed to have become thinner. Simply because he stood in the middle of the marketplace, he had also witnessed all the miseries of the era, and no one gets fat from such a sight. I was as if in a dream and thought of the fairy tale of the enchanted cities, and I hastened out to the gate lest I awake too soon. I missed many a tree in the court garden, and many had grown crooked with age, and the four large poplars that once seemed to me like green giants had become small. Some pretty maidens dressed as gaily as ambling tulips were going for a walk. And I had known these tulips when they were but little bulbs; for ah, they were the neighbor's children with whom I had once played princess in the tower. But the fair maidens whom I had once known as blooming roses were now faded roses, and Saturn had cut deep wrinkles with his scythe into many a high brow whose pride had once charmed my heart. And now for the first time and, alas, too late, I understood what the glances they had cast at the adolescent boy were supposed to mean; in other countries I had meanwhile noticed many parallels in other beautiful eyes. I was deeply moved by the humble bow of a man whom I had once known to be wealthy and distinguished and who had since sunk to being a beggar. After all, everywhere in the world it can be seen that people, once they are falling, as if in accordance with Newton's law, descend ever faster and faster into misery. The person, however, who seemed to me completely unchanged was the little Baron, who tripped as merrily as ever through the court garden, holding up his left coattail with one hand, swinging his slim cane with the other; it was the same friendly face whose rosiness was somewhat concentrated around the nose, it was still the old conical hat, it was still the old pigtail, only some of the hairs that stuck out of it were white. But as cheerful as he looked, I knew nonetheless that the old Baron had in the interval suffered much sorrow; his face tried to conceal it from me, but the white hairs of his pigtail betrayed it to me behind his back; yet the pigtail would gladly have denied it and really wagged merrily yet sadly.

I was not tired, but I did get a desire to sit once more on the wooden bench on which I had once carved the name of my love. So many new names had been carved over it that I could hardly find it again. Ah, I had once fallen asleep on this bench and dreamed of happiness and love. "Dreams are fluff." The old children's games, even the old, charming fairy tales again came to mind; but a new, treacherous game and a new, ugly tale always resounded through them, and it was the story of two poor souls who were untrue to one another and went so far in their faithlessness that they even broke faith with the good Lord. It is an evil story, and if there is absolutely nothing better to do, one can weep over it. O Lord, once the world was so pretty, and the birds sang your eternal praise, and little Veronica looked at me with silent eyes, and we sat in front of the marble statue at the castle courtyard. On one side is an old, devastated castle, which is haunted and where at night a headless lady in long, trailing, black silken garments with a long, rustling train wanders about; on the other side is a high, white building in whose upper rooms colorful paintings in golden frames gleamed wonderfully and on whose ground floor were so many thousands of mighty books that I and little Veronica often looked at with curiosity when good Ursula lifted us up to the window. In later years when I had become a big boy, I climbed every day to the highest rung of the library ladder and fetched down the topmost books and read them so long that I no longer feared anything, least of all headless ladies, and I became so smart that I forgot all the old games and fairy tales and pictures, and little Veronica and even forgot her name.

But while I, sitting on the old bench in the court garden, dreamed my way back into the past, behind me I heard confused voices of people lamenting the fate of the poor Frenchmen who, dragged to Siberia as captives during the Russian war, had been detained there for several long years even after there was peace and who only now were returning home. As I looked up, I actually glimpsed these orphan children of fame. Through the tears in their tattered uniforms peered naked misery; in their weathered faces were deep, plaintive eyes, and though mangled, weary, and mostly lame, they nonetheless remained in a kind of military step, and strangely enough a tambour major with a drum tottered ahead, and with inner horror I was gripped by the memory of the saga of soldiers who during the day had been killed in battle and who by night rose up again from the battlefield, and with the drummer in the lead, marched back to their native city. The old folk sing songs about them:

> He beat on the drum with might and main:
> To their old night quarters they go again;
> > Through the lighted street they come:
> > Trallerie, trallerei, trallera,
> They march before Sweetheart's home.

> Thus the skeletons return ere break of day,
> Like tombstones white in their cold array,
> > And the drummer he goes before;
> > Trallerie, trallerei, trallera,
> She can see him come once more.

Truly the poor French tambour major seemed to have risen half putrified from the grave. He was but a small shadow in a dirty, ragged gray capote; a dead, yellow face with a large moustache that hung down sorrowfully over his faded lips; the eyes were like burnt-out tinder in which only a few sparks still glimmered, and yet by one of those sparks I recognized Monsieur Le Grand.

He also recognized me, and pulled me down to the grass, and there we sat as of old when he taught me French and modern history on the drum. It was still the well-known old drum, and I could not wonder enough how he had preserved it from Russian greed. He now drummed again as of old, but without speaking while doing so. Although his lips were uncannily pressed together, his eyes spoke all the more, lighting up triumphantly as he drummed the old marches. The poplars near us trembled as he again thundered forth the red guillotine march. And, as of old, he drummed the old liberation battles, the ancient fights, the deeds of the Emperor, and it seemed as though the drum itself were a living creature that enjoyed being able to express its inner pleasure. I again heard cannon thunder, the whistling of bullets, the noise of battle; I again saw the undauntable courage of the Garde; I again saw fluttering flags, I again saw the Emperor on his horse— but gradually a melancholy tone slipped into that most joyous whirl; from the drums came sounds in which the wildest jubilation and the most horrible grief were mysteriously mingled; it seemed simultaneously a victory march and a funeral dirge. Le Grand's eyes opened spookily wide, and I saw in them nothing but a broad, white field of ice covered with corpses—it was the battle of Moscow.

I would never have thought that the hard old drum could give forth such painful sounds as Monsieur Le Grand now was able to entice from it. They were drummed tears, and they sounded ever softer and softer, and like a melancholy echo deep sighs escaped from Le Grand's breast. And he became ever more feeble and ghostlike; his withered hands trembled from cold; he sat as in a dream and moved only the air with his drumsticks and listened as if to distant voices; and finally he looked at me with a profound glance, a beseeching glance that was as deep as an abyss—I understood him—and then his head sank down onto the drum.

Monsieur Le Grand never drummed again in this life. And his drum never gave forth another sound; it was not to serve any enemy of freedom for their servile roll call; I had understood the last beseeching glance of Le Grand very well and immediately drew the rapier from my cane and pierced the drum.

Chapter 11

Du sublime au ridicule il n'y a qu'un pas, madame! But life is basically so fatally serious that it would be unbearable without such a connection between the pathetic and the comic. Our poets know that. The most horrible images of human madness are shown to us by Aristophanes only in the laughing mirror of wit. Only in the doggerel of a puppet show does Goethe dare to utter the great pain of the thinker who comprehends his own nothingness, and Shakespeare puts the gravest indictment about the misery of the world into the mouth of a fool who is anxiously rattling his cap and bells.

They all learned it from the great primeval poet who in his thousand-act world tragedy knows how to drive humor to the utmost, as we see every day: after the departure of the heroes come the clowns, and *graciosos* enter with their fool's clubs and whips, and after the bloody scenes of the Revolution and imperial actions the fat Bourbons waddle forth again with their stale old jokes and tender-legitimate *bon mots,* and the old *noblesse* gracefully hop past with their starved smiles, and behind them wander the pious Capuchins with candles, cross, and church banners. Comical traits customarily slip into even the highest pathos of the world tragedy. The despairing republican who, like a Brutus, plunged a knife into his heart first smelled it perhaps to make certain it had not also been used for cutting herring—and on this great stage of the world, things happen just the same as on our beggarly stages. On it, too, there are drunken heroes, kings who forget their parts, stage scenery that gets stuck, booming prompters' voices, *danseuses* who create astonishing effects with the poetry of their *derrières,* costumes that dazzle as the main attraction. And meanwhile up in heaven in the first row of the boxes sit the dear angels and look through their lorgnettes at us comedians here below, and the good Lord sits earnestly in his large loge and is perhaps bored or figures that this theater cannot survive much longer, because this one gets too high a fee and the other too little, and everyone acts much too poorly.

Du sublime au ridicule il n'y a qu'un pas, madame! While I was writing the end of the last chapter, telling you how Monsieur Le Grand died and how I conscientiously executed the *testamentum militare* contained in his last glance, someone knocked at my door, and in walked a poor old woman who pleasantly inquired if I were a doctor. And when I said yes, she asked me in quite a friendly manner to go home with her to trim her husband's corns.

Chapter 12

The German censors ——— ——— ——— ——— ———
——— ——— ——— ——— ——— ——— ——— ———
——— ——— ——— ——— ——— ——— ——— ———
——— ——— ——— ——— ——— ——— ——— ———

———— ———— ———— ———— ———— ———— ———— ————
———— ———— ———— ———— ———— ———— ———— ————
———— ———— ———— blockheads ———— ———— ————
———— ———— ———— ———— ———— ———— ———— ————
———— ———— ———— ———— ———— ———— ———— ————
———— ———— ———— ———— ———— ———— ———— ————
———— ———— ———— ———— ———— ———— ———— ————

Chapter 13

Madame, the whole Trojan War was already hatched under Leda's productive hemispheres, and you can never understand Priam's famous tears if I do not first tell you about the ancient swan eggs. For this reason, please do not complain about my digressions. In all previous chapters there is not a line that does not belong to the topic. I write concisely, I avoid all superfluity, often I even neglect the necessary. For instance, I have not yet once properly quoted—I do not mean geniuses; on the contrary, I mean authors—and yet quoting from old and new books is the chief pleasure of a young author, and so a few truly erudite quotations adorn the whole man. Do not believe, madame, that I lack familiarity with book titles. Moreover I am familiar with the knack of those great minds who know how to pick out the currants from their rolls and quotations from their lecture notes. I also know where Barthel gets his new wine. In an emergency I could negotiate a loan of quotations from my learned friends. My friend G. in Berlin is, so to speak, a little Rothschild of quotations and will gladly lend me a few million, and if he does not happen to have them handy, he can easily muster them together from some other cosmopolitan bankers of the intellect. But I do not yet have need of a loan. I am a man in good standing and have annually my ten thousand quotations to devour. In fact, I have even discovered the art of passing off wrong quotations for genuine. If any wealthy, learned person—for instance, Michael Beer—wants to buy this secret from me, I will gladly sell it for nineteen thousand talers at the present exchange rate. I am also willing to bargain. I do not wish to withhold another one of my inventions for the benefit of literature and will impart it gratis.

Namely, I consider it advisable to include the house numbers along with quotations from all obscure authors.

These "good people and bad musicians," as the orchestra is termed in *Ponce de Leon*—these obscure authors almost invariably still possess a copy of their long out-of-print books, and to track these down it is therefore necessary to know their house numbers. If I wanted, for example, to quote Spitta's *Song Book for Journeymen,* my dear madame, where would you go about finding it? But if I cited: "vide *Song Book for Journeymen* by P. Spitta, Lüneburg, Lüner Street, no. 2, make a right turn at the corner"—then, madame, if you considered it worth the trouble, you could track down the book. But it is not worth the trouble.

Moreover, madame, you can have no idea of the facility with which I quote. Everywhere I discover opportunities to parade my profound learnedness. If I speak of eating, for example, I remark in a note that the Greeks, Romans, and Hebrews also ate; I quote all the delightful dishes prepared by Lucullus's cook—woe is me that I was born a millennium and a half too late. I also remark that these communal meals were called thus and thus among the Greeks and that the Spartans ate bad black soups. It is good, after all, that I was not yet alive in those days; I can imagine nothing more terrible than if I, poor soul, had become a Spartan; soup is my favorite dish. Madame, I am considering going to London soon, but if it is really true that no soup is to be had there, a longing will soon drive me back to the soup-meat pots of my fatherland. I could also discourse at length about the foods of the ancient Hebrews and proceed to the Jewish cuisine of the modern era. On this occasion I quote the entire Steinweg. I could also cite how humanely many Berlin scholars have expressed themselves about Jewish cuisine. I would then come to the other achievements and superiorities of the Jews, to the inventions to their credit—as, for instance, bills of exchange and Christianity. But wait! We do not want to give them too much credit for the latter, since we actually have not made much use of it—I believe that the Jews themselves have not profited so much by it as by their invention of bills of exchange. While on the topic of the Jews, I could also quote Tacitus: he says that they honored asses in their temples—and on the topic of asses a broad field of quotation opens up to me! How many strange things can be cited about ancient asses as opposed to the modern! How reasonable were the former, and, ah, how stupid the latter! How reasonably, for instance, Balaam's ass speaks (vide Pentat. Lib. —— —— —— —— —— —— — —— —— ——), madame, I do not have the precise work in hand and want to leave this passage open to be filled in later. On the other hand, with reference to the tastelessness of modern asses, I quote: "Vide —— —— —— —— —— —— —— — ——." No, I also want to leave this passage open, otherwise I myself will be cited—namely, *injuriarum*. The modern asses are great asses. The ancient asses, who had such a high place in civilization (vide Gesneri, *De antiqua honestate asinorum*, in comment. Götting. T. II. p. 32)—they would turn over in their graves if they were to hear how people talk about their descendants. Ass was once an honorable name, meaning as much as Court Councilor, Baron, Doctor of Philosophy. Jacob uses it for comparing his son Issachar, Homer uses it for comparing his hero Ajax, and it is now used for comparing Mr. von ——. Madame, while speaking of such asses, I could immerse myself deeply in literary history. I could quote all the great men who have been in love— for example, Abelardum, Picum Mirandulanum, Borbonium, Curtesium, Angelum Politianum, Raymundum Lullum, and Henricum Heineum. On the topic of love I could again mention all the great men who did not smoke, for example, Cicero, Justinian, Goethe, Hugo, and I. By chance it happens that all five of us are also lawyers to some extent. Mabillon could not even endure the smell of an unfamiliar pipe. In his *Itinere Germanico* he complains about German inns: "*Quod molestus ipsi fuerit tabaci grave olentis foetor.*" On the other hand, an extraordinary preference for tobacco has been ascribed to other great men. Raphael Thorus wrote a hymn to tobacco. Madame, perhaps you do not yet know that Isaac Elzevirius published it in quarto in 1628 at Leyden, and Ludovicus Kinschot wrote a preface to it in verse. Graevius even composed a sonnet about tobacco. The great Boxhornius also loved tobacco. Bayle, in his *Dict. Hist. et Critiq.*, reports of having been told that the great Boxhornius while smoking wore a large hat with a hole in the front part of the brim through which he often stuck his pipe so it would not hinder him in his studies. Apropos of the great Boxhornius, I could also cite all the great learned people who let themselves be intimidated and who ran away. But

I refer merely to Joh. Georg Martius: *De fuga literatorum, etc., etc., etc.* If we go through history, madame, we find that all great men had to take to their heels once in their lives: Lot, Tarquin, Moses, Jupiter, Madame de Staël, Nebuchadnezzar, Benjowsky, Mahomet, the whole Prussian army, Gregory VII, Rabbi Yitzchak Abarbanel, Rousseau—to which I could add very many other names, for instance, those whose names are posted on the blackboard of the stock exchange.

So you see, madame, that I am not wanting in thoroughness and profundity. Only in systematology do I not fare so well. As a true German I should have opened this book with a full explanation of its title, as is the custom and tradition in the Holy Roman Empire. Phidias, it is true, made no preface to his Jupiter; just as little as on the Medicean Venus—I have observed her from all sides—a quotation can be found; but the old Greeks were Greeks, and the likes of us is an honest German and cannot deny his German nature, and accordingly I must still get around to expressing my thoughts about the title of my book.

Madame, I shall proceed to speak

I. of ideas
   A. of ideas in general
      a. of reasonable ideas
      b. of unreasonable ideas
         α. of ordinary ideas
         β. of ideas covered with green leather.

These will again be divided into . . . But we shall arrive at that in due course.

Chapter 14

Madame, do you have any idea about an idea? What is an idea? "There are some good ideas in this coat," my tailor said to me as he looked with earnest attention at the overcoat, dating from my elegant Berlin period, that is now to be made into a respectable dressing gown. My washerwoman complains that the Reverend S. has been putting ideas into her daughter's head, as a result of which she has become silly and won't listen to reason. The coachman Pattensen grumbles on every occasion, "That's an idea! That's an idea!" Yesterday, however, he became truly annoyed when I asked him what he imagined an idea to be. And he crossly growled, "Well, well, an idea is an idea! An idea is any stupid thing that is thought up." The word is used in this meaning as the title of a book by Court Councilor Heeren in Göttingen.

The coachman Pattensen is a man who knows how to find his way at night or in fog across the broad Lüneburg Heath; Court Councilor Heeren is a man who likewise with unerring instinct can locate the ancient caravan routes of the Orient and, once he is there, plod about for days and years as safely and as patiently as any camel of antiquity. Such people can be trusted, such people can be followed, and for this reason I have entitled this book *Ideas*.

The title of this book therefore means as little as the title of its author. It was not chosen by him out of learned arrogance and should be interpreted as anything but vanity. Madame, accept my most sorrowful assurance that I am not vain. This remark, as you yourself were about to observe, is necessary. I am not vain—I would not become so even if a forest of laurels grew on my head and a sea of incense were poured into my young heart. My friends and other contemporaries in time and space have fully taken care of that. You know, madame, that old women have a way of giving their children a slight putdown when anyone praises their beauty, lest praise harm the little darlings. You know, madame, that in Rome when the triumphator, crowned with glory and adorned in purple, rode his golden chariot drawn by white horses from the Campus Martius; when he like a god towered above the festive procession of lictors, musicians, dancers, priests, slaves, elephants, trophy bearers, consuls, senators, and soldiers—it was then that the rabble trailing behind sang all manner of mocking songs. And you know, madame, that in our beloved Germany there are many old women and much rabble.

As stated, madame, the ideas being discussed are as remote from those of Plato as Athens is from Göttingen, and you should as little have great expectations of the book itself as of the author. In fact, how the latter could ever have excited such expectations is as inconceivable to me as to my friends. The Countess Julia wants to explain the matter and avows that if the author in question occasionally utters anything really witty and original, this is merely deception by him, and basically he is as stupid as the others. That is false. I do not deceive at all. I do not mince matters; I write in all innocence and simplicity whatever comes to mind, and it is not my fault if that is something sensible. At any rate, I have better luck in writing than in the Altona lottery—I wish it were the reverse—and from my pen come many bull's-eyes, many thoughts that hit the jackpot, and that is done by God; for He, who denies the most devout Elohist psalmists and edifying poets all beautiful thoughts and all fame in literature, lest they be too much praised by fellow mortals and thereby forget heaven, where the angels are already preparing accommodations for them—He is in the habit of blessing us other profane, sinful, heretical authors, for whom heaven is as good as nailed shut, all the more with excellent thoughts and earthly fame, and this He indeed does more from divine grace and mercy so that the poor soul, who has been created anyway, does not leave completely empty-handed and can feel, at least down here on earth, a portion of that joy that is denied him up there (vide Goethe and the writers of tracts).

So you see, madame, that you may read my writings; they testify to God's grace and mercy. I write in blind trust in His omnipotence. In this respect I am a genuinely Christian author and, to speak like Gubitz, while I am starting this very sentence I do not yet know how I shall end it and what I actually should say, and for this I rely on the good Lord. And how indeed could I write without this pious trust? The fellow from Langhoff's printing office is now standing in my room waiting for manuscript, and the hardly born word wanders warm and wet to press, and what I think and feel at this moment can already be printer's waste by noon.

It is easy for you to talk, madame, when you remind me of the Horatian maxim *nonum prematur in annum*. This rule, like many others of its kind, may be very good in theory but is worth nothing in practice. When Horace provided the author with that famous rule of letting his works lie nine years in his desk, he should also at the same time have provided him with the recipe for going nine years without food. When Horace invented this rule, he was perhaps sitting at the table of Maecenas, eating roast turkey with truffles, pheasant pudding with venison sauce, lark cutlets with teltower turnips, peacock's tongues, Indian bird's nests, and Lord knows what all, and everything for free. But we, we unlucky latecomers, live in a different era. Our art patrons have entirely different principles: they believe that authors and medlars flourish best if they lie for a period of time on straw; they believe that the dogs would not be fit for hunting metaphors and thoughts if they were fed too well; and if they nonetheless occasionally feed a poor dog, then it is the wrong dog who least deserves the scraps: for example, the dachshund who licks hands or the tiny Italian toy spaniel who knows how to cuddle up into the lady's perfumed lap or the patient poodle who has learned a practical trade and can fetch and carry, dance and drum. While I am writing this, my little pug is standing behind me barking. Quiet, Ami! I did not mean you, for you love me and accompany your master in need and in danger, and you would die on his grave, as faithful as many other German dogs who, banished abroad, lie before the gates of Germany, starving and whimpering. Forgive me, madame, for digressing for the purpose of vindicating the honor of my poor dog. I shall now return to the Horatian rule and its inapplicability in the nineteenth century, when poets cannot dispense with the petticoat-pension of the muse. *Ma foi,* madame, I could never survive that rule for twenty-four hours, let alone nine years. My stomach has no understanding of immortality. I have already thought about the matter, and I want to be only half immortal and completely satiated. And if Voltaire wanted to give three hundred years of his eternal fame for one good digestion of a meal, I offer twice as much for the meal itself. And oh, what manner of beautiful, abundant food there is in this world! The philosopher Pangloss is right—this is the best world! But it is necessary to have money in this best of all worlds—money in the pocket, not manuscripts in the desk. The innkeeper at the King of England, Mr. Marr, is himself an author and also knows the Horatian rule, but I do not believe that if I were to put it into practice he would feed me for nine years.

And when all is said and done, why should I practice it? I have so many good things to write about that I do not need to dawdle. As long as my heart is full of love and the head of my fellow man is full of foolishness, I shall never lack subject matter for writing. And my heart will love as long as there are women; if it cools for one, it immediately fires up over another; just as in France the King never dies, so, too, in my heart the Queen never dies, for my heart's motto is *la reine est morte, vive la reine!* In like manner, the foolishness of my fellow man will never die out. For there is only one kind of cleverness, and it has definite limits; but there are a thousand illimitable follies. The learned casuist and pastor Schupp even says, "There are more fools than people in the world" (vide Schupp's *Instructive Writings,* p. 1121). Considering that the great Schuppius lived in Hamburg, this statistical detail is no exaggeration at all. I am now in that very city and can say that I really feel exceptionally well when I realize that all these fools I see here can be used in my writings. They constitute a cash honorarium, ready money. I am really in the clover. The Lord has blessed me. The crop of fools has turned out particularly well this year and, like a good manager, I consume only a few—I select the most yielding ones and save them for the future. People often see me out on the promenade looking happy and cheerful. Like a rich merchant who, rubbing his hands with pleasure, strolls about among the chests, barrels, and bales of his warehouse—that is how I stroll among my people. You are all my own! You are all equally dear to me, and I love you just as you yourselves love your own money, and that is saying a lot. I had to laugh heartily when I recently heard that one of my people had expressed some concern and that he did not know what I lived on—and yet he himself is such a capital fool that I could live from him alone as if from invested capital. Many a fool is, however, to me not only ready money, but I have already determined the specific purpose of the ready cash I can get from writing about him. Thus, for instance, from a certain well-padded, fat millionaire I shall purchase a well-padded chair that is called a *chaise percée* by French women. From his fat millionairess I will buy myself a horse. When I see the fat gentleman—a camel will sooner get into heaven than that man through the eye of a needle—when I see him waddling along the promenade, I become curiously anxious. Although he is not acquainted with me, I involuntarily greet him, and he returns the greeting so heartily, so invitingly, that I would like to make use of his kindness on the spot and nonetheless become embarrassed because of the many well-dressed people just passing by. His wife is by no means a bad-looking woman. She has, it is true, only one eye, but it is consequently all the greener; her nose is like the tower facing Damascus; her bosom is as large as the ocean, and all sorts of ribbons flutter above it like the flags of the ships that have entered the harbor of this ocean bosom—even the sight of it makes one seasick—her neck is quite pretty and as plumply rounded as . . . (the image for the comparison will be found below), and on the violet-blue curtain covering this image thousands and thousands of silkworms have surely spun away their lives. You will see, madame, what a steed I shall acquire! When this lady meets me on the promenade, my heart truly rejoices. It is as if I could already swing upward into the saddle. I flick my riding crop, I snap my fingers, I cluck with my tongue, I make all sorts of riding movements with my legs—Giddap, giddap! Whoa, whoa!—and the dear woman looks at me so soulfully and with such inner understanding: she neighs with her eye, she flares her nostrils, she flirts with the croup, she curvets and suddenly breaks into a slow canter. And I stand there with folded arms, complacently looking back at her, thinking about whether I will ride her with a curb or on the snaffle, whether I should give her an English or a Polish saddle, etc. People who see me standing there cannot understand what there is about this woman that so attracts me. Tale-bearing tongues have already tried to make her husband uneasy and insinuated that I looked at his wife with the eye of a *roué*. But my honest, soft, leather *chaise percée* is reputed to have answered that he regards me as an innocent, even slightly bashful youth who looks at him with a certain uneasiness, like someone who feels the need of making closer contact but is restrained by a blushing timidity. My noble horse thinks, on the contrary, that I have a free, independent, chivalric air and that my eager politeness merely signifies the wish to be invited to dine with them sometime.

You see, madame, I can use everybody, and the city directory is actually the inventory of my property. And I consequently can never go bankrupt, for I would transform my creditors themselves into sources of income. Moreover, as already stated, I really live very economically—damned economically! For instance, while I write this I am sitting in a dark, gloomy room on Dismal Street, but I cheerfully endure it. In fact, I could, if I only wanted to, sit in the most beautiful garden just as well as my friends and loves. I would merely need to cash in on my schnaps clients. These latter, madame, consist of deteriorated hairdressers, down-and-out pimps and restaurant owners who themselves no longer have anything to eat, poor scoundrels who know the way to my apartment and who, for a substantial tip, will relate to me the *chronique scandaleuse* from their part of town. Madame, you wonder why I do not once and for all show such folks the door? Why, madame, what can you be thinking of? These people are my flowers. Someday I shall describe them in a beautiful book and use the royalties to buy myself a garden. Their red, yellow, blue, and variegated countenances already appear to me like the flowers of that garden. What do I care if other noses assert that these flowers smell only of kümmel, tobacco, cheese, and depravity! My own nose, my head's chimney, in which fantasy climbs up and down like a chimney sweep, asserts the contrary; it detects no smells in these people except the fragrance of roses, jasmine, carnations, and violets. Oh, how comfortably will I sit in my garden some morning, listening to the song of the birds and warming my limbs in the blessed sunshine, inhaling the fresh breath of the leaves, and be reminded of the old scoundrels by the sight of the flowers!

For the time being, though, I am still sitting in my dark room on dark Dismal Street and in its midst content myself with hanging the greatest obscurantist of the country. *"Mais est-ce que vous verrez plus clair alors?"* Apparently, madame, but do not misunderstand me; I do not mean that I am hanging the man himself but merely the crystal lamp that I intend to buy with the royalties earned from writing about him. Meanwhile, I believe it would be still better and that it would become bright in the entire country if the obscurantists could be hung *in natura*. If the people cannot be hung, however, they must be branded—I am again speaking figuratively, I brand them *en effigie*. It is true that Herr von Weiss— he is as white and unblemished as a lily—tried to whitewash himself when I asserted in Berlin that he had really been branded. For this reason, the fool had the authorities inspect him and provide him with written confirmation that no coat of arms was printed on his back, and he considered this negative coat-of-arms certificate a diploma that would secure him admission into the best society and was astonished when they nonetheless kicked him out. And now he is screaming death and murder at me, poor soul, and wants to shoot me with a loaded pistol wherever he finds me. And what do you suppose, madame, that I do to prevent that? Madame, from this fool, that is, from the royalties I will earn from writing about him, I will buy myself a good barrel of Rüdesheimer Rhine wine. I mention this so you will not believe it is malicious delight that makes me appear so merry whenever I encounter Herr von Weiss on the street. In fact, I see in him only my blessed Rüdesheimer; as soon as I set eyes on him I become delighted and pleased and automatically begin to hum, "Upon the Rhine, 'tis there our grapes are growing." "This picture is enchantingly fair." "O White Lady." Then my Rüdesheimer looks horribly sour, enough to make one believe he might consist only of poison and gall; but I assure you, madame, it is a genuine vintage. Although the attestation is not etched onto it, the connoisseur nonetheless can appreciate it. I will cheerfully tap this cask, and should it ferment all too threateningly and show signs of exploding in a dangerous manner, in compliance with regulations it will have to be secured by several iron bands.

You see, therefore, madame, that you need not do anything for me. I can calmly look at everything in this world. The Lord blessed me with earthly goods, and even if he did not quite conveniently deliver the wine to the cellar, he at least allows me to work in his vineyard. I only need gather the grapes, press them with my feet, squeeze them, barrel them, put them in the cellar, and I then have the clear heavenly gift. And although fools do not exactly fly roasted into my mouth but run at me rather raw and not even half-baked, still I know how to turn them on a spit, stew them and pepper them until they are tender and tasty. O madame, you will enjoy it when I someday give a grand fête! Madame, you will praise my cooking. You will have to admit that I can entertain my satraps as pompously as once did the great Ahasuerus, who, when he was king from India to the Moors, ruled over 127 provinces. I will slaughter whole hecatombs of fools. That great Philoschnaps who, like Jupiter, woos Europe's favor in the form of an ox, will supply the ox stew; a sad tragedian who showed us a tragical Alexander on a stage representing a tragical Persian kingdom will supply my table with a splendid pig's head, grinning sourly sweetly as usual with a slice of lemon in his mouth and shrewdly covered with laurel leaves by the artistic cook. The singer of coral lips, swan necks, bounding, snowy, little hills, little things, little legs, little Mimis, little kisses, and little assessors, namely, H. Clauren, or as the pious Bernardine sisters on Frederick Street call him, "Father Clauren, our Clauren!"—this original will supply me with all those dishes that he knows how to describe so divinely in his annual little pocket brothels with the imagination of a nibbling kitchen maid. And he shall even give us an altogether special little dish with a small plate of celery "for which the little heart bounds with love!" A shrewd, dried-up maid of honor whose head only is palatable will give us a similar dish, namely asparagus; and there will be no shortage of Göttingen sausages, Hamburg smoked beef, Pomeranian geese breasts, ox tongues, steamed calves' brains, "cheek," salt fish, all sorts of jellies, Berlin jelly doughnuts, Vienna tarts, confections . . .

Madame, in my imagination I have already overeaten! The devil take such gluttony. I cannot stand much; my digestion is poor; the pig's head has the same effect on me as on the rest of the German public. Afterward I must eat a Willibald Alexis salad, which purges and purifies. Oh, the wretched pig's head with the still more wretched sauce that tastes neither Grecian nor Persian but, on the contrary, like tea with new soap! Summon me my plump foolionaire!

Chapter 15

Madame, I observe a faint cloud of displeasure on your lovely brow, and you seem to ask: is it not wrong that I prepare the fools in this manner, stick them on the spit, that I carve and grease them and even butcher many that must lie undevoured and that must now serve as prey to the sharp beaks of the jokers while widows and orphans weep and wail?

Madame, *c'est la guerre!* Now I want to solve the whole riddle for you. I myself am by no means one of the reasonable ones, but I joined their party, and we have now been waging war against the fools for 5588 years. The fools believe that they have been wronged by us, asserting that there is only a limited quantity of reason in the world, that the reasonable people—Lord knows how—have usurped the whole amount and that it is an outrage to see how one single person has appropriated so much reason for himself that the other people and the whole country have become utterly obscure. This is the secret cause of the war, and it is truly a war of extermination. The reasonable people show themselves, as usual, to be the calmest, most moderate, and most reasonable; they sit securely fortified behind their ancient Aristotelian works, have much artillery, and also enough ammunition—for they themselves invented gunpowder—and now and then they throw a well-aimed bomb among their foes. But unfortunately the latter are by far the more numerous, and their shrieking is terrible, and they commit atrocities every day—for in reality every stupidity is an abomination to the reasonable person. Their military stratagems are often of a very shrewd kind. Some of the leaders of the large army surely guard against admitting the secret causes of the war. They have heard that a well-known deceitful man who advanced so far in the art of falsehood that he ended by writing false memoirs—namely Fouché—once asserted that *les paroles sont faites pour nous cacher nos pensées;* therefore they talk a great deal, make long speeches, and write big books in order to conceal the fact that they have no thoughts at all; and if anyone is listening, they praise the sole blessed source of thoughts—namely reason; and if anyone is looking at them, they work away at mathematics, logic, statistics, mechanical improvements, public spirit, stable fodder, and so forth. And just as a monkey becomes more ridiculous the more he resembles man, these fools also become more ridiculous the more reasonably they behave. Other leaders of the great army are more openhearted and admit that their own share of reason turned out to be very slight and that perhaps they never had any reason at all. Meantime, they cannot refrain from asserting that reason is very sour and basically of little value. This may perhaps be true, but unfortunately they do not have enough reason to prove it. They therefore resort to all manner of aid, discover new strengths within themselves, explain that these are quite as effective as reason and, in certain emergencies, even more effective—for instance, feeling, faith, inspiration, etc.—and they console themselves with this surrogate reason, with this mangold reason. I, poor thing, am especially hated by them; they assert that I originally was one of them, that I am an apostate, a deserter who has broken the holiest ties, that I am now even a spy who secretly reveals what they, the fools, have garnered together for the purpose of exposing them to the laughter of my new associates and that I myself am so stupid that I do not realize that the latter are all the while laughing at me and will never regard me as one of their own. And about this the fools are perfectly right.

It is true that they do not consider me to be one of their own and that I am often the object of their secret giggling. I know that well, although I do not show it. My heart bleeds inwardly, and when I am alone my tears flow. I know very well that my position is unnatural, that everything I do is considered foolish by the reasonable and atrocious by the fools. They hate me, and I feel the truth of the saying "A stone is heavy, and the sand is weighty; but a fool's wrath is heavier than them both." And they are not wrong to hate me. It is perfectly true that I have torn asunder the holiest ties; according to God and law, I would have had to live and die among the fools. And, oh, I would have had it so easy among them! Even now, if I would repent, they would still receive me with open arms. They would be able to tell from my eyes if they could do anything to please me. They would invite me to dinner every day and would include me in their tea parties and clubs in the evening, and I could play whist with them, smoke, talk politics, and if I yawned from time to time, they would say behind my back, "What beautiful feelings! A soul full of faith!" Permit me, madame, that I offer up a tear of emotion here. Ah, and I would drink punch with them until the proper inspiration came, and then they would bring me home in a sedan chair, anxiously concerned that I might catch a cold, and one would promptly bring me my slippers, another my silk dressing gown, a third my white nightcap, and finally they would make me a professor extraordinarius or president of a missionary society or supreme calculator or director of Roman excavations; for I would be just the man they could use in all professions inasmuch as I can very accurately distinguish the Latin declensions from the conjugations and am not so apt as other people to mistake a Prussian riding boot for an Etruscan vase. My sentiment, my faith, my inspiration could, in addition, accomplish much good at prayer meetings— namely, for myself—and then my remarkable poetic talent would stand me in good stead on the birthdays and at the weddings of the great; nor would it be bad if I were to laud in a great national epic all those heroes of whom we know with certainty that from their decayed corpses crept worms that now claim to be their descendants.

Many men who are not born fools and who once were gifted with reason have, because of such advantages, gone over to the fools and live in a veritable fool's paradise; those follies toward which they initially were somewhat reluctant have now already become second nature—they are in fact no longer to be regarded as hypocrites but as true believers. One of them in whose head total darkness does not as yet prevail is really fond of me; and recently when I was alone with him he closed the door and spoke to me in an earnest voice: "Oh, fool! You who play the wise man and have not, after all, as much sense as an unborn child! Do you not know that the great in the land only elevate someone who humiliates himself and praises their blood as better than his own? And now you even spoil it with the pious people of the country. Is it really so difficult to roll your soulful eyes in holy rapture, to tuck your piously crossed arms into your coat sleeves, to let your head hang down like a lamb of God and to whisper Bible sayings by heart? Believe me, no gracious highness will reward you for your godlessness; men of love will hate, slander, and persecute you, and you will never make a career either on earth or in heaven."

Ah, that is all true! But I, after all, have this unfortunate passion for reason. I love it even though it does not favor me by returning my love. I give it everything, and it grants me nothing. I cannot tear myself away from it. And just as once the Jewish King Solomon in his Song of Songs exulted the Christian Church and, in fact, used the image of a black, passionate maiden so that his Jews might not suspect anything, so have I in my countless songs lauded just the contrary—namely, reason—and even used the image of a white, cold maiden who attracts and repels me, who now smiles at me, then scorns me, and ultimately turns her back on me. This secret of my unfortunate love, which I reveal to none, provides you, madame, with a measure of appreciation for my foolishness. You can see from it that it is an extraordinary kind and that it magnificently towers over the ordinary foolish doings of mankind. Read my *Radcliffe,* my *Almansor,* my *Lyrical Intermezzo*—reason, reason, nothing but reason—and you will be horrified at the height of my folly. In the words of Augur, the son of Jakeh, I can say, "Surely I am more brutish than any man, and have not the understanding of a man." High into the air rises the forest of oaks, high above the oaks soars the eagle, high above the eagle sweep the clouds, high above the clouds shine the stars—madame, is that getting too high for you? *Eh bien,* high above the stars hover the angels, high above the angels rises—no, madame, my foolishness cannot manage to go any higher. It reaches heights enough. It gets dizzy from its own sublimity. It makes me into a giant with seven-mile boots. At noon I feel as though I could devour all the elephants of Hindustan and then pick my teeth with the spire of the Strasbourg Cathedral; in the evening I become so sentimental that I would like to guzzle down the Milky Way without reflecting how indigestibly the small, fixed stars would remain in my stomach; and at night the spectacle really starts up. In my head there is then a congress of all the peoples of the past and of the present; there assemble the Assyrians, Egyptians, Medes, Persians, Hebrews, Philistines, Frankfurters, Babylonians, Carthaginians, Berliners, Romans, Spartans, Turks, and Yokels. Madame, it would take too long to describe all these people to you. Just read Herodotus, Livy, the magazine of Haude and Spener, Curtius, Cornelius Nepos, the *Companion.* Meanwhile, I want to have breakfast. This morning I am not getting ahead very well with my writing; the good Lord leaves me in the lurch. Madame, I even fear—yes, yes, you noticed it before I did myself; yes, I see—the right kind of divine aid has not even arrived today. Madame, I want to start a new chapter and tell you how I arrived in Godesberg following the death of Le Grand.

Chapter 16

When I arrived in Godesberg, I sat down again at the feet of my beautiful friend, and near me lay her brown dachshund, and we both looked up into her eyes.

Ah, Lord, in those eyes was all the splendor of the earth and an entire heaven besides. I could have died with rapture as I gazed into them, and had I died at that instant my soul would have flown directly into those eyes. Oh, those eyes are indescribable! I want to have some poet who went mad from love brought here from a lunatic asylum to fetch from the abyss of his madness an image to be compared with those eyes. Just between you and me, I myself would be mad enough not to require any help in such an undertaking. "God d--n!" an Englishman once said. "When she quietly looks at a man from head to foot, it is enough to melt one's copper coat buttons and one's heart to boot." "F——e!" said a Frenchman. "Her eyes are of the largest caliber, and when she shoots one of her thirty-pound glances—crack!—there you are in love!" There was a red-headed lawyer from Mainz who said her eyes look like two cups of black coffee. He wanted to say something sweet, for he always put a barbaric amount of sugar into his coffee. Bad comparisons. I and the brown dachshund lay motionless at the feet of the fair lady and gazed and listened. She sat beside an old iron-gray soldier, a man of knightly appearance with lateral scars on his furrowed brow. They both spoke of the Seven Mountains illuminated by the evening sunset and of the blue Rhine, which quietly and impressively flowed nearby. What did we care about the Seven Mountains and the sunset and the blue Rhine and the boats as white as sails that swam on it and the music coming from one boat or the jackass of a student who, seated in the boat, sang so mellifluously and beautifully? I and the brown hound both gazed into the eyes of our friend and looked at her countenance, which shone forth rosy-pale from her black braids and curls like the moon from dark clouds. The features were of the noblest Grecian type, the lips boldly arched with a trace of melancholy, rapture, and childish mood; and when she spoke, the words were breathed forth deeply almost in a sigh, yet were pushed out impatiently and rapidly; and when she spoke and her speech floated down like a warm, genial flower shower from her lovely mouth—oh, then the crimson of evening covered my soul and memories of childhood jingled triumphantly through my mind; but, above all, like a small bell there resounded within me the voice of the little Veronica, and I grasped the lovely hand of my friend and pressed it to my eyes until the sound in my soul was no more. And then I leaped up and laughed, and the dachshund barked, and the brow of the old general wrinkled up more sternly, and I sat down again and clasped again the beautiful hand and kissed it and told and spoke of little Veronica.

Chapter 17

Madame, you want me to describe the appearance of little Veronica. But I will not. You, madame, cannot be compelled to read more than you please, and I, on the other hand, have the right to write exactly what I choose. But I now want to tell you about the appearance of the lovely hand that I kissed in the previous chapter.

First of all, I must confess I was not worthy of kissing that hand. It was a lovely hand, so tender, transparent, perfumed, brilliant, sweet, soft, loving—really I must send to the apothecary for twelve shillings' worth of adjectives.

On the middle finger was a ring with a pearl—I never saw a pearl that played a more lamentable part. On the marriage finger she wore a ring with an antique blue gem—I have studied archaeology in it for hours; on the forefinger she wore a diamond—it was a talisman; as long as I looked at it, I was happy; for where it was, there too was the finger with its four colleagues, and she often struck me on the mouth with all five of them. Having been thus hand-polished, I firmly believe in animal magnetism. But she did not strike hard, and when she struck I always deserved it for some godless turn of phrase; and as soon as she had struck me, she at once repented it and took a cake, broke it in two, and gave half to me and the other half to the brown dachshund, smiled, and said, "You two have no religion, and you will never be blessed, so you must be fed cakes in this world, since no place will be set for you at the table in heaven." And she was more than half right; in those days I was very irreligious and read Thomas Paine, the *Système de la Nature,* the *Westphalian Advertiser,* and Schleiermacher, letting both my beard and my understanding grow, and considered joining the rationalists. But when that lovely hand swept over my brow, my understanding came to a halt and sweet dreams filled me, and I again thought I heard gentle songs of the Virgin Mary, and I thought of little Veronica.

Madame, you can hardly imagine how pretty little Veronica looked as she lay in her little coffin. The burning candles surrounding it cast a glow on the pale, smiling little face and on the red silk roses and rustling gold spangles that adorned her small head and the small white shroud. Pious Ursula had led me in the evening into the quiet room, and when I saw the small corpse laid out amid lights and flowers on the table, I at first believed that it was a pretty saint's image in wax. But I soon recognized the dear face and smilingly asked why little Veronica was so still. And Ursula said, "That is death's doing."

And when she said, "That is death's doing"—but I don't want to tell this story today, it would be too long; besides I would first have to speak of the lame magpie that limped about the castle courtyard and that was three hundred years old, and then I could become truly melancholy. I have suddenly gotten a desire to tell another story, and it is amusing and also just suits this place, for it is the real story that was supposed to be told in this book.

Chapter 18

There was nothing but night and pain in the knight's breast. The dagger thrusts of slander had really hit their mark in him, and as he walked across Saint Marcus Square, he felt as though his heart must burst and bleed to death. His feet staggered from weariness—the noble quarry had been chased all day long, and it was a hot summer day—sweat stood on his brow, and as he climbed into the gondola he sighed heavily. He sat unthinkingly in the black cabin of the gondola; unthinkingly the soft waves rocked him and bore him along the familiar route toward the Brenta; and as he stepped out in front of the famous palace, he heard that Signora Laura was in the garden.

She stood leaning on the statue of the Laocoon beside the red rose tree at the end of the terrace near the weeping willows that hung down mournfully over the river flowing past. There she stood smiling, a gentle image of love, engulfed by the fragrance of roses. He awakened as from some dark dream and was suddenly transformed into mildness and longing. "Signora Laura," he said, "I am wretched and tormented by hatred and distress and falsehood." And then he faltered and stammered, "But I love you." And then a tear of joy darted into his eye, and with moist eyes and flaming lips he cried, "Be mine—and love me!"

This hour is covered by a veil of dark mystery; no mortal knows what Signora Laura replied, and when her guardian angel in heaven above is asked about it, he hides his face and sighs and is silent.

The knight stood alone by the statue of the Laocoon for a long time; his own face was just as distorted and white; unconsciously he plucked all the roses from the rose tree; he even crushed the young buds. The tree never again bore blossoms; in the distance a mad nightingale lamented, the willows whispered anxiously, the cool waves of the Brenta murmured gloomily; night with its moon and stars rose on high—a lovely star, the loveliest of all, fell down from heaven.

Chapter 19

Vous pleurez, madame?

Oh, may the eyes that now shed such lovely tears long light up the world with their rays, and may a warm and loving hand close them in the hour of death! A gentle kiss of death, madame, is also a good thing at the hour of death, and I hope you will not be without it when that time comes and when the fair, weary head sinks down and the black curls tumble over the paling visage. Oh, then may God repay you those tears that have flowed for me, for I myself am the knight for whom you wept; I myself am that errant knight of love, the knight of the fallen star!

Vous pleurez, madame?

Oh, I know those tears! For what purpose the protracted dissimulation? You, madame, you yourself are the beautiful woman who even in Godesberg wept so sweetly when I told the dreary tale of my life. Like pearls on roses the beautiful tears ran down your beautiful cheeks—the dachshund was silent, the evening bells in Königswinter faded away, the Rhine murmured more softly, night covered the earth with its black mantle, and I sat at your feet, madame, and looked up into the starry heaven. At the beginning I took your eyes for two stars as well. But how can anyone confuse such beautiful eyes with stars? These cold lights of heaven cannot weep about the misery of a person who is so wretched that he can no longer weep.

And there were some other special reasons that I could not fail to recognize these lovely eyes—in these eyes dwells the soul of little Veronica.

I have checked back, madame; you were born on the very day on which little Veronica died. Johanna in Andernach predicted that I would find little Veronica again in Godesberg, and I recognized you at once. That was a bad idea, madame, that you should die just as the charming games were supposed to get started. Since pious Ursula said to me, "That is death's doing," I have gone about alone and solemnly in the big painting galleries, but the paintings no longer seemed to please me as much as formerly; they seemed to have suddenly faded; there was only one work that retained color and brilliance; you know, madame, which work I mean:

It is the Sultan and Sultana of Delhi.

Do you recall, madame, how we often stood for hours in front of it and how pious Ursula smirked so strangely when people noticed that the faces in that picture so much resembled our own? Madame, I find that your likeness is admirably caught in that painting, and it is incomprehensible how the artist portrayed you even to the clothing you wore at that time. It is said that he was insane and dreamed your image. Or was his soul perhaps in the large, sacred ape who waited on you in those days like a jockey? In that case, he must certainly have remembered the silver-gray veil he spoiled by spilling red wine onto it. I was glad that you dismissed him; he did not dress you particularly well, and at any rate the European dress for women is much more becoming than the Indian. Beautiful women are admittedly lovely in any dress. Do you remember, madame, that a gallant Brahmin—he looked like Ganesa, the god with an elephant's trunk, who rides on a mouse—once paid you the compliment that the divine Menaka, as she descended Indra's golden castle to the royal penitent Visvamitra, was surely not more beautiful than you, madame?

Do you no longer remember that? Why, it can hardly be three thousand years ago that this was said to you, and beautiful women are not usually inclined to forget delicate flattery so quickly.

For men, however, the Indian dress is far more becoming than the European. Oh, my rosy-red lotus-flowered pantaloons of Delhi! Had I worn you when I stood before Signora Laura and besought her love, the previous chapter would have sounded different! But, alas! At that time I wore straw-colored pantaloons woven by some unimaginative Chinese in Nanking; my ruin was woven into them—and I became miserable.

Often there is a young man sitting in a small German coffee-house, quietly drinking his cup of coffee; and meanwhile in far-away, distant China his ruin is growing and flourishing and is spun and woven there and, despite the great wall of China, it knows how to find its way to the youth who thinks it is merely a pair of Nanking trousers, unsuspectingly dons them, and is made misera-ble. And, madame, so much misery can be and can remain con-cealed in the small breast of a person that the poor creature him-self does not feel it for days and is happy as a lark and merrily dances and whistles and trills: lalarallala, lalarallala-la-la-la.

Chapter 20

"She was lovable, and he loved her. He, however, was not lov-able, and she did not love him."   —*Old Play*

And because of this stupid incident, you wanted to shoot your-self? Madame, if a person wants to shoot himself, he always has ample reasons for it—you may be certain of that. But the question is whether he himself knows what these reasons are. Until the final moment, we play a comedy with ourselves. We even mask our misery, and while dying of a chest wound complain of a tooth-ache.

Madame, you surely know a remedy for a toothache?

But I had a toothache in my heart. That is the worst misfortune, and a filling of lead and tooth powder invented by Berthold Schwartz alleviates it quite effectively.

Misery gnawed and gnawed at my heart like a worm—the poor Chinese was not to blame; I brought this misery with me into the world. It lay with me even in the cradle, and when my mother rocked me, she rocked it with me, and when she sang me to sleep, it fell asleep with me, and it awoke as soon as I opened my eyes again. When I grew up, it, too, grew until it was finally quite large and burst my . . .

Now we want to speak of other things—of bridal wreaths, masked balls, of joy and nuptial bliss: lalarallala, lalarallala, lalaral-la-la-la.

Translated by Charles Godfrey Leland
and adapted by Robert C. Holub
and Martha Humphreys

Part Three

EPIC
POETRY

Germany: A Winter's Tale

1

It was in November, that dreary month;
The days were growing shorter;
The winds ripped all the leaves from the trees;
And I came to the German border.

And as I reached the borderline
A stronger pulse began
To throb within me; down my cheeks
I think some teardrops ran.

And when I heard the German tongue
Strange feelings thrilled my spirit;
It almost seemed as though my heart
Would burst with joy to hear it.

A little harp girl sang. Her voice
Was strong, though out of key;
Still I was deeply stirred to hear
A German melody.

She sang of love and the pain of love,
Of sacrifice on earth,
And meetings in that better world
Where sorrows change to mirth.

She sang of this earthly vale of tears,
Of pleasures that soon run dry;
How the soul will feast on eternal joys
—Transfigured in the sky.

She sang a heavenly lullaby,
The song of renunciation
By which the people, that giant clown,
Is lulled from its lamentation.

I know the authors, I know the tune,
I know it line for line—
In public, water is all they preach;
While in secret they guzzle wine.

A new song, and a better song,
O friends, I'll sing for you.
Here on earth we mean to make
Our paradise come true.

We mean to be happy here on earth—
Our days of want are done.
No more shall the lazy belly waste
What toiling hands have won.

Wheat enough for all mankind
Is planted here below;
Roses and myrtle, beauty and joy,
And green peas, row upon row.

Yes, green peas enough for every man,
As soon as they break their pods.
We gladly leave to the angels and birds
The dainties of the gods.

And, after our death, if wings should sprout
We'll visit you up there,
And eat the holiest tarts and cakes
That angel cooks prepare.

A new song, and a better song!
It rings like fiddle and flute.
The *miserere* sounds no more;
The bells of death are mute.

Young Europe's betrothed to Liberty,
That genius of beauty and grace.
They lie in each other's passionate arms,
They feast on their first embrace.

And although they lack the blessing of priests,
Theirs is a proper wedding.
Long live the bridegroom and his bride
And the children of their begetting!

An epithalamium is my song;
A new, a better creation!
Within my soul arise the stars
Of highest consecration.

Inspired stars! They blaze out wild;
In torrents of flame they spill;
I feel that my powers have wondrously grown;
I could shatter an oak at will.

Through my veins, since treading on German soil,
Magical juices flow—
The giant has touched his mother again,
And his power begins to grow.

2

While the young harp girl was trilling her song
Of heaven's eternal pleasures,
Prussian customs officials searched
My trunk for its hoard of treasures.

They sniffed at everything, rummaged around
To see if jewels were hidden;
They dug through breeches, handkerchiefs, shirts,
For lace, or a book that's forbidden.

You fools, who search inside my trunk!
There's nothing that you can find.
The contraband that journeys with me
I've stuck away in my mind.

I've lace that the laces of Mecklenburg
And Brussels can hardly match.
Just wait till my needlepoints are unpacked;
You'll feel them prick and scratch.

The future's bright crown diamonds
Are glittering in me:
The temple gems of the great unknown,
The God that is to be.

And I carry many books in my head—
Solemnly I state it:
My head is a bird's nest twittering
With books to be confiscated.

Believe me, there can be nothing worse
On the bookshelves of the Devil—
Even von Fallersleben's books
Are on a safer level.

A passenger who stood nearby
Paused kindly to explain
That this was the Prussian *Zollverein*,
The mighty customs chain.

"The *Zollverein*," the gentleman said,
"Will be our true foundation,
And bind the dismembered fatherland
Into one great nation.

It will bring us material unity:
An outwardly welded state;
While union of soul, on the other hand,
Our censors will create.

They'll bring internal unity:
No room for minds that doubt.
We need a united Germany:
United within and without."

3

Carolus Magnus lies entombed
In Aachen's ancient dome.
Don't confuse him with Karl Mayer, who
Makes Swabia his home.

I'd hate being emperor under that dome,
Too dead and buried to know it;
I'd much rather live where the Neckar flows,
As Stukkert's puniest poet.

Milling around on Aachen's streets
The dogs were humbly imploring:
"O stranger, give us a little kick!
Life has become so boring."

An hour or so in this dull nest
I aimlessly wandered around;
Saw Prussian military again:
They'd changed but little, I found.

Gray cloak, with collar high and red,
Is still the dress of these henchmen.
(Körner sang in earlier days:
Red's for the blood of Frenchmen.)

Still the same wooden, pedantic folk:
With stiff right angles they move;
And frozen plainly on every face
The same, undimmed self-love.

They stalk around so stiltedly,
So sprucely bolt upright,
As though they'd swallowed the whipping rod
That bloodied their backs last night.

The whip has never quite disappeared;
They keep it within them now;
One still remembers the "he" of old
When hearing the intimate "thou."

In truth, the long moustache is just
The pigtail's newer phase;
The pigtail that formerly hung behind
Hangs under the nose these days.

The new costume of the cavalry
Is fine—I was quite impressed,
Especially by the bright spiked helm,
With its point of steel at the crest.

This is chivalric, recalling the past:
So far off and romantic;
The Chatelaine Jeanne de Montfaucon,
The Barons Fouqué, Uhland, Tieck.

It calls to mind the squires and knights
Of those lovely feudal years
Who carried loyalty high in their hearts
And a coat of arms on their rears.

It reminds me of tourneys and crusades,
When men were noble-hearted;
When faith was more than a printed word—
Before the first journal was started.

It springs from the very highest wit;
Yes, yes, this helmet I like!
It was a notion befitting a king,
Not lacking a point, a spike!

But should a storm arise, I fear
The sky will be drawn by your spike,
And down upon your romantic head
Most modern lightning will strike.

In Aachen, I saw on the post-office shield
The bird that I despise.
It still sat glaring down at me
With poison-flaming eyes.

O hateful bird, if you should fall
Into my hands one day,
I'll pluck each feather from your back
And chop your claws away.

And after this, high in the air
I'll build a perch for you,
And call the huntsmen of the Rhine
To show what they can do.

He who shoots the eagle down
Shall instantly be crowned
And we shall cry, "Long live the King!"
While guns and trumpets sound.

4

Late in the evening I came to Cologne,
And I heard the Rhine as it moved.
The air that fanned me was German air,
And its influence improved

My appetite. The dish of ham
And omelettes tasted fine.
And since it was salted very well
I washed it down with wine.

Still like gold in the sea-green glass
The Rhine wine brightly glows;
If you drink a couple of pints too much
It climbs up into your nose.

It starts an itching so sweet in your nose,
You are overcome with delight!
It drove me into the echoing streets,
Into the darkening night.

The houses of stone looked down at me
As though they would like to unfold
Tales of Cologne, the holy town,
Forgotten tales of old.

Yes, here the clergy used to go
Upon their pious ways.
Here the black men von Hutten described
Were lords in other days.

Here the nuns and friars danced
The can-can of the Dark Ages.
Here Hochstraaten, the Menzel of Cologne,
Spat out his poisoned pages.

Here the flames of the funeral pyre
Devoured books and people;
Kyrie Eleison accompanied this,
And bells rang out from the steeple.

Here malice and stupidity
Like street curs used to mate;
The descendants can still be recognized
By their sectarian hate.

But see! Clear in the moonlight there
That mighty comrade of stone!
He looms up high, so devilish black:
The Cathedral of Cologne.

It was meant to be the mind's Bastille,
And the Romish plan was clever:
"In this great prison the German mind
Will pine away forever."

Then Luther came upon the scene,
And spoke his mighty "Stay!"
And so Cologne's Cathedral stands
Unfinished to this day.

It never was finished—and that is good.
Its very unfinished condition
Makes it a landmark of German strength
And of the Protestant mission.

Poor wretches of the Cathedral Guild:
You, with your powerless hands,
Hope to revive the halted task
Till the finished stronghold stands.

Oh, silly illusion! All in vain
Your alms bag is hungrily shaken:
Begging of heretics, even of Jews;
It is all so fruitless, mistaken.

Though great Franz Liszt performs for you,
In vain is his contribution;
And in vain a talented king will use
His power of elocution.

It will never be finished, the spire of Cologne,
Though Swabian fools may send
A ship all loaded up with stones
To bring the job to an end.

It will never be finished, despite the great
Outcry of owl and raven,
Old-fashioned birds, who like to make
A high church tower their haven.

Yes, instead of being done,
A darker fate approaches:
Its inner crypt will be a stall
For horses and for coaches.

"But if the Cathedral turns to a stall
We'll have a problem to tackle:
What shall be done with the three holy kings
Who rest in the tabernacle?"

Such questions are asked. But need we be
So fretted in our day?
The three holy kings of the East can find
Some other place to stay.

In Münster, high on Saint Lambert's tower,
There hang three cages of iron.
Take my advice, there's no better place
For the three holy kings to lie in.

The king of the tailors sat there once
With his ministerial pair,
But we'll take other majesties
And give them shelter there.

Sir Melchior shall hang at the left,
Sir Balthasar at the right,
Between them Sir Gaspar—when they were alive
God knows where they spent the night!

The holy alliance of the East
That is canonized today
May not have always behaved itself
In a fair and pious way.

Sirs Balthasar and Melchior
May have committed the crime
Of pledging their subjects a better law
At some distressing time—

And later failing to keep their word—
Sir Gaspar may've repaid
His people with a bloody thanks
For trusting the vows he'd made.

5

And when I reached the great Rhine bridge
Where the forts of the harbor lie,
There in the moonlight I could see
Old Father Rhine flow by.

Greetings, greetings, my Father Rhine!
How has your world been turning?
Many times I've thought of you,
With hunger and with yearning.

I spoke, and I heard in the water's deep
A strangely sullen rumbling;
It sounded like an old man's cough,
A sickly groaning and grumbling.

"Welcome, my son! I'm glad to hear
That I've not been forgotten.
You've been away these thirteen years;
As for me—things have been rotten.

I swallowed stones at Biberich;
And, son, was that an ordeal!
But the verses of Nicholas Becker made
An even lumpier meal.

He praised me as though I were still a maid
Without a stain upon her
Who won't let anybody lift
Her little crown of honor.

I feel like plucking out my beard
When his stupid rhymes resound;
I could almost bid the world goodbye
And in myself be drowned.

That I am not a stainless maid
The Frenchmen long have known.
So often has their victor's reek
Been mingled with my own.

That stupid song, and that stupid man!
He slandered me with his rot.
And, in a sense politically,
He put me in a spot.

For if the French come back again,
My cheeks will blush and burn,
I who so often prayed to God
That they might soon return.

I've always loved the French so well,
Those darling little dears!
Are their pants still white? Do they sing and spring
As they did in other years?

I'd like to see them once again,
But what a ribbing I'd face
Because of that accursed song,
Because of that disgrace!

That urchin, Alfred de Musset,
Will lead the march, I fear;
He might be the drummer boy, and drum
His bad jokes into my ear."

Thus poor Father Rhine complained:
Hopelessly sad and frightened.
I offered him many a comforting word,
Hoping his heart would be lightened:

"Oh, never fear, my Father Rhine,
The mockery of France;
These French are not the French of old,
They even wear different pants.

Their pants are red, instead of white;
New buttons are now in season;
No more do they sing, no more do they spring;
Their heads have grown heavy with reason.

They're thinkers; now Hegel, Fichte, and Kant
Are all their conversation.
They smoke tobacco, guzzle beer,
And bowl for recreation.

They're smug philistines, just like us,
And carry it to extremes:
They're beginning to follow Hengstenberg;
Voltaire is through, it seems.

De Musset, it's true, has always been
A rogue, and a rogue he remains.
But have no fear; one of these days
We'll put his tongue in chains.

And if he drums you an evil jest,
We'll whistle an uglier air:
We'll whistle aloud what happened to him
Among his ladies fair.

You can rest untroubled, Father Rhine,
Don't let the bad songs grieve you.
Soon you'll be hearing a better song.
Farewell; for a while I leave you."

6

With Paganini always came
A *spiritus familiaris,*
Sometimes in the shape of a dog, sometimes
In the form of the late George Harris.

Napoleon saw a scarlet man
Before each grave occasion.
Socrates had his demon, too;
It was no hallucination.

And at night, while sitting at my desk,
I also used to see
A visitor, in a weird black hood,
Standing in back of me.

Something was hidden under his cloak,
And when I saw, it seemed
An axe—an executioner's axe—
Because of the way it gleamed.

He looked to be of dumpy size;
Each eye was like a star.
He never disturbed me as I wrote,
But quietly waited afar.

For years this singular guest of mine
Had been leaving me alone,
When all at once I found him here
In the moonlit night of Cologne.

I was thoughtfully strolling along the streets,
And back of me he came,
As though my shadow—and every time
I stopped, he did the same.

He halted in his tracks, and stood
With an expectant air;
And when I continued, he followed me
Till we reached Cathedral Square.

I couldn't stand it; I turned and said:
"Now tell me by what right
You follow my footsteps everywhere
Here in the desolate night?

We always meet when thoughts of the world
Are sprouting in my heart,
When inspiration fires my brain
And flashes of lightning dart.

You stare with such relentless eyes—
What is it you want of me?
And what have you got there under your cloak,
That glitters so ominously?"

But he replied in a monotone
That was dry, and a bit phlegmatic:
"Don't exorcise me, if you please,
And don't be so emphatic!

I am no scarecrow, no ghost of the past
Out of the grave arising;
And I am no friend of rhetoric,
Do little philosophizing.

I'm of a practical character:
The calm and silent kind.
But know: I'll carry out, I'll do
All that you've had in mind.

And even though the years go by,
I find no satisfaction
Till thought becomes reality;
You think, and I take action.

You are the judge; the headsman am I,
Who stands and awaits your will;
And whether your judgment be right or wrong,
Obediently I kill.

The axe of the consul in ancient Rome
Went first, may I remind you.
You've got your 'lictor,' too; but now
The axe is carried behind you.

I am your 'lictor'; with shiny axe
I follow close behind
On all your travels—I am the deed,
The offspring of your mind."

7

I wandered home, and slept with songs
Of angels in my head.
In Germany your bed is soft,
For it's a feather bed.

In the nights of exile, how many times
For these kind pillows I yearned,
When on those hard French mattresses
I sleeplessly tossed and turned!

In German feather beds you sleep
And dream exceeding well.
Here at last the German soul
Escapes its earthly cell.

The soul escapes, and goes soaring up
To the loftiest realms of the sky.
O German soul, in your nightly dreams
How haughtily you fly!

The gods grow pale at your approach!
And everywhere you go
With beating pinions you snuff out
Many a starlet's glow.

The French and the Russians rule the land;
The British rule the sea;
But in the realms of dream we own
Unchallenged mastery.

Here we become one mighty state,
Here, in dreams, we are crowned—
While other peoples build their realms
Upon the level ground . . .

And as I fell asleep, I dreamed
That once again I strolled
In moonlight, on the streets of Cologne,
The echoing streets of old.

And once again behind me came
My comrade, darkly hooded.
Ever on we went, although
I stumbled, weary-footed.

On we went! And in my breast
My heart was torn and bruised.
And from the deep wound of my heart
The drops of scarlet oozed.

Sometimes I plunged my fingers in,
And sometimes I would spread
Over the doorposts, as I passed,
A smear of bloody red.

And every time I marked a house
In such a way, there fell
Moaning sadly and softly afar
The sound of a tolling bell.

In heaven, though, the moon turned pale:
Soon it was out of sight.
The frenzied clouds came racing past,
Like horses of the night.

And always with his hidden axe
The hooded figure stalked
In back of me—and in this way
For quite a while we walked.

We walked and walked, until we reached
Cathedral Square at last.
The gates were standing open wide,
And through their arms we passed.

Only silence and death and night
Ruled in that giant room;
Hanging lamps burned here and there
The better to show the gloom.

Along the pillars long I walked,
Only my comrade's pace
Rang in my ears, as step for step
He followed me through the place.

At last we came to a dazzling room
And saw a bright display
Of silver, gold, and precious stones;
Here the three kings lay.

But wonder of wonders! The three holy kings
Who'd been content to lie
So still, were sitting upright now
On their sarcophagi.

Three skeletons, in fantastic dress,
With scepters in their hands;
Atop their wretched, yellowed skulls
Were crowns of the Eastern lands.

Like jumping jacks they moved their bones,
That had slept for ages there;
A smell of incense and of mold
Arose and fouled the air.

One of the monarchs moved his mouth
And delivered a long oration,
Explaining why he'd a right to demand
My awe and admiration.

First, because he was a corpse,
Second, because a king,
And third, because he was a saint—
But it didn't mean a thing.

Laughing aloud, I answered him:
"Your speech was very clever,
But I can see that you belong
To a time that is gone forever.

Out! Out of here! You should have crawled
Down to your graves before.
Life is now coming to confiscate
This chapel's treasure store.

The future's joyous cavalry
Shall here at last be housed.
And if you're not willing, I'll turn to force:
I'll club you till you're deloused!"

So I spoke, and wheeled around;
I saw the terrible glint
Of my silent lictor's terrible axe—
He understood the hint.

He came up close and savagely
Smashed them, scepter and crown;
And with one blow those bones of false
Belief came tumbling down.

Horribly boomed through all the vaults
The echo of that stroke.
Streams of blood shot from my breast,
And suddenly I awoke.

8

The fare from Cologne to Hagen is
Five dollars, six Prussian cents.
I had to take the open coach:
—No room in the diligence.

A late fall morning, damp and gray,
The coach groaned through the mud;
But despite the nasty weather and way
I'd never felt so good.

This is truly my native air!
It touched my cheeks, and they glowed!
And this is the muck of my fatherland:
This mud of the country road!

The horses seemed old friends of mine—
Their tails so cordially swung.
Atalanta's apples were not as fair
As their little cakes of dung.

We drove through Mülheim: a pretty town;
Its people get things done.
I saw them last in the month of May,
In eighteen thirty-one.

Everything then was blossom-crowned;
Sunbeams were laughing then;
Full of longing sang the birds;
And there were hopeful men.

"Soon the lean barons will ride away,"
The people used to think,
"And long-necked bottles will be drained
For a departing drink.

And freedom will come with song and dance,
With her banner, the white-blue-red;
Perhaps she'll even be able to fetch
Napoleon from the dead."

My God! The barons still are here!
And many who came this way—
Gawky fellows, dry as bone—
Carry big bellies today.

They looked like love and faith and hope,
Those pale invading swine;
Since then their noses have grown red
From too much German wine.

And freedom has sprained an ankle—no more
Can she leap as in other days.
From the towers of Paris the tricolor droops
With a melancholy gaze.

Since then the Emperor's risen again,
But he had been taught to behave
By the English worms; with his own consent
Once more he's laid in the grave.

I saw his funeral myself,
And the coach that solemnly rolled
With the golden victory goddesses
Who carried the coffin of gold.

All along the Champs Elysées,
And through the Triumphal Arch,
Right through the mist, right over the snow,
Advanced the funeral march.

The music was shockingly dissonant;
The musicians numb with frost.
The eagles on the standards seemed
Sorrowful and lost.

And the people were lost in memories,
So ghostly did they seem!
Once again was conjured up
Their old imperial dream.

I couldn't help but weep that day:
My eyes grew dim with tears
When that old cry, *"Vive l'Empereur!"*
Resounded in my ears.

9

The following morning I left Cologne;
It was only a quarter of eight.
We came to Hagen almost at three.
In Hagen they always eat late.

Here was the good old German style
Of cooking I knew so well.
Hail to thee, dear sauerkraut!
How goodly is thy smell!

Stuffed chestnuts in green cabbage leaves,
As if they'd been cooked by mother.
O native codfish, my greetings to you!
How smartly you swim in the butter!

To feeling hearts the fatherland
Remains forever precious—
Eggs and herrings stewed dark brown
Are also most delicious.

How the sausages danced in sizzling fat!
The thrushes, those deeply pious
Broiled angels, chirped in the applesauce:
"We're glad you've come to try us!"

They twittered: "Welcome, countryman!
It's long since we've seen your face;
You've roved around with foreign birds
So long in a foreign place!"

Upon the table stood a goose:
A quiet, genial thing.
She may have loved me once, when we
Were both still young of wing.

Her gaze was so deeply significant,
So fervent, so pained, so true!
She surely possessed a noble soul;
But she wasn't easy to chew.

In a pewter dish the head of a swine
Was afterward brought out.
We still adorn with laurel leaves
The swine's uplifted snout.

10

As we rode from Hagen, darkness fell;
The evening air was raw.
Only at Unna, in the inn,
My bones began to thaw.

I found a pretty maiden there
Who brought me punch and was friendly.
Her curly hair was like yellow silk;
Her moonlit eyes shone gently.

I heard the lisping Westphalian speech
With pleasure once again.
Sweet memories rose in the steam of the punch;
I thought of those fine young men,

Those dear Westphalians, with whom I drank
Far more than we were able,
In Göttingen, and were so moved
We ended under the table.

Those dear, those good Westphalians
Have always been my friends.
They're all so firm, so sure, so true:
No bragging, no pretense.

How splendidly in the fencing hall
They stand—those lion hearts!
So rightly aimed, and so precise
Their tierces and their quartes!

They duel well, they guzzle well,
And when these friendly folk
Shake hands with you, they always cry:
They're sentimental oaks.

Heaven preserve you, valiant race,
Bless your harvest and seed,
Keep you always from war and fame,
From hero and heroic deed!

May God forever grant your sons
Exams that they can pass,
And may He grant a handsome match
To each Westphalian lass!

11

This is the forest of Teutoburg
Of Tacitus' report.
This is the classical morass
Where Varus was stopped short.

Here he was faced by the Cheruscan chief,
Hermann, of noble blood;
And here the German nation rose
Victorious from the mud.

If Hermann hadn't won the fight
At the head of his fierce blond hordes,
There'd be no more German liberty—
We'd have bowed to the Roman lords.

Our fatherland would now be ruled
By the Roman tongue and tunic;
Swabians would be Quirites now;
There'd be vestal virgins in Munich.

They'd make a diviner of Hengstenberg;
He'd delve, both day and night,
In the entrails of oxen. Neander would watch
And interpret the swallows' flight.

Birch-Pfeiffer'd be drinking turpentine
Like the Roman ladies of old.
(Because of this their urine smelled
Especially sweet, we're told.)

No German rascal would Raumer be
But a Roman rascalatius.
Freiligrath would use no rhyme,
In the manner of Flaccus Horatius.

The barbarous beggar, Father Jahn,
They'd call Barbarianus.
Massmann'd speak Latin. Me Hercule!
Marcus Tullius Massmannus!

The friends of truth would have to fight
Wild beasts in the arenas—
Not against dogs in the small-time press,
But lions, jackals, hyenas.

Instead of three dozen sovereigns,
One Nero would keep us in chains.
Defying the henchmen of slavery
We would all cut open our veins.

Schelling would be a Seneca;
And he'd be Nero's victim.
To our painter Cornelius we would say:
"*Cacatum non est pictum.*"

Thank God! The Romans were driven away;
The victory was Hermann's.
Varus and all his hordes succumbed,
And we—we still are Germans.

We speak the German we used to speak;
Everything stayed the same.
An ass is an ass—not *asinus.*
The Swabians kept their name.

The Prussian Eagle is Raumer's prize—
He keeps to the German path—
We haven't done away with rhyme:
No Horace is Freiligrath.

Massmann speaks no Latin. Thank God!
Birch-Pfeiffer only writes plays.
She guzzles no dreadful turpentine
Like the ladies of Roman days.

O Hermann, we give you thanks for this!
And, to honor you and your tribe,
In Detmold they're building a monument.
I was one of the first to subscribe.

12

The coach bumps on through the darkened woods.
But a wheel has broken away;

And suddenly: Crash! We stop in our tracks.
This isn't very gay.

The coachman dismounts and hurries to town;
And alone in the woods I prowl.
It is the middle of the night;
I hear wild creatures howl.

They are the wolves that howl so wild;
I know their famished cries.
Like candles blazing in the dark
Glimmer their fiery eyes.

They've heard of my coming, I've no doubt;
They set the woods afire
In honor of my visit there—
And greet me with their choir.

It is a serenade they sing—
For me—their celebration!
Deeply moved, I draw myself up
And deliver a grateful oration:

"Fellow wolves! I'm proud and thrilled
To spend this night among
Such noble souls who howl to me
Their tender welcome song.

At this auspicious moment, friends,
My feelings can't be measured;
Believe me, till the day I die
This hour shall be treasured!

I thank you for the confidence
With which you honor me
And which you've proved in trying times
By acts of loyalty.

You never doubted me, fellow wolves,
Never would let them persuade you,

Those villains who called me a renegade,
Who said that I had betrayed you,

Sold out to the dogs, and soon would be
Chief shepherd dog in the fold.
It was far beneath me to contradict
The lies that you were told.

Believe me, though I sometimes wore
A coat of wool to keep
The cold away, I was never convinced
To fight in the cause of the sheep.

I am no sheep, no shellfish, no dog;
I play no councilor's part;
I've stayed a wolf through all the years,
With wolfish teeth and heart.

I am a wolf, and with the wolves
I'll howl my whole life through.
Yes, count on me and help yourselves;
Then God will help you too."

That was the speech I made, without
The slightest preparation.
Kolb's *Allgemeine* printed it
With the usual mutilation.

13

The sun rose over Paderborn
With a very sullen expression.
Bringing light to the stupid earth—
A wearisome profession!

As soon as he's brightened one corner up
He carries his radiant light
With glittering speed to the other side,
While the first sinks down into night.

The stone rolls back on Sisyphus,
The deep Danaid tun
Is never filled, and the ball of earth
Is lighted in vain by the sun!

And as the morning mists dissolved
I thought that I could see
An image of the Son of Man
Who bled upon the tree.

Poor cousin of mine, I'm filled with woe
Whenever I see your face.
You hoped to save the world—you fool!
Friend of the human race!

They've given you a dirty deal,
Those lords of high estate.
Who told you to speak so recklessly
Against the church and the state?

Too bad for you, the printing press
Was a yet unknown device.
You would have written a book, no doubt,
On the problems of paradise.

The censor would have stricken out
The most offensive section,
And you'd have not been crucified—
Thanks to his kind protection.

Had you left that Sermon on the Mount
To be preached by later messiahs,
You'd still have had spirit and talent enough,
And could have spared the pious!

You scourged the bankers, the changers of gold,
You drove them out of the temple.
Luckless crusader, now on the cross
You hang as a warning example.

14

Moist wind, dry land; the carriage limps
Through mud; but an old refrain
Keeps singing and ringing in my soul:
"Sun, thou accusing flame!"

It is the refrain of the ancient song
My nurse so often sang—
"Sun, thou accusing flame!" like the call
Of a hunting horn it rang.

There is a murderer in the song:
A carefree, happy fellow;
At last they find him in the woods—
Hanging from a willow.

His death decree was nailed to the trunk,
That anyone who came
Might see the word of the Vehmic court:
"Sun, thou accusing flame!"

The sun was plaintiff, his voice of doom
Had called the murderer's name;
Dying, Ottilie had screamed:
"Sun, thou accusing flame!"

When I think of the song, I also think
Of my nurse, so dear and old;
I see her brown face once again,
With every wrinkle and fold.

Her birthplace was in Münster-land,
And often I heard her tell
Ghost stories, fables, and fairy tales—
And she knew the old songs well.

How my heart would throb, when my
   dear old nurse

Told of the Princess fair
Who sat alone on the lonely heath
And combed her golden hair!

There she had to tend the geese,
And when, at eventide,
She drove them through the gate once more
She always stopped and cried.

For she could see a horse's head
Nailed where the town gate stands.
This was the head of the wretched horse
Who'd borne her to distant lands.

The Princess sighed, "O Fallada,
That you should be hanging so!"
The horse's head cried down, "Alas,
That you ever wished to go!"

The Princess sighed, and deeply sighed,
"If my dear mother knew!"
The horse's head cried sadly down,
"Her heart would break for you!"

I used to listen with bated breath
When, gravely whispering,
My dear old nurse began to tell
Of Redbeard, our hidden King.

She'd have me believe the scholars wrong,
She said he was living still
Together with his comrades-in-arms—
Hiding in a hill.

Kyffhäuser is the name of the hill;
A cave's within its walls.
A spectral light of hanging lamps
Creeps through the gloomy halls.

The first room is a royal stall,
And in this room you see
Thousands of horses in their cribs,
All harnessed brilliantly.

They're saddled well, and bridled well,
But of this fine array
There's none that stirs; as though of steel
They neither stamp nor neigh.

Lying on straw in the second room
Warriors can be seen:
Thousands of soldiers: bearded folk
With warlike, defiant mien.

They're fully armed from head to toe,
But all these men of war
Are motionless; they make no sound;
They lie asleep on the floor.

And in the third room, piled up high,
Weapons and arms are stored:
Armor and helmets of silver and steel,
Battle axe, spear, and sword.

Very few cannon, yet enough
To form a trophy. Behold!
Above them a banner flutters high:
Its color is black-red-gold.

And in the fourth room lives the King—
For ages he's been there:
His head on his arm, at the table of stone,
Set on the same stone chair.

His flowing beard is red as flame;
At times his old eyes twinkle;
But there are times when worry seems
To make his forehead wrinkle.

Is he asleep, or does he muse?
The answer isn't clear;
But he shall mightily stir himself
When the proper hour is here.

Then shall he seize the worthy flag
And cry: "To war! To war!"
His troops will wake, and leap from the ground
With a tremendous roar.

And each will swing upon his horse
That will neigh, and trample the ground.
They'll ride out into the echoing world
And how their trumpets will sound!

They'll gallop well, they'll battle well;
They'll have slumbered out their time.
The King's tribunal will be severe:
The killers will pay for their crime—

The killers who once thrust their sword
With foul assassin's aim
Through golden-haired young Germany—
"Sun, thou accusing flame!"

There's many a man who thinks himself safe,
And, laughing, sits in his tower,
Who shall not escape the avenging rope
At Redbeard's awakening hour!

How lovely they sound, how sweet they sound,
The tales of that dear old dame!
My superstitious heart exults:
Sun, thou accusing flame!

15

Like needlepoints came prickling down
A fine, an icy rain.

Sadly the horses swished their tails;
I watched them sweat and strain.

I heard the toot of the coachman's horn,
Just as I used to hear it.
"There ride three riders out to the gate!"
Dusk came over my spirit.

I drowsed and fell asleep; and lo!
My dreams went wandering;
They brought me into the magic hill
Before our great old King.

No more did he sit at the table of stone
On his chair of stone—erect.
And he seemed less venerable now
Than one had been led to expect.

He waddled around through the rooms with me
And spoke in an intimate way.
He showed me, with a collector's pride,
The treasures on display.

The art of clubbing he explained
With a few well-chosen words.
He tenderly rubbed, with his ermine fur,
The rust from several swords.

With a peacock fan he dusted helms
Until they shone like new;
He polished many coats of mail,
And some spiked helmets, too.

He dusted off the flag, and said:
"It makes me feel so good
To think that moths haven't touched the silk,
And there's nary a worm in the wood!"

And as we came upon the room
Where soldiers, armed for the fight,

Were lying fast asleep on the floor,
The old man spoke with delight.

"Here we must softly speak and tread,
To drive no dreams away.
Once more a hundred years have passed,
And they're to be paid today."

And lo! He tiptoed up to them,
Held out a golden ducat
And stuck one quietly away
In every soldier's pocket.

And as I watched him in surprise,
He grinningly began:
"At the close of every century
I pay them one ducat per man."

And in the room where horses stood
In long and silent file,
Old Redbeard gaily rubbed his hands
And smiled a mysterious smile.

He counted the horses one by one,
And patted their ribs, approving;
He counted and counted; with anxious haste
His silent lips were moving.

"That still is not the proper count,"
He said at last with regret.
"I've plenty of soldiers, and weapons, too,
But not enough horses yet.

I've sent my grooms to the ends of the earth
To purchase all they are able;
They'll buy me the finest horses they see;
I've already a splendid stable.

I'm waiting till the count's complete,
Then I'll attack—and free

My fatherland, my German folk
That loyally waits for me."

So spoke the King, but I cried out:
"Attack, old fellow, attack!
If your soldiers have not horses enough,
Let them ride on an ass's back!"

"One doesn't rush into attack,"
Redbeard replied with a smile;
"Rome was not built up in a day;
All good things take a while.

Who comes not now, comes later on;
Oaks don't grow in a day;
And *chi va piano, va sano,* my friend;
That's what the Romans say."

16

A jolt of the carriage woke me up,
But soon I slept again,
And dreamt of Redbeard, the ancient King,
Among his sleeping men.

Again we chatted and strolled about
Through each resounding hall;
He asked me this, he asked me that,
And bade me tell him all.

Not a syllable from the upper world
These many, many years,
—Since the Seven Years' War, not a single word
Had reached the monarch's ears.

He asked about Moses Mendelssohn,
And Karschin; dropped a query
About old Countess Dubarry, too,
Louis the Fifteenth's dearie.

O King, I cried, how backward you are!
Many a year has passed
Since Moses died—son Abraham, too,
Has long since breathed his last.

With Leah, Abraham begot
A fine son, Felix by name
Who's gone quite far in the Christian world:
A conductor of great fame.

The aged Karschin is also dead,
And her granddaughter, Klencke, is gone;
Her daughter, Helmine Chezy, though,
Has not as yet passed on.

As long as Louis the Fifteenth ruled,
Dubarry's life was gay.
By the time she went to the guillotine
She'd grown quite old and gray.

King Louis the Fifteenth died in bed,
His passing was serene;
The Sixteenth, though, was guillotined
With Antoinette, his Queen.

The Queen, as befits a royal wife,
Went with a brave demeanor;
Dubarry, though, shed tears and shrieked,
When they came to guillotine her.

Redbeard suddenly stood still:
"By God, what does it mean?"
He looked at me with staring eyes,
"What is this guillotine?"

Guillotining—I explained—
Is a method we're now applying
To people of every circumstance:
It expedites their dying.

268 · Heinrich Heine

In this new method we employ
A newly developed machine;
Monsieur Guillotin invented it,
So it's called the guillotine.

First they strap you to a board:
It drops—they quickly shove you
Between two posts—a three-cornered axe
Hangs directly above you;

They pull a cord, then downward shoots
The spritely blade—and crack!
Your head immediately drops
Into a waiting sack.

The King broke in on my words: "Shut up!
Enough of your machine!
God forbid that I should come
To use a guillotine!

The King, you say! And his royal Queen?
Strapped! Onto a plank!
That goes against all etiquette
And all respect of rank!

And who are *you*, that you dare be
So intimate with me?
I'll clip your impertinent wings, young scamp!
Just wait, just wait and see.

When I listen to the things you say
My very innards are stirred.
Your breath is itself a crown offense;
High treason's in every word!"

Since Redbeard flew into such a rage,
And could only snarl and shout,
I, too, forgot to hold my tongue,
And my inmost thoughts burst out:

"Sir Barbarossa!" I cried out loud—
"You're a mythical creation.
Go, get some sleep! Without your help
We'll work out our salvation.

The republicans would scoff at us
If a ghost with scepter and crown
Came marching at the head of our ranks—
They'd laugh us out of town.

And I don't care much for your flag these days;
No longer am I thrilled
By your black-red-gold—I got sick of it
In the days of the student guild.

It would be best if you stayed at home
Here in your mountain hall—
Considering how matters stand,
We need no King at all."

17

I wrangled with the King in dreams,
Only in dreams, of course,
Awake, we answer majesty
With no such bold retorts.

Only while dreaming ideal dreams
Does the German dare impart
The German opinion he has held
So deep in his loyal heart.

We were passing a forest when I awoke;
The sight of all those trees,
Their naked, wooden reality—
Expelled my fantasies.

The oak trees gravely nodded their heads;
The birches, cautioning,
Shook their twigs—and I cried out:
"Pardon, my dear old King!

Forgive, oh, Redbeard, my hasty words!
I haven't your sensible mind.
My patience is short—but come, O King,
On the fastest horse you can find!

And if you don't care for the guillotine,
We'll do it the old way again:
The rope for burghers and farmers in smocks;
The sword for noblemen.

But switch it around from time to time:
Let peasants die by the sword,
And let the nobility be hanged—
We're creatures all of the Lord . . .

Bring back the laws of Charles the Fifth,
Set up the gallows again,
And divide the people in guilds and estates
As they were divided then.

Let the Holy Roman Empire rule,
Just as in ancient days;
Bring back its moldiest trumpery,
And all its foolish ways.

The Middle Ages I'll endure,
No matter how dark they be—
If only from that hybrid thing
You'll promise to set us free;

From that new-fangled chivalry,
A nauseating dish
Of Gothic illusion and modern lie,
That's neither foul nor fish.

We'll shut down all the theaters
And chase the clowns away
Who parody the olden times—
O King, we await your day!"

18

A mighty fortress is Minden town:
Its arms and bulwarks are fine.
But Prussian fortresses are not
Favorite places of mine.

We got there in the hour of dusk,
And when we rolled across,
The old planks of the drawbridge groaned;
The dark moats gaped at us.

The lofty bastions glowered down
As though they expected war;
The great gate clattered open wide
And clattered shut once more.

Alas! My soul grew sorrowful,
As once Odysseus' soul
Grew dark when Polyphemus shoved
The rock in the cavern's hole.

A corporal neared, and asked our names
In a voice of brash defiance.
No-man's my name; I'm an oculist:
I open the eyes of giants.

I felt still worse when I got to the inn;
I had no appetite.
Went straight to bed—but I didn't sleep—
The bed gear won the fight.

It was an ample feather bed,
With curtains of damask red;
The canopy of faded gold—
And a dirty fringe at the head.

Accursed fringe! That all night long
Robbed me of my repose!
Like the sword of Damocles it hung
Menacing over my nose.

It sometimes seemed a serpent's head
And I heard it hiss at me:
"You're in the fortress, and here you'll stay—
And never again be free!"

If only I were home—I sighed—
If I could be back there
In Paris with my darling wife
On the Faubourg Poissonière!

It seemed as though some eerie thing
Was passing over my head,
Just like a censor's icy hand—
And then my reason fled.

Policemen, draped in burial shrouds,
A crowd of ghosts, surrounded
My bed; and as they weirdly moved
A clang of fetters sounded.

Alas! The specters dragged me off.
I found myself at last
Upon a steep and rocky wall:
There they bound me fast.

That evil, filthy canopy fringe!
I found it here once more—
But it seemed to be a vulture now,
Of death-black feather and claw.

It looked like the Prussian eagle now,
And clutched me close, and ripped
The liver out of my gaping breast;
I groaned, and bitterly wept.

I'd been weeping long—when a rooster crowed
And the fevered vision fled.
I lay at Minden, in sweaty sheets,
With the tassel over my head.

I traveled on by special post;
And the first free breath I found
Was outside in the open air
On good old Bückeburg ground.

19

O Danton, you were wrong indeed,
And paid for being wrong!
On his heels, on his feet, a man can take
His fatherland along.

Half the Duchy of Bückeburg
Was pasted to my boots;
Such muddy roads I've never seen
In all my wide pursuits.

When we reached the city of Bückeburg
I took the time to get down
And look at my grandfather's place of birth—
Hamburg was grandmother's town.

I reached Hanover close to noon,
And gave my boots a cleaning.
I went at once to see the town,
—I like my tours to have meaning.

My word! This is a pretty place!
The streets are very clean.
I saw some splendid buildings here—
A most imposing scene.

I especially liked a great wide square
Surrounded by buildings of state:
The King lives there, his palace is there—
It's a joy to contemplate!

(I mean the palace.) At either side
Of the gate, a sentry stands.
Fierce and menacing redcoats watch
With muskets in their hands.

"This is Ernst Augustus' home,"
My Cicerone said;
"A high Tory lord, a nobleman:
He's old—but far from dead.

His life is right idyllical—
No satellite can guard it
As well as the fear in our loving friends—
Spineless and chickenhearted!

I sometimes see him; and then he gripes
How deadening to the mind
The Kingship of Hanover is,
To which he's now confined.

He finds the life too narrow here,
Being used to the British way;
He's plagued by the spleen; he's even afraid
He'll hang himself some day.

He was stooped by the fire two days ago,
Awake before the sun;
He was cooking a cure for his ailing dogs,
Unhelped by anyone."

20

From Harburg to Hamburg's an hour's ride;
Dusk had beaten me there.
The stars in heaven greeted me;
I felt the cool, mild air.

And when I opened mother's door
She nearly fainted for joy;
She clapped her wrinkled hands, and cried:
"My darling, darling boy!

It has been all of thirteen years
Since you left home, my sweet.
You surely must be wild for food—
Now, what would you like to eat?

I have some fish, and goose meat, too—
And lovely oranges."
Then give me fish, and goose meat, too—
And lovely oranges.

And while I ate with growing zest
Mother was gay as could be;
She asked me this, she asked me that;
Some questions embarrassed me.

"My darling boy! Now tell me the truth—
Are you well tended in France?
Does your wife know how to manage the house?
Does she mend your shirts and pants?"

The fish is good, dear motherkin,
But 'twere better that no one spoke.
You really mustn't bother me now:
I might swallow a bone, and choke.

And when I'd devoured the excellent fish
She brought out the goose, and served me.

Again she asked me this and that;
Some of her questions unnerved me.

"My darling boy! In which of the lands
Do you find that life is cheerier?
Here or in France? And of these two folk
Which would you call superior?"

The German goose, dear motherkin,
Is good—but the Frenchmen do
A better job of stuffing geese;
Their sauces are better, too.

And when the goose had taken her bow,
The oranges came into sight.
They tasted so sweet—I'd never dreamed
They could give me such delight.

But mother cheerfully began
Her questions; and she harassed me
By bringing up a thousand things—
Some of her questions embarrassed me.

"My darling boy! And what are your views?
Do you still take note of the trends?
What party do you belong to now?
What sort of folks are your friends?"

The oranges, dear motherkin,
Are good—and with genuine zeal
I swallow down the last sweet drop,
And lay aside the peel.

21

Hamburg, half of it burned away,
Is slowly being reborn;
The doleful city looks just like
A poodle halfway shorn.

So many streets are here no more
That I keep thinking of!
Where is the house in which I kissed
My first sweet kiss of love?

Where is the printer's where I took
My *Reisebilder* to press?
The oyster cellar, where first I knew
An oyster's tenderness?

And the Dreckwall? Where has the Dreckwall gone?
In vain I search the street!
Where's the pavilion, where I had
So many cakes to eat?

And the City Hall, in which were throned
The elders of the town?
Prey to the flames! The fire burned
Even the holiest down.

The people still were sighing with fear,
And with a mournful gaze
Recounted the terrible history
Of that gigantic blaze.

"It started in every quarter at once!
There was nothing but smoke and flame.
The high church towers flared up wild
And, crashing, down they came.

The old exchange was burned to the ground,
Where once our fathers stood
And dealt with each other for centuries
As honestly as they could.

The bank, the city's silver soul,
And the book in which was listed
The bank account of every man—
Thank God! The fire missed it.

Thank God! They raised a fund for us
In all the farthest lands—
An excellent business—eight million marks
Came pouring into our hands.

The money filled our open hands—
It flowed from every nation;
We also accepted stores of food;
Rejected no donation.

They sent us clothes and beds enough,
And bread, and meats, and soups!
The King of Prussia was kind enough
To offer us his troops.

The material damage has been repaid,
That could be estimated—
But for the fright, the fright we felt,
We'll never be compensated!"

"Dear people," I said to cheer them up,
"You mustn't wail and weep;
Troy was a better city than yours,
Yet it fell in a blazing heap.

Dry your puddles, restore your homes,
And if you're set on vengeance
Let it take the form of better laws
And better fire engines.

Go easy on pepper in mock turtle soup;
And learn to scale your fish—
Unscaled carp, when it's cooked in grease,
Is not a healthy dish.

Turkey cocks can't do much harm,
But you might be led to disaster
By the treacherous bird that laid its egg
In the wig of the burgomaster.

This nasty bird's identity
It's needless to announce—
Whenever I remember him—
My lunch begins to bounce."

22

Even more striking than the town's
Was the people's transformation.
Like wandering ruins they walk around
In pain and tribulation.

The thin ones are even thinner now,
The fat ones even fatter;
The children are old, the older folk
Return to childish chatter.

Many that I'd left as calves
Were oxen when I found them;
Many goslings had grown into geese,
With haughty plumage around them.

Old Gudel looked like a siren still,
With her paint and powder and pearls;
She'd purchased teeth of dazzling white,
And a mop of pitch-black curls.

My friend, the stationer, had best
Preserved his youthful air;
He looks like John the Baptist, with
His halo of blond hair.

I saw ——— only from far,
He swiftly fled from view;
I hear his mind was burned away,
But Biber'd insured it, too.

I saw my friend, the censor, again—
We met in the marketplace.
He was stooped and wandering in a fog
With a troubled look on his face.

We shook hands, and his eyes were moist.
He felt such deep delight
At seeing his poet once again!
It was a moving sight—

I didn't find them all. Some friends
Had left this earthly shore.
Alas! My Gumpelino, too,
Shall smile at me no more.

The noble fellow had lately died:
And now, with wings full-grown,
He must be hovering—seraph-white—
Around Jehovah's throne.

In vain I sought through Hamburg's streets,
In every possible spot,
For the bent Adonis who hawked his cup
And porcelain chamber pot.

Sarras the faithful poodle's dead;
The heaviest loss in years!
If three score writers passed away
Campe would shed less tears.

The population of Hamburg State
Consists—from its founding day—
Of Jews and Christians; the latter, too
Give very little away.

All of the Christians are pretty good,
They've good strong appetites, too.
And they're sure to pay up every bill
Even before it's due.

And as for the Jewish community,
It seems to have split in two:
The old ones pray in the synagogue,
And a temple houses the new.

The new Jews feast on pork, and stand
In constant opposition—
They're democrats; the old belong
To aristoscratchy tradition.

I love the old, I love the new,
But I swear by God above
There are certain fish we call smoked sprats
For which I've a greater love.

23

The republic of Hamburg was never as great
As those of Venice and Florence;
But the oysters of Hamburg can't be beat—
They're best in the cellars of Lorenz.

When I went down there with good old Campe
The evening air was fine;
We were bent on wallowing once more
In oysters and Rhine wine.

A good crowd sat there; and I was glad
To find, among the others,
Many old cronies, like Chaufepié,
And many new-sworn brothers.

Here's Wille, whose face is a register;
His academic foes
Had signed inscriptions in that book
Too legibly—with blows.

Here was that thorough pagan, Fuchs,
A personal foe of Jehovah—
Devoted to Hegel, and also, perhaps,
To the Venus of Canova.

My Campe had turned Amphitryon,
And smiled in great delight;
Like a transfigured Madonna's now
His eyes were blessedly bright.

I ate and drank with zest, and thought:
"This Campe's a perfect gem—
There may be other good publishers—
But he's the best of them.

Where another publisher perhaps
Would have let me starve in hallways,
This fellow even buys me drinks;
I'll have to keep him always.

I thank the mighty Lord on high
Who made the sap of the vine,
And permitted such a publisher
As Julius Campe to be mine!

I thank the mighty Lord on high
Whose glorious word gave birth
To oysters in the ocean world
And wine of the Rhine on earth!

He made the lemons grow, with which
Our oysters are bedewed—
Now, Father, see that I may well
Digest this evening's food!"

The Rhine wine always mellows me,
And soothes my strife-torn mind,
And kindles there a mighty urge,
An urge to love mankind.

It makes me leave my lonesome room;
It drives me from street to street;
I look for a garment soft and white,
A soul for my soul to meet.

At moments like these I nearly melt
With sadness and desire;
All cats are gray, all women then
Are Helens, and set me afire.

And as I came where the Drehbahn runs
I saw the moon illumine
A woman, splendid and sublime,
A wondrously high-breasted woman.

Her face was round, and hale, and sound;
Her eyes were turquoise blue;
Her cheeks were like roses; like cherries her mouth—
And her nose was reddish, too.

Her head was covered with a white
And well-starched linen bonnet;
It looked like a crown, with towerlets
And jagged pinnacles on it.

She wore a white tunic down to her calves,
And oh, what calves they were!
The bases of two Doric columns
Couldn't be lovelier!

The most earthly unaffectedness
Could be read upon her face,
But her superhuman rear betrayed
She belonged to a higher race.

Stepping up to me, she said:
"Welcome to Elbe's shore—
After an absence of thirteen years—
I see you're the same as before.

Perhaps you seek those lovely souls
Who often met you here
And reveled all night long with you
In a passed, a perished year.

That hundred-headed hydra, Life,
Long since devoured them all—
The old times and the girls you knew
Are lost beyond recall!

You'll find those pretty flowers no more,
That you loved when your heart was warm;
Here they bloomed—they are withered now,
And their leaves are ripped by the storm.

Withered, stripped, and trampled down
By destiny's brutal feet—
My friend, such is the earthly fate
Of all that is lovely and sweet!"

"Who are you?" I cried. "You look at me
Like a dream that once I knew—
Majestic lady, where do you live?
May I accompany you?"

At this the woman smiled and said:
"Sorry! But *I'm* refined;
I'm a respectable, moral sort;
Sorry! I'm not that kind.

I'm not that kind of a mademoiselle,
A Loretta with open bodice—
Know then: I am Hammonia,
Hamburg's protecting goddess!

You start, and even seem afraid;
You—such a valiant singer!
Are you still so anxious to come with me?
Well, then! No need to linger!"

But noisily I laughed, and said:
"I'll come along—proceed!
I'll come along, though hell's the place
To which your footsteps lead!"

24

How I got up her narrow stairs
I really couldn't say;
Perhaps a few invisible ghosts
Carried me part of the way.

Here in Hammonia's little room
The hours went swiftly by.
The goddess confessed, her opinion of me
Had always been quite high.

"You see," she said, "before your time
My heart was set afire
By one who praised the Messiah's works
Upon his pious lyre.

My Klopstock's bust is standing yet
On the bureau, there by the clock,
Though recently I've been using it
In place of a milliner's block.

Now you're my pet; your picture hangs
On the wall above my bed.
And see, a fresh green laurel wreath
Adorns your handsome head.

And yet, the way you've often nagged
My sons, I must admit,
Has sometimes deeply wounded me;
Let's have no more of it.

I trust that time has cured you of
Such naughty occupation,
And taught you even to look on fools
With greater toleration.

But tell me! Winter's almost here—
What could have been your reason
For starting on a journey north
In such a draughty season?"

"O my goddess!" I replied,
"Thoughts lie slumbering deep
Within the core of the human heart,
That may suddenly wake from their sleep.

On the surface things went pretty well,
But something within oppressed me,
And day by day that oppression grew—
Homesickness possessed me.

The air of France, that had been so light,
Now smothered me with its weight;
I had to breathe some German air
Or I would suffocate.

I longed for German tobacco smoke,
For the fragrance of our peat.
My foot grew faint with eagerness
To step on a German street.

I longed to see my old lady again,
And all through the night I'd sigh;
She lives beside the gate of the dam;
Lottchen lives nearby.

That old and noble gentleman
I also longed to see;
He never failed to bawl me out,
Yet always took care of me.

'Stupid fellow!' he used to say.
Once more I wanted to hear it—
It always echoed like a song,
A sweet song, through my spirit.

I longed for the bluish chimney smoke
That rises from German stoves;
For the nightingales of Saxony;
For quiet beech tree groves.

I even hungered for those spots
Where grief had bowed me down;
Where once I dragged the cross of youth,
And wore a thorny crown.

I wanted to weep again, where once
My bitterest tears fell burning—
Love of country, I believe,
Is the name of this foolish yearning.

I do not like to speak of it;
It's only a disease;
Modest, I never permit the crowd
To see my agonies.

I have no patience with the bunch
That hopes to stir your heart,
By putting its patriotism on show
With every abscess and wart.

Shameless, shabby beggars are they
That kneel and whine for charity—
Give Menzel and his Swabians
A penny of popularity!

O goddess mine, you've found me today
In a very sensitive state;
I'm somewhat ill, but if I take care,
I'll soon recuperate.

Yes, I am ill, and you could help
To raise my spirits some,
By serving a cup of good hot tea;
I'd like it mixed with rum."

25

She brewed some tea, mixed it with rum,
And poured a cup for me.
But she herself drank down the rum
Without a drop of tea.

Against my shoulder she leaned her head
(The bonnet was somewhat crushed
As a result of her carelessness)
And she spoke in a tone that was hushed:

"Often I've anxiously thought of you
In Paris, that sinful place,
Living without a watchful friend
Among that frivolous race.

You stroll along those avenues
And haven't at your side
A loyal German publisher
To be your mentor and guide.

And it's so easy to be seduced!
Those boulevards are lined
With sickly sylphs; and all too soon
One loses peace of mind.

Don't go back, but stay with us!
Here morals and breeding still stand—
And many a quiet pleasure blooms
Here in the fatherland.

Stay with us in Germany;
You'll find things more to your liking;
You've surely seen with your own eyes
That progress has been striking.

And the censorship is harsh no more—
Hoffmann grows milder with age;
No more will he mutilate your books
As he did in his youthful rage.

You, too, are older and milder now—
Less eager for a fight;
You'll even see the bygone days
In a more propitious light.

To say that things were hopeless here
Is gross exaggeration;
You could break your chains, as they did in Rome,
By self-extermination.

The populace had freedom of thought,
The greatest number possessed it;
Only the few who published books
Were ever really molested.

Lawless tyranny never ruled;
Demagogues—even the worst—
Never lost their citizenship,
Without being sentenced first.

And even in the hardest times
Evil did not prevail—
Believe me, no one ever starved
In any German jail!

So many fine examples of faith
And kindness could be found
Blossoming here in days gone by!
Now doubt and denial abound.

Practical, outward liberty
Will one day drag to its doom
The ideal that grew in our breasts—it was pure
As the dream of the lily in bloom!

Our beautiful poetry also dies,
Today it's a flickering fire;
Freiligrath's King of the Moors goes down
With the other kings that expire.

Our grandsons will eat and drink enough,
But their thoughtful silence is gone;
The idyll is over, and in its stead
A spectacle play comes on.

Oh, could you be silent, I'd open for you
The book of destiny;
In my magic mirrors I'd let you view
Things that are to be.

I'd like to show you what no one else
Has seen before this day—
The future of your fatherland—
But ah! You'd give it away."

"My god, O goddess!" I cried, enrapt,
"Nothing could be so sweet!
Show me the future of Germany—
I am a man and discreet.

I'll pledge my silence by any oath
That you may wish to hear;
I guarantee my secrecy—
Tell me, how shall I swear?"

The goddess answered, "Swear to me
In Father Abraham's way,
When Eleazar prepared for his trip—
Now heed whatever I say!

Lift up my gown, and lay your hand
Down here on my thigh, and hold it,
And swear that this secret, in speech and in books,
Shall never be unfolded."

A solemn moment! I felt as though
The breath of a buried day
Blew on me as I swore the oath,
In the ancient patriarch's way.

I gravely lifted Hammonia's gown,
And laid my hands on her hips,
And vowed the secret would never escape
From my writing quill or my lips.

26

The rum must have reached Hammonia's crown—
(Her cheeks became so red)
And with a sigh she turned to me
And sorrowfully said:

"I'm growing old; I was born on the day
That Hamburg rose from the ground.
As queen of the shellfish, here at the mouth
Of the Elbe, my mother was crowned.

My father was a mighty king,
Carolus Magnus by name.
Friedrich the Great of Prussia had not
Such wisdom, power, and fame.

His coronation chair is still
At Aachen; but the chair
On which he used to sit at night
Was left in mother's care.

Mother willed this chair to me;
You see—it's old and faded;
But should Rothschild offer me all his wealth
I'd never agree to trade it.

Do you see, there in the corner stands
A chair from an earlier day;
The leather is torn from its back, and moths
Have eaten the cushion away.

But if you go up close and lift
The cushion from the chair,
You'll see an oval opening;
A pot is hidden there—

It is a magic pot, in which
The magical powers brew;
Stick in your head, and future times
Shall be revealed to you—

Germany's future, like waving dreams,
Shall surge before your eyes;
But do not shudder, if out of the mess
Foul miasmas arise!"

She spoke, and laughed peculiarly,
But there was no fear in my soul;
With curiosity I ran
To stick my head in the hole.

The things I saw, I won't betray—
I promised never to tell.
I'm barely permitted to report:
God! O God! What a smell!

Against my will those cursed, vile
Aromas come to mind:
The startling stink, that seemed to be
Old cabbage and leather combined.

And after this—O God!—there rose
Such monstrous, loathsome stenches;
It was as though the dung were swept
From six and thirty trenches—

I know very well what Saint-Just said
Of late to the welfare board—
Neither with attar of roses nor musk
Can the great disease be cured.

But all other smells were put to shame
By this prophetic scent—
No longer could my nostrils bear
That vile presentiment.

My senses swooned, and when I woke
I was still Hammonia's guest—
My head was resting comfortably
Upon her ample breast.

Her nostrils quivered, her lips were aglow,
Her look was a shower of lightning;
With a bacchanal hug of the poet, she sang
In an ecstasy fierce and frightening:

"I love you, stay in Hamburg with me;
We'll gaily eat and drink
The wines and oysters of today,
And forget tomorrow's stink!

Put back the cover! And spare our joy
From the horrible smells below it—
I love you as never a woman before
Has loved a German poet!

I kiss you—and your genius fills
My soul with inspiration;
And suddenly I'm overcome
By a grand intoxication.

I feel as though I hear the song
Of watchmen on the street—
They sing a prothalamium,
My comrade-in-joy, my sweet!

And now the mounted lackeys come,
With torches richly burning;
They dance the torch dance solemnly,
Hopping, and waddling, and turning.

Here come the worthy senators,
And the elders in their glory;
The burgomaster clears his throat
For a trial of oratory.

The diplomatic corps appear
In dress befitting their stations;
With reservations, they wish us well
In the name of the border nations.

With rabbis and pastors arm in arm
God's delegation appears—
But alas! Here comes Herr Hoffmann, too,
Wielding his censor shears!

The shears are rattling in his hand;
He comes with savage heart—
And cruelly cuts into your flesh—
It was the choicest part . . ."

27

And in that night of miracle
Whatever else took place
I'll let you know another time,
In warmer summer days.

Hypocrisy's old race, thank God!
Dissolves before our eyes.
It slowly sinks into the grave,
Killed by its cancer of lies.

There is a new race growing up:
Unrouged, unsinning youth!
Freedom of thought, and freedom of joy—
I'll let them know the truth.

They understand a poet's pride,
And know the worth of his art;
They bathe in the warmth of his sunlit mind,
And heed the pulse of his heart.

My heart is loving as the light,
And pure and chaste as fire;
The noblest of the graces tuned
The strings of my golden lyre.

This is the very lyre that once
My father made resound,
The late Lord Aristophanes
Whom the Graces loved and crowned.

Upon this lyre he sang a tale
That every schoolboy knows,
Of a Greek who sued for Zeus's child
And, winning her love, arose.

In the previous chapter I made an attempt
To imitate the end
Of Aristophanes' *The Birds;*
—It's the finest play he penned.

The Frogs is also excellent.
They're playing it in translation
Upon the stage of Berlin right now
For royal gratification.

The King's enchanted. That shows a taste
For the art of a day that's gone.
Father would laugh far more to hear
Our own frogs carrying on!

The King's enchanted. But were the bard
Alive, who wrote this play,
I'd stop him at Prussia's borderline
And warn him to turn away.

For the real Aristophanes things would be bad:
He'd soon be marched before us,
Clinking his chains and accompanied
By a huge policemen's chorus.

The crowd would soon be allowed to jeer
Instead of wagging its tail;
And soon the police would be aroused
To get on the poet's trail.

O King! I wish you very well,
And here's the advice I give:
Pay your respects to the poets who've died,
But spare the ones who live!

Do not offend the living bards;
They've weapons and conflagrations
More dreadful than all the lightnings of Jove
—Which were only a poet's creations.

Offend the gods, both old and new,
The whole Olympian lot,
And high Jehovah leading the rest—
But the poet—offend him not!

The gods, to be sure, are very hard
On wrongs that people do;
The fires of hell are rather warm:
There one must fry and stew—

But there are certain saints, who pray
Until the sinner is freed;
Through gifts to churches, and requiems,
Heaven will intercede.

And Christ will descend on the final day
And break the hell gates down,
And though his judgment may be severe,
Some will be spared his frown.

But there are hells from whose confines
No amnesty avails—
No prayers will help, and even the word
Of our redeemer fails.

Have you not heard of Dante's hell,
The tercets that flamed from his pen?
He whom the poet imprisons there
Can never go free again—

No God, no savior, can free him from
This conflagration of rhyme!
Beware, lest we hold you in such a hell
Until the end of time!

Translated by Aaron Kramer

Index of Titles and First Lines

(Titles indicated by bold-face type)

(GERMAN)

(ENGLISH)

ACKNOWLEDGMENTS

Every reasonable effort has been made to locate the owners of rights to previously published translations reprinted here. We gratefully acknowledge permission to reprint the following material:

All translations by Aaron Kramer of lyric poems and *Germany: A Winter's Tale* from *The Poetry and Prose of Heinrich Heine*, edited by Frederic Ewen. Copyright © 1969 by Citadel Press Inc. Published by arrangement with Lyle Stuart Inc. Translation of "Remembering Krähwinkel's Reign of Terror," from *Heinrich Heine: Paradox and Poet: The Poems* by Louis Untermeyer. Copyright© 1937 by Harcourt, Brace and Co. By permission of Harcourt Brace Jovanovich, Inc. Translations of "A spruce is standing lonely," "My heart, my heart is saddened," "Which way now?" "Course of the world" by Max Knight from *Heinrich Heine: Selected Works,* edited by Helen M. Mustard, copyright © 1973 by Random House, Inc. Translation of "Die Götter Griechenlands" by Vernon Watkins from *Heinrich Heine: The North Sea,* edited by Vernon Watkins, London, Faber & Faber, n.d. By permission of G. M. Watkins. Translation of "Maria Antoinette" by Margaret Armour from *Heine's Prose and Poetry,* edited by Ernest Rhys, London, J. M. Dent and Sons Ltd. By permission of William Heinemann Ltd. Translation of "Ich habe verlacht" by Charles Godfrey Leland from *The Works of Heinrich Heine,* edited by Charles Godfrey Leland, New York, E. P. Dutton and Co., 1906. By permission of William Heinemann Ltd. Translation of *Ideas—Book Le Grand* by Charles Godfrey Leland. From *The Sword and the Flame, Selections from the Prose of Heinrich Heine,* edited by Alfred Werner. By permission of the publisher. Copyright© 1960 by A. S. Barnes & Company, Inc. All rights reserved.